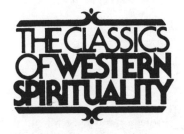

THE CLASSICS OF WESTERN SPIRITUALITY
A Library of the Great Spiritual Masters

Francis and Clare
The Complete Works

TRANSLATION AND INTRODUCTION BY
REGIS J. ARMSTRONG, O.F.M. CAP.
AND
IGNATIUS C. BRADY, O.F.M.

PREFACE BY
JOHN VAUGHN, O.F.M.

PAULIST PRESS
NEW YORK • MAHWAH

Cover Art—
The artist, JOSEPH DORNIAK, is a Franciscan friar from Bridgeport, Connecticut.

Library of Congress
Catalog Card Number: 82-62693

ISBN: 0-8091-2446-7

Published by Paulist Press
997 Macarthur Boulevard
Mahwah, New Jersey 07430

Printed and bound in the
United States of America

Contents

CONTENTS

Editors of This Volume

REGIS J. ARMSTRONG, O.F.M. Cap., is a member of the Order of Friars Minor Capuchin. He obtained a doctorate in spiritual theology from Fordham University in 1978. His doctoral dissertation was a study of the spiritual theology of the Legenda Major, the major life of Saint Francis of Assisi, by Saint Bonaventure. He was directed in this project by Dr. Ewert H. Cousins and Fr. Ignatius Brady, O.F.M. Father Regis also holds a degree in pastoral counseling obtained through the Division of Pastoral Counseling of Iona College, New Rochelle, New York. In addition to his teaching, he has traveled extensively throughout Japan, Korea, the Philippines, Latin America, England, Wales, Ireland, Italy, and the United States and has lectured in these countries on the writings of Saint Francis and Saint Clare and the spiritual theology of the Franciscan tradition.

He is presently a member of the Franciscan Institute of Saint Bonaventure University, Saint Bonaventure, New York, and is also a member of the staff of the Program of Spiritual Development of the Archdiocese of New York as well as of the faculty of Maryknoll Seminary, Maryknoll, New York.

IGNATIUS BRADY, O.F.M., one of the world's leading authorities on Bonaventure and early Franciscan spirituality, is prefect of the theology section of the Franciscan research center Collegio S. Bonaventura at Grottaferrata near Rome. Father Ignatius was assigned to this post in 1961, when the center was located at Quaracchi in Florence. It was at this center that the critical text of Bonaventure's work was edited and published from 1882 to 1902. Following in the distinguished tradition of the Quaracchi editors, Father Ignatius has produced as his major scholarly achievement the critical text of *The Sentences of Peter Lombard* and has written important articles on the authenticity and textual status of works of Bonaventure. Born in Detroit in 1911, he entered the Order of Friars Minor, receiving the Franciscan habit in 1929, and was ordained a priest in 1937. From the Pontifical Institute of Mediaeval Studies, Toronto, he received a licentiate in medieval studies in 1941; and from the University of Toronto, a master of arts degree in 1940 and a doctorate in philosophy in 1948. He has taught at Duns Scotus College, Detroit; the Franciscan Institute of St. Bonaventure University; the Catholic University of America; and the Antonianum, the international university of the Friars Minor in Rome. In 1962 the Friars Minor conferred on him the title Lector Jubilatus, the highest recognition afforded to their teachers. A recognized authority on Franciscanism, he has attended General Chapters of his Order, has been appointed a member of pre–General Chapter committees, and was assigned as theological consultant to the Union of Major Superiors. He has been increasingly in demand in many parts of the world to conduct Franciscan study weeks and retreats and to give conferences on Franciscan spirituality, especially in the Far East, Italy, England, Ireland, and the United States.

In addition to his textual work, he has translated a number of books and has published numerous articles for journals and encyclopedias on early Franciscan history, philosophy, theology, and spirituality.

Author of the Preface

JOHN VAUGHN, O.F.M., a Franciscan friar and a Roman Catholic priest, is a native of California and is 53 years old. He studied Spanish language and literature at the University of Southern California in Los Angeles, and spiritual theology at the Institute of Spirituality of the Gregorian University in Rome. Besides being engaged in pastoral ministry in Mexico and California, he was also a member of the Franciscan Formation Staff and later Minister Provincial of the Franciscan Province of Saint Barbara. At present he lives in Rome, where he serves as Minister General of the Order of Friars Minor.

Preface

At one time in Assisi, for a brief period as history goes, one could have spoken of Francis, the son of the merchant Pietro di Bernardone, without thinking also of the Lady Clare, daughter of the rich house of Offreduccio di Bernardino, nobility of the Umbrian town. If the people of Assisi knew him, it was as a noisy lad, affable, kind, generous, a leader among his own, yet somewhat of a profligate who, in the words of Thomas of Celano in his first work on Saint Francis (n. 2), wasted his life until he was almost twenty-four. If Clare indeed knew anything of this fickle young man, it was probably more by hearsay and gossip than by sight. After all, he was some twelve years older than she, from another part of town, and of the merchant class.

Yet his dreams were of higher things than those of a tradesman's son: He would be a knight and attain renown and glory. Glory indeed! He ended in the prison of Perugia, and returned home a sick young man. Long weeks in bed brought a change in him as he began to assess his life to that point. When he ventured forth, leaning on a cane, the whole world around him seemed changed; only slowly did he realize that the change was in himself. Nonetheless, he still sought earthly glory, urged on by a dream one night of his father's house transformed into a palace filled with all manner of armor, soldiers to follow him, and a bride of great beauty. The accounts differ in detail, but he came to know that somehow he was to be a knight of Christ and herald of the Great King, yet only after a great change in himself.

Of this he bears witness in the plain unvarnished account of his "conversion" in the first lines of his Testament. Henceforth he would live unto God in Christ through the power of the Spirit, seeking ever the things that are above. God's words became a lamp for his steps and a light for his path (Ps 119:105) as he strove to follow the teachings and the very footprints of our Lord Jesus Christ (see *The Earlier Rule*, I, 1; XXII, 2; and *The Second Version of the Letter to the Faithful*, 13).

That Francis was indeed a man possessed of the Spirit of the Lord is revealed in everything he wrote: admonitions, letters, rules; and in many a spoken word, when, for example, in a moment of exaltation, or perhaps of desolation, he came to see that the true Minister

General of the Order is the Holy Spirit (cf. Thomas of Celano, *Second Life of Saint Francis*, n. 193), whose presence and action in them all the friars must ever desire and show by their response to His guidance (*Later Rule*, X, 8).

It follows that the writings of Saint Francis are in reality instruments of the Spirit for all his sons and daughters, and indeed for all who would deepen their Christian vocation. It is good to know the history, if possible, of each writing or dictate of the Seraph of Assisi; but of much more profit to recognize that he (or, truly, Christ through him) is speaking today to us who profess to follow him, and to a host of admirers the world over. He calls us to revitalize our lives and those of others, and indeed to renew the very life of the Church in these times of crisis. "Repair My Church" today! Stir up new dreams, seek a fresh outlook! "Brothers, let us begin," said Francis then and now: "Let us begin, for until now we have done little or nothing!"

On our part is it too much to strive to have his Catholic spirit, evident in his words, his actions, his writings; to share his deep attachment to the Church of Rome (remembered in the great statuary group that faces the Cathedral of Rome, the Church of the Lateran); his heartfelt desire to carry Christ "to the Saracens and other nonbelievers" (*Later Rule*, XII) and to the Christians of Europe, and, finally, to the whole world, by the word and example of his sons: "Let all the brothers preach by the works they do" (*Earlier Rule*, XVII)?

For all, not only the friars, clerics, and sisters, but likewise our brothers and sisters in Christ the world over, a deeper knowledge of the words and the writings of Francis under the guidance of the Spirit will go far toward our daily renewal in the ways of the Lord as we seek to walk with Francis in the footsteps of Christ. "Brothers, let us begin!"

On her part, Saint Clare has left us just enough in writing to make us hunger for more: her Rule for the Sisters at San Damiano in Assisi (approved on her deathbed), her Testament, four most remarkable letters to Blessed Agnes of Prague, and a Blessing (not too well authenticated, I am told). We must remember, however, that though she had "committed herself wholly to the guidance of Francis, considering him to be after God the director of her steps" (*The Legend of the Virgin Saint Clare*, c. 3, n. 6), the saint gave her much freedom, knowing that the Spirit was guiding her. Both had assuredly a deep faith in His presence and action in them, a presence that gave Clare the strength and the will to follow in her own way of the Gospel life after the death of Francis. Totally given over to prayer, contemplation, and a rigorous form of life, her heart's concern was first and foremost for her sisters at San Damiano, and only remotely for the nuns of other monasteries who sought to follow their example and form of life.

The four letters to Blessed Agnes, daughter of the king of Bohemia, are certainly an exception, for which we must be truly grateful to the Spirit (we may suspect that there may have been more). Would that we had those of Blessed Agnes to Saint Clare, that the exchange might be complete! Nonetheless, the letters of Clare and at least one document of Pope Gregory IX well reveal the earnest desire of Blessed Agnes to follow closely the pattern of life permitted at San Damiano.

We welcome this volume, sure that it reveals not only the scholarship needed to produce more accurate texts and some writings unknown to earlier editors (admittedly dependent on the researches of the late Kajetan Esser, O.F.M., who died July 10, 1978 and his collaborators), but also an adequate rendition into English of the Latin of the writings and dictated works of the Blessed Francis. The definitive Latin text is best represented by the small volume *Opuscula Sancti Patris Francisci Assisiensis* (ed., K. Esser, O.F.M., Grottaferrata, 1978), which is based in large part on Father Esser's octavo volume *Die Opuscula des Heiligen Franziskus von Assisi* (Grottaferrata, 1976), in which are examined all the works ever attributed to Saint Francis. Of these, some twenty-four or more are found to be either doubtful or clearly not authentic, including the Prayer for Peace—"Lord, make me an instrument of Your peace," ascribed to Saint Francis in the last forty years or more. Earlier—in a small Italian prayerbook, the first known printing—it is ascribed to William the Norman! In addition, the Capuchin Willibrord van Dyke is said to have found it on a holy card ascribed to William the Conqueror!

Thus amused and content, I welcome this volume and its contribution to the celebration of the eight hundredth anniversary of the birth of Saint Francis, and pray that it will be a means whereby both Francis and Clare will bring many today closer to Christ and to His Church.

ACKNOWLEDGEMENTS

We wish to express our gratitude to the most high, all-powerful Father for the opportunity of collaborating on this volume. In His continuing goodness to us, He has enabled us to deepen our spiritual bonds with Saint Francis and Saint Clare and to renew our commitment to the Gospel way of life that we profess with them. We also thank Him for strengthening the bonds of brotherhood and friendship through this work.

It is an honor to have the Preface of this volume written by Father John Vaughn, O.F.M., Minister General. The contribution of his time and talents to our undertaking is greatly appreciated.

We wish to thank Father Joachim Giermek, O.F.M. Conv., who read our translations and contributed invaluable insights. His presence, encouragement, and assistance enabled us to present a volume that reflects the spirit of the three families of the First Order of Saint Francis: the Order of Friars Minor, the Order of Friars Minor Conventual, and the Order of Friars Minor Capuchin.

Furthermore, we wish to thank the staff and students of the Franciscan Institute, especially Father Conrad L. Harkins, O.F.M., Director, and Noel Riggs, who typed the manuscript, as well as the friars of Saint Bonaventure University, Saint Bonaventure, New York. Their patience and enthusiasm were inspiration and support for our work.

And we are grateful for the patience and understanding of the staff of Paulist Press, especially John Farina, who dealt with two friars on both sides of the Atlantic and harmonized their efforts.

Finally, we wish to express our gratitude to all our students, past and present. They have deepened our enthusiasm, given us strength, and challenged us to live authentically in the spirit of Saint Francis.

Foreword

The persons of Saint Francis of Assisi (c. 1182–1226) and Saint Clare of Assisi (c. 1193–1253) are prominent in the history of Christian spirituality. Both saints have captured the hearts and imaginations of men and women of all nationalities and creeds through the centuries. Both saints shared a vision of faith in the most high, all-powerful Lord Whose generosity and love could be seen in every aspect of life. Due to that faith, they responded to the promptings of the Holy Spirit by embracing lives of ever-deepening poverty and humility. And, as a result, they became effective instruments of the Holy Spirit in promoting the kingdom of peace that Christ had come to establish.

This volume contains translations of the patrimony of writings that these saints of Assisi left to their followers. The relatively few pieces that have survived the vicissitudes of history have become unwitting witnesses to the attitudes of both Saint Francis and Saint Clare that there is nothing in this world to which a person should cling and by which he should be distracted from that Love which is God. Thus the paucity of their writings is another example of the poverty that is at the heart of the Franciscan charism.

It is curious that the friars allowed so many of the writings of Saint Francis to be lost, for the Seraphic Father had been eager to have many of his letters and admonitions copied and preserved. Nonetheless, the manuscript tradition is weak in many instances or is filled with many discrepancies. The oldest manuscript, the Assisi Codex 338, which has been classified as a mid-thirteenth century piece, contains only half of the saint's writings. The manuscript collections of the fourteenth century indicate a wide variety of writings, many of which have been authenticated, and others that have been brought into serious doubt.

The condition of the writings of Saint Clare is even more deficient. With the exception of the Rule of Saint Clare, which was discovered in its original manuscript in 1893 wrapped in a habit of Saint Clare and hidden in a reliquary in the Proto-monastery of Santa Chiara in Assisi, only four other writings have been authenticated. These are the four letters that Saint Clare sent to Blessed Agnes of

FOREWORD

Prague. There have been substantial arguments raised concerning the authenticity of the Testament of Saint Clare, as well as a letter sent to Sister Ermentrude of Bruges, and the Blessing.

This volume represents the first attempt in the English-speaking world to combine the writings of both Saint Francis and Saint Clare in one volume. It is our hope that this presentation will deepen the appreciation of the spiritual vision of both saints and will enable readers to perceive the penetrating depths of their love of God. A study of the writings of these two saints of Assisi, presented in such close proximity, will provide tools for demythologizing many of the popular stories that have developed concerning their relationship. The simplicity of these writings will encourage readers to realize the utterly simple focus of the lives of Saint Francis and Saint Clare: the all-absorbing vision of the Lord Jesus Christ.

The basic texts from which this translation comes are those of Father Kajetan Esser, O.F.M., and Father Ignatio Omaechevarria, O.F.M. Father Omaechevarria's *Escritos de Santa Clara y Documentos Contemporaneos* is a scholarly work in which a detailed study and critical publication of the writings of Saint Clare was presented in 1970. *Die Opuscula des Heiligen Franziskus von Assisi* of Father Esser, first published in a German-Latin edition in 1976 and subsequently in a Latin edition in 1978, is a work that absorbed most of his life. After consulting and evaluating 181 manuscript collections, Father Esser made a major contribution to contemporary studies of Saint Francis of Assisi. The editors of this volume hope that the translation of the writings of Saint Francis and Saint Clare will underscore the dedication and scholarship of both of these friars.

The introductions that precede each text reflect the scholarship of many friars who have been studying the writings of these saints with a renewed enthusiasm within the past few years. As a result of their studies and publications, the textual work of Father Esser and Father Omaechevarria has produced the fruit of a broader consciousness of the richness of the Franciscan spiritual heritage. What remains is the challenge of translating the spirit of Saint Francis and Saint Clare into the daily lives of contemporary readers of their writings.

Francis of Assisi

INTRODUCTION

I   Introduction

G. K. Chesterton wrote in his reflections on the life of Saint Francis of Assisi: "It is the highest and holiest of the paradoxes that the man who really knows he cannot pay his debt will be forever paying it."[1] No person has ever lived that paradox as fully as the Saint of Assisi, whose vision of the world, its history, and his role in it was characterized by a consciousness of the loving God Who has bestowed on him "every good and perfect gift" (Ja 1:17). Saint Francis spent all his energies attempting to respond to the generosity of God and even as he was dying he exhorted his followers: "Let us begin, brothers, to serve the Lord our God for up to now we have made little or no progress."[2] He was a man overwhelmed by the goodness of a loving God. He was a mystic whose faith had so transformed his vision that he perceived that the entire world was redolent with the power, wisdom, and goodness of the Creator. He was a medieval Italian saint who from the earliest years of his spiritual awakening captured the attention and imagination of men and women of every age and every place. Biographies of Saint Francis of Assisi exist in almost every language and devotion to him crosses the barriers of all faiths.

Francis was born in the small Umbrian city of Assisi in the year 1181 or 1182 of Pietro di Bernardone, a wealthy textile merchant, and Pica, of a distinguished French family, probably from Picardy. His wealth and love of life made him the leader of Assisi's youth and filled him with dreams of grandeur. In the intercity feuding between Assisi and Perugia he enlisted, entered the battle of Collestrada, and was imprisoned when the troops of Assisi lost. After his release, he returned to Assisi and turned his back on a military career and a promising profession in the business world in order to respond to the impulses of the Lord that moved mysteriously within him. A meeting with a leper and hearing a voice from the cross of San Damiano re-

---

1. G. K. Chesterton, *Saint Francis of Assisi* (New York: George H. Doran Company, 1924), p. 117.
2. Cf. Thomas of Celano, *First Life*, n. 103, *Saint Francis of Assisi: Omnibus of Sources* (Chicago: Franciscan Herald Press, 1973), pp. 317–318. (Hereafter, referred to as *Omnibus of Sources*).

sulted in his conversion, the renunciation of his possessions, and a project of rebuilding churches.

On February 24, 1208, the feast of Saint Matthias, Francis was working in the little church of Santa Maria degli Angeli, the Portiuncula, and heard the missionary discourse of Matthew's Gospel. He responded immediately and embarked on the life of a poor, itinerant preacher proclaiming a message of penance and peace. Shortly afterward, his first followers joined him and formed a brotherhood dedicated to an intense living of the Gospel life. Within a short period of time, Francis and his brothers set out for Rome to have a simple rule—made up of Gospel texts and a few prescriptions helpful for their common life—approved by Pope Innocent III. This document was approved orally by the Pope. The biographers of the saint tell us that Francis also wrote a Gospel plan for sisters (the Poor Ladies of San Damiano), and another for men and women, single and married, who remained in their homes and among their daily secular concerns and strove to live an intense Christian life.

The Spirit of the Gospels impelled Francis to reactivate the Church's missionary activity. He attempted to go to Syria in 1212, but was shipwrecked in Dalmatia. A second journey, to Morocco, was thwarted by his illness in Spain (1213–1214). But in 1219, during the Fifth Crusade, Francis traveled to Damietta, where he tried in vain to convert the Sultan of Egypt, Malik-al-Kamil. During all of these years, however, Francis and his brothers and sisters witnessed and proclaimed the Gospel and became a strong force of renewal in the Church of Europe.

The life of the Poor Man of Assisi is characterized best by his total identification with the mysteries of Christ. On December 25, 1223, at Greccio, he further developed the dramatic presentations of the birth of Christ and brought the crib scene into popular spirituality. His biographers tell of his intense devotion to the mystery of the Eucharist, in which Francis saw the Lord of all creation assume poverty and humility each day so that all men and women might be reconciled with God and one another. The crucified Christ, however, absorbed the saint's attention to a great degree so that the last years of his life became caught up in the mystery of the Cross. On September 14, 1224, while Francis was immersed in a long period of prayer, he received the stigmata, which he carried until his death.

During the last years of his life he was blind and seriously ill. Yet this did not deter him from undertaking a series of preaching missions, ministering to the lepers, and relentlessly encouraging his brothers to give themselves to the ideals of the Gospel. Francis died at Santa Maria degli Angeli, the Portiuncula, on October 3, 1226. Less than two years later, on July 16, 1228, he was canonized by Pope Gregory IX. In 1939 he was proclaimed the patron of Italy and in 1980 he was proclaimed patron of ecology by Pope John Paul II.[3]

It may come as a surprise that so many biographies, whether medieval or modern, pass over almost entirely the writings and dictates of Saint Francis. His Rule, Testament, Canticle of Brother Sun, and, perhaps, his well-known story of true and perfect joy are the few excerpts that attract the consistent attention of historians. His actions often spoke louder than his words. He delighted in dramatizing his responses to the actions or thoughts of his brothers or the ideals to which his heart clung. Indeed, the heart of Franciscan spirituality seems to be caught up in the mystery of the human person of Francis and has been transmitted throughout history not only in his own biography but in the lives and stories of so many of his followers. The Poverello left no lengthy Rule or expositions on the spiritual life; he provided no plan for spiritual exercises or methods of prayer. It is simply the person of Francis of Assisi that captures the heart, so that the phrase of Cardinal Thomas of Capua (†1242) expresses most clearly the saint's position in the history of spirituality: the *Forma Minorum*, the pattern, the Form of the Minors.[4]

Yet to pass over the few writings that he personally composed or the others he dictated is to neglect his deepest thoughts on the Christian life, the relations he developed among his brothers, sisters, and other creatures that came from the hand of God, and the life of poverty and humility that enabled him to embrace the entire world. These few writings of the Saint of Assisi carry "spirit and life," as he himself described them in the words of John's Gospel (Jn 6:63).[5]

---

3. Innumerable biographies of Saint Francis exist. The *Omnibus of Sources* contains many, although not all, of the biographies written in the thirteenth and fourteenth centuries. It also contains a thorough bibliography of contemporary studies of the saint, the Franciscan Order, its history, spirituality, etc.

4. Cardinal Thomas of Capua, *Officium S. Francisci, Antiphonae ad Benedictus et Magnificat infra Octavam et pro Commemoratione S. Francisci, Analecta Franciscana X, Legendae S. Francisci Assisiensis Saeculis XIII et XIV conscriptae a patribus Collegii* (Quaracchi: Collegium S. Bonaventurae, 1926–1941), p. 387.

5. *The First Version of the Letter to the Faithful*, I, 21.

THE WRITINGS

One problem that faces the reader of any of the great mystics is that of language. Many great spiritual writers have struggled with expressions of the experience of God, particularly those that have come from their own interior lives, and have fallen back on the ineffable mystery that surrounds these moments. Language becomes for many mystics an impediment, a stumbling block, and, at best, only a tool that leads to the expectancy of an experience of God and not to the experience itself. This is particularly true of Saint Francis of Assisi. The style of his writings is extremely simple and utterly unobtrusive. No other mystic had so intense an encounter with God as that of the Poverello on Mount La Verna. He was marked with the signs of the stigmata and was left unable to speak of what he had experienced. Yet he gave to Brother Leo, his companion during those days on Mount La Verna, a precious relic that indicated the vision of God he enjoyed. "You are holy, Lord, the only God, You do wonders," it proclaims; "You are strong, You are great, You are the most high."[6] The words reveal an utterly simple vision. They never point to themselves but clearly and spontaneously direct our attention to God. The Poverello emerges through his writings as eager to have his readers move quickly beyond himself and his words to the reality of God. Thus his writings are deceptively simple, yet marvelously profound.

Saint Bonaventure mentions the elementary education Saint Francis received at the parochial school of San Giorgio.[7] More than likely, he received the basic rudiments of Latin in his early years. The Chronicle of Thomas of Eccleston, *The Coming of the Friars Minor to England*, VII, 28, comments on his very poor Latin and Francis's writings themselves show that he was no man of letters. He had little knowledge of the art of writing and of the rules of composition. Many sentences contain long and run-on phrases, clauses, and thoughts as well as poor grammatical construction. This sometimes prompts a question of the authenticity of a particular writing or the suggestion of a friar's attempting to reword it at a later date. The writings themselves and his early biographers suggest frequent dictation. The Testament, for example, confirms his use of dictation in the

---

6. *The Parchment Given to Brother Leo, Side One: Praises of God*, 1,2.
7. Bonaventure, *Life of Saint Francis*, XIV, 1, trans. Ewert Cousins, The Classics of Western Spirituality (New York: Paulist Press, 1978), p. 324.

way he describes the writing of the Rule: "And I had this written down simply and in a few words."[8] Throughout his biographies four secretaries appear: Leo of Assisi,[9] Caesar of Speyer,[10] Benedict of Pioraco,[11] and Bonizzo of Bologna.[12]

Twenty-eight writings have been firmly established as composed by Saint Francis. In addition to these, there are five dictated letters or blessings transmitted through the biographical tradition. For the most part his writings are short and without any great style. Many of them simply echo the teachings of the Church, particularly the Fourth Lateran Council, and the reflections that emerged from his gatherings with the brothers. Nonetheless, Francis considered the content of his writings to be important. He asked that certain of them be copied exactly, without any addition or subtraction, for example, the Testament. Others he wanted preserved and passed on not only to the friars but to all people, for example, the *Letters to the Clergy* and the *Letter to the Rulers of the Peoples*. He even promised special blessings for those who copied them, for example, the *Letters to the Faithful*, the *Letter to the Entire Order*, and the *Letter to the Clergy*.

Despite these wishes of Saint Francis, many of his writings have been lost: the letters to Cardinal Hugolino,[13] to Saint Clare,[14] to Saint Elizabeth of Hungary,[15] to a mother who desired a cure for her son.[16] Furthermore, the manuscript tradition—other than the two autographs—*The Parchment Given to Brother Leo* and the short *Letter to Brother Leo*—shows the failure of copiers to heed the saint's request to have his writings copied exactly. The critical editions published by Father Kajetan Esser in 1976 and 1978 present 1,028 variations in the manuscripts.[17]

Various approaches have been used to classify the writings of

---

8. *Testament*, 15.

9. Cf. *Legend of Perugia*, 113, *Omnibus of Sources*, p. 1087.

10. Cf. *Chronicle of Jordan of Giano*, 15, *Thirteenth Century Chronicles*, trans. Placid Hermann, O.F.M. (Chicago: Franciscan Herald Press, 1961), p. 30.

11. Cf. *Legend of Perugia*, 17, *Omnibus of Sources*, p. 993.

12. Cf. *Legend of Perugia*, 113, *Omnibus of Sources*, p. 1087.

13. Cf. Thomas of Celano, *First Life*, 100, *Omnibus of Sources*, p. 315.

14. Cf. *Testament of Saint Clare*, 10.

15. Cf. *Chronicle of Nicholas Glassberger*, *Analecta Franciscana*, II, 33.

16. Cf. Bartholomew of Pisa, *De Conformitate Vitae B. Francisci ad Vitam Domini Jesu*, *Analecta Franciscana*, V, 18.

17. Kajetan Esser, O.F.M., *Die Opuscula des Hl. Franziskus von Assisi* (Grottaferrata: Collegium S. Bonaventurae, 1976); and, *Opuscula Sancti Patris Francisci Assisiensis* (Grottaferrata: Collegium S. Bonaventurae, 1978).

Saint Francis. In many of the editions of this century, the threefold division of Father Leonard Lemmens is followed.[18] He classified the writings according to legislative works, spiritual advice, and expressions of prayer and praise. In 1940 John R. H. Moorman, later Bishop of Ripon, divided the writings into three categories: (1) those in which Saint Francis expresses himself freely and spontaneously, uninhibited by a sense of responsibility (e.g., the *Canticle of Brother Sun* and other prayers); (2) those urging some cause or conveying some particular message, and therefore written with a sense of responsibility (e.g., *Letters, Testament*); and (3) those in which Saint Francis is joined by those sharing control of the Order and who induced him to write things with which he did not agree (e.g., *The Earlier Rule* and *The Later Rule*).[19] These two ways of classifying the writings have their limitations. The first suggests preconceived notions concerning the importance of certain writings, and the second reflects some historical prejudice concering the development of the Order.

It is more profitable to examine the writings of Saint Francis in a chronological manner. This enables the reader to reflect on the personal and spiritual growth of the saint and his corresponding experience in the development of the Order. Furthermore, the chronological classification provides the advantage of seeing the writings set against the historical background of the Church, which, for example, was experiencing the tremendous impact of the Fourth Lateran Council, the "Great Council," as it has been called. This approach likewise has a weakness, because a number of the writings cannot be dated. The circumstances in which they were written have not been recorded nor are there any clues provided within the writings themselves (e.g., *The Salutation of the Virtues* and *The Salutation of the Blessed Virgin Mary*). Nonetheless, these undated writings may be examined profitably in a separate category, for they reveal the rich, simple, and timeless ideals of Saint Francis. Thus the following division is suggested:

---

18. [Leonard Lemmens, O.F.M., ed.], *Opuscula Sancti Patris Francisci Assisiensis*, Bibliotheca Franciscana Ascetica Medii Aevi, I (Quaracchi: Collegium S. Bonaventurae, 1904).

19. John R. H. Moorman, *The Sources for the Life of Saint Francis of Assisi* (Manchester, 1940).

INTRODUCTION

If a study of the writings of Saint Francis is undertaken in this manner, the simplicity of his vision, the tensions and difficulties of his life as the Order developed, and his journey into the mystical prayer of Mount La Verna come clearly into focus.

For the sake of order, however, the editors of this volume have chosen to follow the example of Father Esser, who presents the writings in a simple alphabetical manner. In this way, the writings are more easily accessible for reference and study.[20]

---

20. Kajetan Esser, O.F.M., in his *Opuscula Sancti Patris Francisci Assiensis*, pp. 37–43, lists the following texts attributed to Saint Francis as spurious or doubtful: (1) *Collatio: "Haec sunt arma"*: contained in the Wadding edition, but, in reality, a series of Patristic sayings. (2) *Collatio*: attributed to Saint Francis; more accurately attributed to Francesco Petrarch, Italian poet and humanist (1304–1374). (3) *Letter to Br. Agnellus of Pisa*: no convincing evidence to support this. (4) *Letter to Br. Bernard*: is found in S. Bonaventure, *Epistola continens viginti quinque memorialia*. (5) *Letter to Br. Elias*: no convincing evidence to support this. (6) *Letter to John of the House of Hanover*: found in only one place—*Annales Historiae illustrium principium Hanoniae*, by Br. James of Guyse (†1389). (7) *Letter to the Hermitages of Portu Vegla*: no convincing evidence. (8) *Prayer: Absorbeat*: taken from thoughts of authors known in the Middle Ages, reported by Ubertino da Casale, who does not confirm its authorship. (9) *Prayer Composed by Saint Francis*. (10) *Daily Prayer of Saint Francis*. (11) *Prayer in Sickness*: from the *Legenda major*, XIV, 2. (12) *Prayers with Five Our Fathers*. (13) *Prayer for obtaining Poverty*: from Ubertino da Casale. (14) *Another Prayer of Saint Francis*. (15) *Prayer: Holy Mother of God*: cannot be proven. (16) *Perfections Given to Brother Juniper*. (17) *Prologue over the Words of St. Francis*. (18) *Prophecy concerning the Order of Minors*. (19) *Rule of Brothers and Sisters of Penance*: in reality, the Rule of Pope Nicholas IV (1298). (20) *Sermon of Francis concerning the Eucharist*. (21) *Sermon of St. Francis to His Brothers*. (22) *Prophetic Words of St. Francis*. (23) *Psalter attributed to St. Francis*. (24) *Prayer: Make Me an Instrument of Your Peace*: can only be found in twentieth-century sources and erroneously attributed to Saint Francis.

II The Spiritual Theology

The words of Saint Paul's First Letter to the Corinthians provide an excellent background against which to reflect on the writings of Saint Francis:

> These are the very things that God has revealed to us through the Spirit, for the Spirit reaches the depths of everything, even the depths of God. After all, the depths of a man can only be known by his own spirit, not by any other man, and in the same way the depths of God can only be known by the Spirit of God. Now instead of the spirit of the world, we have received the Spirit that comes from God, to teach us to understand the gifts that he has given us. Therefore, we teach, not in the way in which philosophy is taught, but in the way that the Spirit teaches us: We teach spiritual things spiritually.[21]

In much the same way, Saint Francis teaches "spiritual things spiritually," that is, according to the ways of the Spirit. The very heart of his view of life seems to be summarized best in *The Later Rule*, X, 8, in which the saint encourages his followers to pursue "what they must desire above all things: to have the Spirit of the Lord and His holy manner of working." Throughout his writings Saint Francis teaches the transparent, inconspicuous, and unassuming ways of the Holy Spirit, and this teaching is expressed through the saint's concern for God his Father, Jesus his Lord and Brother, his fellow human beings, and the marvels of God's creation. He already begins to cultivate an atmosphere or environment in which the "school" of Franciscan theology of the spiritual life develops and focuses on that love, the medium of the Holy Spirit, which teaches us "to understand the gifts that he has given us" (1 Cor 2:12).

Many commentaries on the writings of Saint Francis have overlooked this aspect because of a weak pneumatology. In this "privi-

---

21. 1 Cor 2:10–13.

11

leged moment of the Holy Spirit," as Pope Paul VI described our age,[22] the rich heritage of Saint Francis is entering a new phase of interpretation. The very use of the word "spirit" is seen best in the Pauline sense, which is, in fact, a Hebraic sense expressing the Spirit of Yahweh overwhelming the spirit of the human person. Thus Francis, like Paul, slips inadvertently from references to the Spirit of God to the spirit of the human person. He perceives the dignity of the human personality, which could become the transparent expression of the divine presence. The many activities of the spiritual life, as Francis describes them, are simply expressions of the Holy Spirit: the spirit of loving obedience, of prayer and devotion, of peace. Thomas of Celano provides an insight into this understanding of the Spirit's activity when he reports that the saint considered the Holy Spirit to be the true Minister General of the Order. "He wanted this thought inserted into his rule," Celano writes, "but since it was already approved by papal bull, this could not be done."[23] The point could not be expressed more clearly, however, as articulating the prominent role of the Holy Spirit in the understanding of the Franciscan life.

A TRINITARIAN LIFE

A superficial glance at one of the earliest writings, *The Form of Life Given to Saint Clare and Her Sisters,* shows the awesome activity of the Holy Spirit drawing us into a relationship with the Triune God. Variations on this same theme can be seen throughout the writings: the vocation to be a child and servant of the heavenly Father, Whose will must always be sought; a brother or sister and spouse of Jesus Christ, Whose life must be imitated through the pursuit of Gospel perfection; a pure dwelling place and vehicle of the Holy Spirit, Whose activity merits careful attention. Francis presents this profound vision of the Christian life to all his followers, his brothers and sisters in religious life, all the faithful, and to all nonbelievers.

Traditionally, Franciscan spiritual writers have identified the approach of Saint Francis as Christocentric. In this Francis was no different from other Christians. What is unique in his writings, however,

---

22. Pope Paul VI, *Evangelii Nuntiandi* 75 (Washington: United States Catholic Conference, 1976), p. 56.
23. Thomas of Celano, *Second Life*, 193, *Omnibus of Sources*, p. 517.

is his intuition of the penetrating character of the Trinitarian life in the daily living of Christian faith. The dramatic declaration to his father before the crowd of Assisi: "From now on I can freely say 'Our Father Who art in heaven,' not father Peter Bernardone ..."[24] seemed to establish the sense of his identity as a son of a loving Father. Hence his entire life became a struggle to conform his life to that of the Son Who revealed Himself in the Gospel. The continuous invocation "Father" echoes throughout all of the writings, most particularly in *The Office of the Passion* and in his written prayers. His words to his brothers in *The Earlier Rule*, XXII, possibly written before his departure to the Near East where he hoped to embrace martyrdom in imitation of Jesus, express this simple drive of his life: "And now that we have left the world, we have nothing else to do except to follow the will of the Lord and to please Him."[25] The life of Saint Francis as seen through his writings is one of maintaining a relationship with his Father, of seeking always to do His will, and of making his way to Him after the model of His son. No better expression of his Trinitarian life can be found than in the prayer at the conclusion of the *Letter to the Entire Order:*

Almighty, eternal, just and merciful God,
grant us in our misery [the grace]
to do for You alone
what we know You want us to do
and always
to desire what pleases You.
Thus,
inwardly cleansed,
interiorly enlightened,
and inflamed by the fire of the Holy Spirit,
may we be able to follow
in the footprints of Your beloved Son,
our Lord Jesus Christ.
And,
by Your grace alone,
may we make our way to You,

---

24. Thomas of Celano, *Second Life*, 12, *Omnibus of Sources*, p. 372.
25. *The Earlier Rule*, XXII, 9.

Most High,
Who live and rule
in perfect Trinity and simple Unity,
and are glorified,
God all-powerful,
forever and ever.
Amen.[26]

The words "by Your grace alone" are significant in understanding the dynamism of the Holy Spirit, which was behind the drive, the unquenchable desire of Francis to be Christ-like. It was the Spirit of a son always eager to please his Father and always receptive to the gifts the Father would give.

Once again there is a Pauline expression of pneumatology in the writings as we examine his frequent use of the phrase "the Spirit of the Lord." In his *Opuscula* Father Esser identifies this as a passage taken from Isaiah 11:2, the passage that Jesus claims as His own in Luke's Gospel (4:16–22).[27] In Paul's epistles, however, there is a clear identification established between the Lord and the Spirit as 2 Corinthians 3:17 indicates: "Now this Lord is the Spirit, and where the Spirit of the Lord is, there is freedom." The Pauline understanding expresses the Spirit of the Lord Jesus Christ, the Spirit of the Son, which is the Spirit of adopted sons enabling us to exclaim "Abba, Father!" It is never "our" Spirit as "Our Father" or "Our Savior," but the Spirit that possesses us and focuses our attention on Jesus the Lord Who is the Revelation of God. This is the understanding Francis manifests in his writings as he repeatedly refers to the Spirit of the Lord and to His evident Christological activities. The *First Admonition* is an excellent example of the profound Christological thoughts of Saint Francis that must be understood through the medium of the Holy Spirit. This short work expresses the totally Spirit-filled person who comes to us through his writings. Furthermore, this Admonition provides us with another dimension of the divine impulses that directed his life.

---

26. A *Letter to the Entire Order*, 50–52.
27. *The First Version of the Letter to the Faithful*, I, 6; *The Second Version of the Letter to the Faithful*, 48.

14

INTRODUCTION

AN ECCLESIAL LIFE

The *First Admonition* leads the reader beyond the mystery of the Incarnate Word of God to the continuing presence of Christ in the Eucharist. Thus there is a sense of the Church in the writings of Francis, which is rooted in his discovery of the Word of God in the Church. The biographers tell us of the simple prayer Francis taught his followers, which also has been transmitted to us through the Testament: "We adore You, Lord Jesus Christ, in all your churches throughout the world, and we bless You, for through Your holy cross You have redeemed the world."[28] This simple prayer expresses the deep faith in the Church that the saint always exhibited.

Many contemporary biographers portray Francis as a man at odds with an institutional Church that stifled his enthusiasm and delivered a death blow to his vision.[29] His writings, however, present a different picture as they portray him eager to respond to the legislation of the Fourth Lateran Council. In a postconciliar era, Francis enthusiastically embraced the disciplinary and liturgical renewal that Honorius III encouraged, and he promoted the missionary outreach to the Saracens that was initiated by the Council.[30] The letters that flow from his own Eucharistic Crusade show his deep love and respect for priests and theologians. Few authors of medieval spirituality have ever written as magnificent an encomium of the priesthood as Francis did in the *Letter to the Entire Order*: "Look at your dignity, you brothers [who are] priests, and be holy since He is holy ... hold back nothing of yourselves for yourselves, so that He Who gives Himself totally to you may receive you totally."[31] These praises of the priesthood become more inspiring when seen in the context of a clergy that undoubtedly had difficulty understanding Francis and his itinerant brothers. The writings hint at possible misunderstanding, rejection, and persecution by the clergy. Yet Francis is insistent on showing respect and devotion to those who minister God's word and sacrament to him.

---

28. *The Testament*, 5.
29. Cf. John Holland Smith, *Francis of Assisi* (New York: Scribner & Sons, 1972), pp. 144, 147, 176; Paul Sabatier, *St. Francis of Assisi*, trans. L. Houghton (New York: Scribner & Sons, 1919), pp. 253–254.
30. Cf. *The Earlier Rule*, XVI, n. 1.
31. *A Letter to the Entire Order*, 23–29.

In his deep love for the Church, Francis became a reformer in the fullest sense of the word. He embraced the foundations of the ecclesial tradition and built his own life firmly on them. The desire that his followers do the same is expressed in so many different ways: the desire that all candidates be examined in the teachings of the Catholic faith and the sacraments, the injunction given to his brothers to think and act as Catholics, and the simple command given to the faithful to be Catholic.[32] Julian of Speyer, in composing the liturgical office for his feast, called Francis "a catholic and totally apostolic man."[33] This is certainly the man that emerges through a study of his writings.

A magnificent insight into his love for the Church can be discovered in a simple phrase of *The Salutation of the Blessed Virgin Mary*. Amid the litany of praises that he articulates for Mary, the Mother of God, Francis extols her who is "the virgin made church."[34] In light of Saint Bonaventure's description of the saint's discovery of the Gospel life in the Portiuncula, where "he prayed to her who had conceived the Word full of grace and truth,"[35] the close relationship existing between the Mother of God and the Church is important to note for an understanding of the spiritual theology of the Poverello. Francis places before his brother, sisters, and all the faithful the concept of becoming "a spouse of the Holy Spirit," thus evoking the maternal aspect of the Gospel life.[36] The themes of conception and birth permeate his writings, particularly in the consciousness of the relationships Francis perceives his followers developing toward one another. There is a profound Marian foundation in the thought of the saint of Assisi, on which he built the life of the Order as well as his personal life of prayer. Francis's view suggests the Mother of God as the model of his spiritual growth, and in his devotion to her the Poverello seems to have intuited the teaching of the Second Vatican Council, in which Mary is presented as the Mother and the Model of the Church. The repeated references to the "dwelling-place," the "tabernacle," the "chosen and consecrated one" who conceived and brought Christ into

---

32. *The Second Version of the Letter to the Faithful*, 32.

33. Julian of Speyer, *Officium S. Francisci, Ad I Vesperas, Antiphonae, Analecta Franciscana*, X, p. 375.

34. *Salutation of the Blessed Virgin Mary*, 1.

35. Bonaventure, *Life of Saint Francis*, III, 1, p. 199.

36. *Office of the Passion*, Compline, Antiphon, 2; *Form of Life Given to Saint Clare and Her Sisters*, 1; *The First Version of the Letter to the Faithful*, I, 7; *The Second Version of the Letter to the Faithful*, 50.

the world, can be seen on two levels in the writings of Francis: the Marian and the ecclesial.

A FRATERNAL LIFE

The Marian and the ecclesial life, so profoundly Trinitarian, was conceived and brought to birth in his own life. He spoke the Word he had conceived and in his dynamic proclamation of the Gospel, the saint received brothers. "The Lord gave me brothers," Francis writes in his Testament, ". . . the Most High Himself revealed to me that I should live according to the form of the Holy Gospel."[37] In the *First Life* of Saint Francis, Thomas of Celano writes of the coming of his first brother, Bernard of Quintavalle: "Saint Francis rejoiced with very great joy over the coming and conversion of so great a man, in that the Lord was seen to have a care for him by giving him a needed companion and a faithful friend."[38] Francis's writings suggest that he understood the gift of brothers as more than simply supportive instruments of the Lord. They were both necessary conditions and necessary expressions of the Gospel life, which demands witness to the Community of God's Love, that is, the Trinity. In order to bring to birth the "spirit of the truth of the Gospel," he needed brothers "according to the Spirit."

Only in this context can the Gospel Life of the Rule of the Friars Minor be understood. *The Earlier Rule* begins quite simply: "This is the life of the Gospel of Jesus Christ."[39] The study of both Rules shows the profound Gospel thought that directs the way the brothers are to live and their behavior and attitude toward each other. Francis rarely uses the abstract term "fraternity." He consistently speaks of his "brothers." His immediate concern is always his brother, the person who is with him and whom the Lord has given to him. His disposition toward any given brother is always characterized by the teaching and example of Christ. Even when he confronts a brother who has sinned, Francis identifies himself with Christ, Who laid down His life for His brothers.[40]

This aspect of Francis's writings becomes more meaningful

---

37. *The Testament*, 14.
38. Thomas of Celano, *First Life*, 24, *Omnibus of Sources*, p. 249.
39. *The Earlier Rule*, Prologue, 2.
40. Cf. *A Letter to a Minister*, 2–8.

when we sense the vision of Christ "who had nowhere to lay his head." Francis's brotherhood was not determined by place, ministry, or nationality. It was a reality determined by the deeper, more penetrating principle of the Holy Spirit. In both Rules Francis expresses a sensitivity to the "itinerant" aspect of a brother's life. The brothers were, indeed, in the world, on the road, and traveling about in order to proclaim the Gospel.[41] Therefore, brotherhood had to be expressed in whatever place they found themselves and intensified through a loving obedience in which the minister and subject were eager to pray with, visit, and serve one another. It is difficult to lose sight of this dynamism of the Gospel brotherhood in the writings of Saint Francis. Yet it is consoling to notice tensions and struggles in expressing the ideal in everyday life. Sin was a reality that Francis saw as an enervating factor in the relationships of the brothers. This destructive force so sapped the vitality of the Spirit of the Lord that a sadness touches the writings of the joyful saint as he deals with the brothers who sin. No more beautiful expression of this consciousness can be found than in the *Letter to a Minister*. The active dynamism of the Spirit once again expresses itself as Saint Francis encourages the ministers to love the sinful brother unconditionally so that he may be drawn to God.

The purity of the Spirit of Love, then, becomes the magnetic force characterizing Francis's vision of the relationships that unite his brothers. As a result of his striving for the purity of expression of that love, the Spirit expanded Francis's relationships with all men and women. The writings embrace men and women from every level of society: his brothers, Saint Clare and her sisters, those with whom he shared a special relationship (the Third Order penitents), the rulers of the people, the clergy. *The Earlier Rule*, XXIII, breaks into an open invitation for everyone to join Francis in proclaiming the marvels of God and expresses that enthusiasm of the Poverello which attracts so many to him.[42] But the poor, the down-trodden, the ever-present lepers of society, hold a special place in his writings. In the early stages

---

41. This is an interesting theme to trace through the writings of Saint Francis. Cf. "pilgrim and stranger," "wherever they may be," etc., as Damien Isabell, O.F.M., suggests in his *Workbook for the Omnibus of Sources* (Chicago: Franciscan Herald Press, 1975), pp. 218–219.

42. *The Earlier Rule*, XXIII, 7.

of his conversion he "went to the lepers and lived with them serving them most diligently for God's sake."[43] This had such an impact on his spiritual vision that in any poor or sick person Francis could see only Christ, "whose noble image he wears, the image of him who made himself poor for us in this world."[44] This consciousness permeated his thought and affection, and he is prompted to tell his brothers that "they must rejoice when they live among people [who are considered to be] of little worth and who are looked down upon, among the poor and the powerless, the sick and the lepers, and the beggars by the wayside."[45] Those who are closest to the earth, the poor and the simple who are dependent on the goodness and generosity of God, teach Francis the true meaning of life. It is this intense identification with their condition that enables him to look on all creatures in a new way. He sees in his relationship to them the all-embracing expression of his relationship to the Spirit. The Spirit universalizes his brotherhood, which embraces not only the friars, the sisters, the clergy, and all the people but also the sun, the moon, the stars, and the elements. He embraces them with the same enthusiasm of affection and love with which he embraces his own brothers and sisters.

In his enthusiasm Francis bursts into song with *The Canticle of Brother Sun,* in which he expresses the profound nature of man. Here he reveals himself as the mystical saint of all ages who penetrates the depths of reality. It is this work that enjoys the largest amount of commentary and has captured the universal appeal of the Poverello. Yet the mystical vision of the work has been understood only sporadically. It takes another mystic, Saint Bonaventure, to capture its truest meaning:

> Aroused by all things to the love of God,
> he rejoiced in all the works of the Lord's hands
> and from these joy-producing manifestations
> he rose to their life-giving
> principle and cause.
> In beautiful things
> he saw Beauty itself

---

43. Thomas of Celano, *First Life,* 17, *Omnibus of Sources,* p. 243.
44. Thomas of Celano, *First Life,* 76, *Omnibus of Sources,* p. 292.
45. *The Earlier Rule,* IX, 2.

and through his vestiges imprinted on creation
he followed his Beloved everywhere,
making from all things a ladder
by which he could climb up
and embrace him who is utterly desirable.[46]

Understood in this light, a deeper meaning of *The Canticle of Brother Sun* surfaces through a careful study of the adjectives used to describe each element of creation. What emerges is a magnificent view of creation (sun, moon, air, fire, etc.,) as an expression of the Trinity, the Most Beautiful, as it is realized in the Church and in the Virgin Mary who receives the fullness of life.[47] Included in the underlying meaning of this great song of praise is Francis's understanding of the human person living in this world. There emerges, through the various adjectives he uses, a description of the Christ-like attitudes that must be assumed before the human person can achieve the blessedness of this mystical vision.[48] In awe before creatures, Francis experiences the intimacy of the Most High and thus his life becomes a passing over, a *transitus*, from the awesome beauty of this world to "Beauty itself." His death is the culmination of that journey and his most radical embrace of what it is to be a creature among creatures: "Praised be You, my Lord, through our Sister Bodily Death, from whom no living man can escape."[49] Death is welcomed as his final created experience of a living sister. It is the way Saint Francis completes his conversion to "serve him with great humility."[50]

46. Bonaventure, *Life of Saint Francis*, IX, 1, trans. Cousins, p. 263.

47. Cf. The recent study of Eloi Leclerc, O.F.M., *The Canticle of Creatures: Symbols of Union*, trans. Matthew J. O'Connell (Chicago: Franciscan Herald Press, 1977).

48. *Canticle of Brother Sun*, 10–11.

49. *Canticle of Brother Sun*, 12.

50. *Canticle of Brother Sun*, 14.

Conclusion

Saint Francis's desire to serve in humility, even in the passing over of his own death, provides the key to understanding the Poverello. His relationship to God, to the Church, to his brothers and sisters, and to all the elements of creation is a relationship of service. *The Admonitions* develop the aspect of what it means to be a servant of God. Francis teaches that service is the way of undoing the sin of Adam, and it is the "holy manner of working" that is the Spirit of the Lord. The Spirit of the Lord always points toward the other, and thus the Spirit-filled person is the true servant. Therein is the poverty and humility of Saint Francis of Assisi.

As a servant of God, entrusted with the Lord's gifts, Francis gives what he has received.[51] The Word he has conceived in the inspiration of the Spirit is proclaimed in his life and deeds. This is his greatest gift. This work of the Spirit in him identifies him with the suffering and crucified Christ, who breathes forth the Spirit. In the total context of his writings, one can perceive Francis, the servant of God marked with the wounds of the Crucified Christ, breathing forth the Spirit that dwells within him. Francis is on the cross in naked embrace. *The First Admonition* develops this continuing identity with Francis and the Incarnate Word in his relationship to the Eucharist, which the Spirit of the Lord dwelling within him continues to receive.

This then is the paradox of the life of Saint Francis. In his total embrace of poverty he is a son and servant of God. He is marked in his identity with the Word of God made flesh, and he is filled with the Holy Spirit. This is his "portion, which leads into the land of the living,"[52] and in this he articulates the fullest, richest call of the human person. It is not, then, Saint Francis of Assisi the medieval Italian mystic who appeals to the world so much as it is the Holy Spirit of the Lord, which penetrated his personality so totally, and continues to inspire every generation with "his holy manner of working" for all the ages yet to come.

---

51. The image of the servant of God is prominent throughout the Admonitions.
52. *The Later Rule*, VI, 5.

Francis of Assisi

THE WRITINGS

The Admonitions

All of the manuscripts of the thirteenth century contain these twenty-eight admonitions and thus indicate their importance in the early Franciscan tradition. The biographers, especially the Anonymous of Perugia, describe the practice of Saint Francis in "giving admonitions, reprimands, or directives, as he thought best, after he had consulted the Lord" (Anonymous of Perugia, 37). These statements were considered so important, Thomas of Celano indicates, that the saint wanted them written down and kept exactly as he had dictated them (cf. First Life, 82). Moreover, two fourteenth-century commentators on the Franciscan spiritual life, Angelo Clareno and Bartholomew of Pisa, underscore the importance of the Admonitions in providing Saint Francis's doctrine on the spiritual life.

It is difficult to determine the circumstances and dates of their composition, but it is likely that they were delivered at the gatherings or chapters of the primitive fraternity in which Saint Francis was accustomed to deliver spiritual exhortations or admonitions (Cf. Thomas of Celano, Second Life, 145, 191).

In an introductory note to the Admonitions in the Opuscula Sancti Patris Francisci Assiensis, *Kajetan Esser, O.F.M., writes: "In these [twenty-eight Admonitions] precious pearls of spiritual wisdom may be discovered which are extremely valuable for Franciscan asceticism and the life of a friar minor." The Franciscan scholar was echoing the thoughts of authors throughout the centuries who saw these short statements as "The Franciscan Sermon on the Mount," "a Mirror of Perfection," or "a precious series of spiritual counsels on the religious life."*

I THE BODY OF CHRIST

1. The Lord Jesus says to His disciples: *I am the way, the truth and the life; no one comes to the Father except through me. 2. If you had known me, you would also have known my Father; and from now on you will know him and have seen him. 3. Philip says to him: Lord, show us the Father and it is enough for us. Jesus says to him: 4. Have I been with you for so long a time and you have not known me? Philip, whoever sees me, sees also my Father* (Jn

14:6–9). 5. *The Father lives in inaccessible light* (cf. 1 Tim 6:16), and *God is Spirit* (Jn 4:24) and, *No one has ever seen God* (Jn 1:18). 6. Therefore He cannot be seen except in the Spirit since *it is the Spirit that gives life; the flesh does not offer anything* (Jn 6:64). 7. But neither, inasmuch as He is equal to the Father, is the Son seen by anyone other than the Father [or] other than the Holy Spirit.

8. Therefore all those who saw the Lord Jesus according to [His] humanity and did not see and believe according to the Spirit and the Godhead that He is the true Son of God were condemned. 9. And now in the same way, all those who see the sacrament [of the Body of Christ], which is sanctified by the words of the Lord upon the altar at the hands of the priest in the form of bread and wine, and who do not see and believe according to the Spirit and the Godhead that it is truly the most holy Body and Blood of our Lord Jesus Christ, are condemned. 10. [This] is attested by the Most High Himself Who says: *This is my Body and the Blood of my new testament [which will be poured out for many]* (cf. Mk 14:22, 24) 11. and *He who eats my flesh and drinks my blood has eternal life* (cf. Jn 6:55). 12. Therefore it is the Spirit of the Lord,[1] Who lives in His faithful, Who receives the most holy Body and Blood of the Lord. 13. All others who do not share in this same Spirit and who presume to receive Him eat and drink judgment to themselves (cf. 1 Cor 11:29).

14. Therefore, *O sons of men, how long will you be hard of heart?* (Ps 4:3) 15. Why do you not recognize the truth and believe in the Son of God? (cf. Jn 9:35) 16. See,[2] daily He humbles Himself (cf. Phil 2:8) as when He came from *the royal throne* (Wis 18:15) into the womb of the Virgin; 17. daily He comes to us in a humble form; 18. daily He comes

---

1. Saint Francis frequently uses the title "Spirit of the Lord" to refer to the Third Person of the Trinity. This qualification reflects a Pauline pneumatology in which the Holy Spirit is described as "the Spirit of Christ" (Rm 8:9), "the Spirit of His Son" (Gal 4:6), and "the Spirit of Jesus Christ" (Phil 1:19). Since the saint perceives the Spirit of the Lord as the dynamic principle of the life of the friars (cf. *Later Rule*, X, 8) it is helpful to understand the Christological implications of these passages.

2. These lines suggest an awareness of Cistercian spirituality, possibly due to the presence of Cardinal Rainerio Cappocci, a Cistercian who was the papal prefect of Umbria. He was present at the Chapter of 1221 (cf. Jordan of Giano, *Chronicle* 16; *Thirteenth Century Chronicles* [Chicago: Franciscan Herald Press, 1961], p. 31). He also preached at the canonization of Saint Francis (cf. Thomas of Celano, *First Life of Saint Francis*, 125). In this instance, the Cistercian text is Pseudo-Bernard, *Tractatus de Corpore Domini* (PL 184:1149–1150).

down from the bosom of the Father (cf. Jn 1:18) upon the altar in the hands of the priest. 19. And as He appeared to the holy apostles in true flesh, so now He reveals Himself to us in the sacred bread. 20. And as they saw only His flesh by means of their bodily sight, yet believed Him to be God as they contemplated Him with the eyes of faith, 21. so, as we see bread and wine with [our] bodily eyes, we too are to see and firmly believe them to be His most holy Body and Blood living and true. 22. And in this way the Lord is always with His faithful, as He Himself says: *Behold I am with you even to the end of the world* (cf. Mt 28:20).[3]

II THE EVIL OF SELF-WILL

1. The Lord said to Adam: Eat of every tree; do not eat of the tree of the knowledge of good and evil (cf. Gen 2:16–17). 2. He was able to eat of every tree of paradise since he did not sin as long as he did not go against obedience. 3. For the person eats of the tree of the knowledge of good who appropriates to himself his own will and thus exalts himself over the good things which the Lord says and does in him;[4] 4. and thus, through the suggestion of the devil and the transgression of the command, what he eats becomes for him the fruit of the knowledge of evil. 5. Therefore it is necessary that he bear the punishment.

III PERFECT OBEDIENCE

1. The Lord says in the Gospel: *He who does not renounce everything he possesses cannot be my disciple* (Lk 14:33); 2. and: *He who wishes to save his life must lose it* (Lk 9:24). 3. That person leaves everything he

---

3. For further insights into this text, consult Oktavian Schmucki, O.F.M. Cap., "Doctrina et Pietas Eucharistica S. Francisci Assisiensis Lumine Primi Verbi Admonitionis Ipsius," *Analecta Ordinis Fratrum Minorum Capuccinorum* 93 (1977): 28–39. For the Eucharistic devotion of Saint Francis, consult B. Cornet, O.F.M., "Le 'De Reverentia Corporis Domini,' Exhortation et Lettre de S. François," *Etudes Franciscaines* 6 (1955): 65–91, 167–180; 7 (1956): 20–35, 155–171; 8 (1957): 35–58; also, E. Franceschini, "L'Eucharistia negli scritti di San Francesco," *L'Eucharistia nella spiritualità francescana* (Quaderni di spiritualità francescana 3), Santa Maria degli Angeli-Assisi (1962): 38–49.

4. A key to understanding Saint Francis's view of the sinfulness of the human person can be found in this concept of appropriation; hence his poverty as the means of undoing sin.

possesses and loses his body who surrenders his whole self to obedience at the hands of his prelate.[5] 4. And whatever he does and says which he knows is not contrary to his [prelate's] will, provided that what he does is good, is true obedience. 5. And should the subject sometimes see that some things might be better and more useful for his soul than what the prelate may command him, let him willingly offer such things to God as a sacrifice; and instead earnestly try to fulfill the wishes of the prelate. 6. For this is loving obedience because it pleases God and neighbor.

7. But if the prelate should command something contrary to his conscience, although [the subject] does not obey him, still he should not abandon him. 8. And if in consequence he suffers persecution from others, let him love them even more for [the love of] God. 9. For whoever chooses to endure persecution rather than be separated from his brothers truly remains in perfect obedience for he lays down *his life* (Jn 15:13) for his brothers. 10. There are indeed many religious who, under the pretext of seeking something better than what the prelate commands, look back (cf. Lk 9:62) and *return to the vomit* of their own will (cf. Prov 26:11; 2 Pet 2:22); 11. these are murderers who cause many souls to perish by reason of their bad example.

IV LET NO ONE APPROPRIATE TO HIMSELF THE ROLE OF BEING OVER OTHERS

1. *I did not come to be served but to serve* (cf. Mt 10:28), says the Lord. 2. Those who are placed over others should glory in such an office only as much as they would were they assigned the task of washing the feet of the brothers. 3. And the more they are upset about their office being taken from them than they would be over the loss of the office of [washing] feet, so much the more do they store up treasures to the peril of their souls (cf. Jn 12:6).

---

5. The Latin word *praelatus* is used frequently by Saint Francis in speaking of the friar who is a "superior." It should be noted that nowhere is the word "superior" used to describe a position of responsibility or authority; "minister" and "servant" are used in general terms to describe this office. In a chronological examination of the writings of Saint Francis, a variety of terms emerge: Minister General, Minister Provincial, Custodian, and Guardian.

V NO ONE SHOULD BOAST IN HIMSELF BUT RATHER GLORY IN THE CROSS OF THE LORD

1. Be conscious, O man, of the wondrous state in which the Lord God has placed you, for He created you and formed you to the image of His beloved Son according to the body, and to His likeness according to the spirit (cf. Gen 1:26). 2. And [yet] all the creatures under heaven, each according to its nature, serve, know, and obey their Creator better than you. 3. And even the demons did not crucify Him, but you together with them have crucified Him and crucify Him even now by delighting in vices and sins.

4. In what then can you glory? 5. For if you were so subtle and wise that you had all knowledge (cf. 1 Cor 13:2) and knew how to interpret all tongues (cf. 1 Cor 12:28) and minutely investigate [the course of] the heavenly bodies, in all these things you could not glory, 6. for one demon knew more about the things of earth than all men together, even if there may have been someone who received from the Lord a special knowledge of the highest wisdom. 7. Likewise, even if you were more handsome and richer than everyone else and even if you performed wonders such as driving out demons, all these things would be an obstacle to you and none of them would belong to you nor could you glory in any of these things. 8. But in this we can glory: in our infirmities (cf. 2 Cor 12:5) and bearing daily the holy cross of our Lord Jesus Christ (cf. Lk 14:27).

VI THE IMITATION OF THE LORD

1. Let all of us, brothers, look to the Good Shepherd Who suffered the passion of the cross to save His sheep. 2. The sheep of the Lord followed Him in tribulation and persecution, in insult and hunger, in infirmity and temptation, and in everything else, and they have received everlasting life from the Lord because of these things. 3. Therefore, it is a great shame for us, servants of God, that while the saints [actually] did such things, we wish to receive glory and honor by [merely] recounting their deeds.[6]

---

6. This Admonition reflects the Cistercian tradition. The theology contained here is that of Godfrey the Abbot, *Declarationes ex S. Bernardi Sermonibus* 65 (PL 184:446C–471D) and Blessed Roger the Abbot, *De Sermone Domini in Ultima Cena, Sermo* I (PL 184, 882D).

VII   GOOD WORKS MUST FOLLOW KNOWLEDGE

1. The Apostle says: *The letter kills, but the spirit gives life* (2 Cor 3:6). 2. Those are killed by the letter who merely wish to know the words alone, so that they may be esteemed as wiser than others and be able to acquire great riches to give to [their] relatives and friends. 3. In a similar way, those religious are killed by the letter who do not wish to follow the spirit of Sacred Scripture, but only wish to know [what] the words [are] and [how to] interpret them to others. 4. And those are given life by the spirit of Sacred Scripture who do not refer to themselves any text which they know or seek to know, but, by word and example, return everything to the most high Lord God to Whom every good belongs.[7]

VIII   THE AVOIDANCE OF THE SIN OF ENVY

1. The Apostle says: *No one can say "Jesus is Lord" except in the Holy Spirit* (1 Cor 12:3); 2. and: *There is no one who does good, not even one* (Rm 3:12). 3. Therefore, whoever envies his brother the good which the Lord says or does in him commits a sin of blasphemy, because he envies the Most High Who says and does every good (cf. Mt 20:15).

IX   TRUE LOVE

1. The Lord says: *Love your enemies [do good to those who hate you, and pray for those who persecute and blame you]* (Mt 5:44). 2. That person truly loves his enemy who is not upset at any injury which is done to himself, 3. but out of love of God is disturbed at the sin of the other's soul. 4. And let him show his love for the other by his deeds.

X   THE CHASTISEMENT OF THE BODY

1. Many people, when they sin or receive an injury, often blame the Enemy or some neighbor. 2. But this is not right, for each one has the [real] enemy in his own power; that is, the body through which he sins. 3. Therefore *blessed is that servant* (Mt 24:46) who, having such an

---

7. Saint Francis uses the phrase "spirit of the divine letter," which the editors have translated "spirit of Sacred Scripture," in an attempt to contrast the literal interpretation of Scripture with the spiritual.

enemy in his power, will always hold him captive and wisely guard himself against him, because as long as he does this, no other enemy, seen or unseen, will be able to harm him.[8]

XI NO ONE SHOULD BE CORRUPTED BY THE EVIL OF ANOTHER

1. Nothing should upset the servant of God except sin. 2. And no matter how another person may sin, if the servant of God lets himself become angry and disturbed because of this, [and] not because of love, he stores up the guilt for himself (cf. Rm 2:5). 3. That servant of God who does not become angry or upset at anything lives justly and without anything of his own.[9] 4. And he is blessed who does not keep anything for himself, rendering *to Caesar what is Caesar's, and to God what is God's* (Mt 22:21).

XII HOW TO DISCERN WHETHER ONE HAS THE SPIRIT OF THE LORD

1. A servant of God may be recognized as possessing the Spirit of the Lord in this way:[10] 2. if the flesh does not pride itself when the Lord performs some good through him—since the flesh is always opposed to every good; 3. rather he considers himself the more worthless in his own eyes and esteems himself less than all others.

---

8. This Admonition inaugurates the study of "the Servant of God," which becomes the focus of the remaining texts. Kajetan Esser, O.F.M., indicates the Biblical source of the text as Matthew 24:45, 46. The image may be extended to embrace the Isaian passages that refer to the Suffering Servant on whom the Spirit rests (Is 11:1–5; 61:1–3). The servant of God is seen as one who identifies closely with Christ and is the ideal Christian in Saint Augustine's *City of God.* In the twelfth-century manuscripts of the *Augustinian Rule,* the title is used frequently to describe the religious. Cf. L. Verheijn, *La Regle de saint Augustin,* 2 vols. (Paris, 1967). Saint Francis uses the term nineteen times in the Admonitions to describe (a) the criteria of a true friar and (b) the beatitudes that form his life.

9. The Latin phrase *sine proprio* used in this passage is the same as that found in the formula of the three vows. It was used as a technical form to describe the vow of poverty. Yet Saint Francis extends its meaning, as this text indicates, and implies that poverty is much more than a material concern. As the doctrine of a life "without anything of one's own" unfolds in the Admonitions, poverty touches on poverty in relationship to (a) one's brothers, (b) one's inner self, and (c) God.

10. Once more the Pauline influence on the writings of Saint Francis can be seen. The Admonition reflects the flesh-spirit tension that pervades the Pauline epistles, especially Romans.

XIII PATIENCE

1. *Blessed are the peacemakers for they shall be called the children of God* (Mt 5:9). The servant of God cannot know how much patience and humility he has within himself as long as everything goes well with him. 2. But when the time comes in which those who should do him justice do quite the opposite to him, he has only as much patience and humility as he has on that occasion and no more.

XIV POVERTY OF SPIRIT

1. *Blessed are the poor in spirit, for the kingdom of heaven is theirs* (Mt 5:3). 2. There are many who, applying themselves insistently to prayers and good deeds, engage in much abstinence and many mortifications of their bodies, 3. but they are scandalized and quickly roused to anger by a single word which seems injurious to their person, or by some other things which might be taken from them. 4. These [persons] are not poor in spirit because a person who is truly poor in spirit hates himself (cf. Lk 14:26) and loves those who strike him on the cheek (cf. Mt 5:39).

XV PEACE

1. *Blessed are the peacemakers, for they shall be called the children of God* (Mt 5:9). 2. The true peacemakers are those who preserve peace of mind and body for love of our Lord Jesus Christ, despite what they suffer in this world.

XVI PURITY OF HEART

1. *Blessed are the pure of heart, for they shall see God* (Mt 5:8). 2. The truly pure of heart are those who despise the things of earth and seek the things of heaven, and who never cease to adore and behold the Lord God living and true with a pure heart and soul.

XVII THE HUMBLE SERVANT OF GOD

1. *Blessed is that servant* (Mt 24:46) who does not pride himself on the good that the Lord says or does through him any more than on

what He says or does through another. 2. That person sins who wishes to receive more from his neighbor then what he is willing to give of himself to the Lord God.

XVIII COMPASSION FOR ONE'S NEIGHBOR[11]

1. Blessed is the person who bears with his neighbor in his weakness to the degree that he would wish to be sustained by him if he were in a similar situation (cf. Gal 6:2; Mt 7:12). 2. Blessed is the servant who attributes every good to the Lord God, for he who holds back something for himself *hides within himself the money of his Lord God* (Mt 25:18), and *that which* he thought *he had shall be taken away from him* (Lk 8:18).

XIX THE HUMBLE SERVANT OF GOD

1. Blessed is the servant who esteems himself no better when he is praised and exalted by people than when he is considered worthless, simple, and despicable; 2. for what a man is before God, that he is and nothing more.[12] 3. Woe to that religious who has been placed in a high position by others and does not wish to come down of his own will. 4. And *blessed is that servant* (Mt 24:46) who does not place himself in a high position of his own will and always desires to be under the feet of others.

XX THE GOOD AND THE VAIN RELIGIOUS

1. Blessed is that religious who takes no pleasure and joy except in the most holy words and deeds of the Lord 2. and with these leads people to the love of God in joy and gladness (cf. Ps 50:10). 3. Woe to that religious who delights in idle and frivolous words and with these provokes people to laughter.

---

11. The editors join Kajetan Esser, O.F.M., in breaking with the customary division of the Admonitions and follow the more solid manuscript tradition in joining Admonition Eighteen with Admonition Nineteen and dividing Admonition Twenty-Five into two separate pieces.

12. Cf. Saint Bonaventure, *Legenda major*, VI, 1: "[Saint Francis] often used to make this statement: 'What a man is in God's eye, that he is and nothing more.'" The phrase is also quoted in *The Imitation of Christ* of Thomas a Kempis, III, 50, 8.

XXI THE FRIVOLOUS AND TALKATIVE RELIGIOUS

1. Blessed is the servant who, when he speaks, does not reveal everything about himself in the hope of receiving a reward, and who is not quick to speak (cf. Prov 29:20), but wisely weighs what he should say and how he should reply. 2. Woe to that religious who does not keep in his heart the good things the Lord reveals to him (cf. Lk 2:19, 51) and who does not manifest them to others by his actions, but rather seeks to make such good things known by his words. 3. He thereby receives his reward (cf. Mt 6:2, 16) while those who listen to him carry away but little fruit.

XXII CORRECTION

1. Blessed is the servant who would accept correction, accusation, and blame from another as patiently as he would from himself. 2. Blessed is the servant who when he is rebuked quietly agrees, respectfully submits, humbly admits his fault, and willingly makes amends. 3. Blessed is the servant who is not quick to excuse himself and who humbly accepts shame and blame for a sin, even though he did not commit any fault.

XXIII HUMILITY

1. Blessed is the servant who is found to be as humble among his subjects as he would be among his masters. 2. Blessed is the servant who remains always under the rod of correction. He is *the faithful and prudent servant* (Mt 24:45) who for all his offenses does not delay in punishing himself, inwardly through contrition and outwardly through confession and penance for what he did.

XXIV TRUE LOVE

Blessed is the servant who would love his brother as much when he is sick and cannot repay him as he would when he is well and can repay him.

THE WRITINGS

XXV [THE SAME POINT]

Blessed is the servant who would love and respect his brother as much when he is far from him as he would when he is with him; and who would not say anything behind his back which in charity he could not say to his face.

XXVI THE SERVANTS OF GOD SHOULD HONOR THE CLERGY

1. Blessed is the servant who has faith in the clergy who live uprightly according to the norms of the Roman Church. 2. And woe to those who look down upon them; for even though they may be sinners, nonetheless no one is to judge them since the Lord alone reserves judgment on them to Himself. 3. For inasmuch as their ministry is greater in that it concerns the most holy Body and Blood of our Lord Jesus Christ, which they receive and which they alone administer to others, 4. so those who sin against them commit a greater sin than [if they sinned] against all other people of this world.

XXVII HOW VIRTUE DRIVES OUT VICE

1. Where there is charity and wisdom
      there is neither fear nor ignorance.
2. Where there is patience and humility,
      there is neither anger nor disturbance.
3. Where there is poverty with joy,
      there is neither covetousness nor avarice.
4. Where there is inner peace and meditation,
      there is neither anxiousness nor dissipation.
5. Where there is fear of the Lord to guard the house (cf. Lk 11:21),
      there the enemy cannot gain entry.
6. Where there is mercy and discernment,
      there is neither excess nor hardness of heart.

XXVIII HIDING A GOOD THING THAT IT MAY NOT BE LOST

1. Blessed is that servant who stores up *in heaven* (Mt 6:20) the good things which the Lord has revealed to him and does not desire to reveal them to others in the hope of profiting thereby, 2. for the Most High Himself will manifest His deeds to whomever He wishes. 3. Blessed is the servant[13] who keeps the secrets of the Lord in his heart (cf. Lk 2:19, 51).[14]

---

13. As he does in other texts, Saint Francis proposes Mary, the Mother of God, as the model Christian. In this instance, she is the ideal servant of God who keeps the secrets of the Lord in her heart.

14. At the end of these Admonitions the manuscripts contain a variety of conclusions that highlight the importance of these pieces: (1) "These are the words of life and salvation; if someone reads them and fulfills them, he will find life and receive salvation from the Lord. Amen." (2) "Blessed is that servant who practices these virtues and who places them in his heart; he will always be wise, for he will have an excellence which the experts will recognize." (3) "These words of Saint Francis are not available for everyone, but are addressed to those who possess the Spirit of God." (4) "The exhortations of our Seraphic Father Francis, the Standard-bearer of Jesus Christ."

The Canticle of Brother Sun

Song, music, and poetry were so deeply a part of the nature of Saint Francis that in times of sorrow and sickness as well as of joy and good health he spontaneously gave voice in song to his feelings, his inspirations, and his prayers. The clearest expression of this aspect of the personality of the Poverello is the Canticle of Brother Sun. G. K. Chesterton, in his reflections on the saint, wrote of this work: "It is a supremely characteristic work and much of Saint Francis could be reconstructed from that work alone."[1] And Eloi Leclercq, O.F.M., has written: "The manner in which Francis here looks at the created world is a key to his inner self, for the Canticle undoubtedly has elements that reveal in a special way the personality of its author."[2] The Canticle of Brother Sun is a piece of spiritual literature that comes at a transition period in the development of language, that is, when Latin was slowly becoming Italian. For this reason, philologists and literary scholars as well as students of spiritual theology have studied this work. In the twentieth century more than five hundred articles have examined the Canticle and within the past twenty years ten books have been written about it.[3]

The Legend of Perugia, 43, narrates the circumstances of the composition of the first section of the Canticle, in which the saint invites all creation to praise its Creator. The author describes the intense suffering of the Poverello in that period after he had received the stigmata. "For his praise," he said, "I wish to compose a new hymn about the Lord's creatures, of which we make daily use, without which we cannot live, and with which the human race greatly of-

---

1. G. K. Chesterton, *Saint Francis of Assisi* (New York: George H. Doran Company, 1924), p. 132.

2. Eloi Leclercq, *The Canticle of Creatures: Symbols of Union*, trans. Matthew J. O'Connell (Chicago: Franciscan Herald Press, 1978), p. 4.

3. For further studies, consult F. Bajetto, "Un trentennio di studi (1941–1973) sul Cantico di Frate Sole. Bibliografia ragionata," *L'Italia Francescana* 49 (1974): 5–62. Vittore Branca, "Il Cantico di Frate Sole," Studio delle Fonti Critiche," *Archivum Franciscanum Historicum* 41 (1948): 3–87; Mario Casella, "Il Cantico delle creature: Testo Critico e Fondamenti di Pensiero," *Studi Mediovali* 16 (1943–1950): 102–134; Giacomo Sabatelli, "Studi recenti sul Cantico di Frate Sole," *Archivum Franciscanum Historicum* 51 (1958): 1–24.

fends its Creator." The second section of the Canticle, consisting of two verses concerning pardon and peace, was composed a short time afterward in an attempt to unite the quarrelling civil and religious authorities of Assisi. The same Legend of Perugia, *44, describes the reconciling power the Canticle had in the resolution of the conflict. The final verses of the work, which constitute the third section, were written at the death of Saint Francis. Once again the* Legend of Perugia, *100, provides the details of the scene at the Portiuncula where the Seraphic Father enthusiastically sang the praises of Sister Death and welcomed her embrace.*

This magnificent hymn expresses the mystical vision of the Saint of Assisi and, since it springs from the depths of his soul, provides us with many insights into the profundity of his life of faith in the Triune God, Who so deeply enters into creation. In this vision, however, the Little Poor Man does not lose himself in space or in the vastness of the created world. He becomes so intimate and familiar with the wonders of creation that he embraces them as "Brother" and "Sister," that is, members of one family. More than any other aspect of the Canticle, this unique feature has enhanced the spiritual tradition of Christian spirituality.

1. Most High, all-powerful, good Lord,
   Yours are the praises, the glory, the honor, and all blessing.[4]
2. To You alone, Most High, do they belong,
   and no man is worthy to mention Your name.
3. Praised be You, my Lord, with all your creatures,
   especially Sir Brother Sun,
   Who is the day and through whom You give us light.
4. And he is beautiful and radiant with great splendor;
   and bears a likeness of You, Most High One.
5. Praised be You, my Lord, through Sister Moon and the stars,[5]
   in heaven You formed them clear and precious and beautiful.

---

4. Cf. Rev 4:9, 11.
5. It is important to penetrate the meaning of the word *per*, which Saint Francis uses throughout the remainder of his first section. It suggests a corruption of the Latin *per*, or the French *pour*, and the developing Italian *par*. Thus it may be translated "for," suggesting an attitude of thanksgiving; "by," expressing a sense of instrumentality; or "through," indicating instrumentality as well as a deeper sense of mysticism in perceiving God's presence in all creation. All translations are acceptable. The editors of this

6. Praised be You, my Lord, through Brother Wind,
   and through the air, cloudy and serene, and every kind of
      weather
   through which You give sustenance to Your creatures.
7. Praised be You, my Lord, through Sister Water,
   which is very useful and humble and precious and chaste.
8. Praised be You, my Lord, through Brother Fire,
   through whom You light the night
   and he is beautiful and playful and robust and strong.
9. Praised be You, my Lord, through our Sister Mother Earth,
   who sustains and governs us,
   and who produces varied fruits with colored flowers and herbs.
10. Praised be You, my Lord, through those who give pardon for
      Your love[6]
   and bear infirmity and tribulation.
11. Blessed are those who endure in peace
   for by You, Most High, they shall be crowned.
12. Praised be You, my Lord, through our Sister Bodily Death,[7]
   from whom no living man can escape.
13. Woe to those who die in mortal sin.
   Blessed are those whom death will find in Your most holy will,
   for the second death shall do them no harm.[8]
14. Praise and bless my Lord and give Him thanks
   and serve Him with great humility.

---

volume, however, accept the final translation, since it is more consistent with the witness of Saint Bonaventure's theology of exemplarism, e.g., *Itinerarium mentis in Deum, Legenda major*, IX, 1.

6. The second section of the Canticle begins with this stanza. Since the human person is not part of the chorus of the previous section, he now enters into the hymn through an identification with the God-man, Jesus Christ, i.e., by suffering weakness and tribulation, pardoning out of love, and enduring in peace.

7. The third section begins with this stanza.

8. Cf. Rev 2:11; 20:6. Saint Fulgentius of Ruspe comments on these verses in his treatise on forgiveness: "Here on earth they are changed by the first resurrection, in which they are enlightened and converted, thus passing from death to life, sinfulness to holiness, unbelief to faith, and evil actions to holy life. For this reason the second death has no power over them. . . . As the first resurrection consists of the conversion of the heart, so the second death consists of unending torment" (cf. Saint Fulgentius of Ruspe, *On Forgiveness*, Liber 2, 11, 2–12, 1. 3–4, *Corpus Christianoum* 91A, 693–695).

The Canticle of Exhortation to Saint Clare and Her Sisters

The Legend of Perugia, *45, describes the events at San Damiano after Saint Francis composed the* Canticle of Brother Sun. *The author narrates the composition of another canticle inspired by the need to console and encourage the Poor Ladies of San Damiano, that is, Saint Clare and her sisters. The text of this piece seemed to have been lost until 1941, when it was published with the* Rule and Constitutions of the Nuns of the Order of Saint Clare. *In 1976, however, Father Giovanni Boccali, O.F.M., discovered a fourteenth-century manuscript in a convent of the Poor Clares in Verona, Italy, and in 1978 published his evidence for its authenticity.*[1] *The text was written in the dialect of the Umbrian Valley and thus is closely associated with the* Canticle of Brother Sun, *which was composed in the same language.*

1. Listen, little poor ones called by the Lord,
       who have come together from many parts and provinces:
2. Live always in truth,[2]
       that you may die in obedience.[3]
3. Do not look at the life outside,
       for that of the Spirit is better.[4]

---

1. Consult: Giovanni Boccali, O.F.M., "Parole di esortazione alle 'poverelle' di San Damiano," *Forma Sororum* 14 (1977): 54–70; idem, "Canto di esortazione di san Francesco per le 'poverelle' di San Damiano," *Collectanea Franciscana* 48 (1978): 5–29. Also, A. Menichetti, "Una 'prosa' volgare di san Francesco," *Studi e Problemi di Critica Testuale* (Bologna) 1979: 5–10; F. Brambilla Ageno, "Proposte al testo della 'prosa' volgare di San Francesco," *Studi e Problemi di Critica Testuale* (Bologna) 1980: 5–8.

2. Cf. 2 Jn 3; 3 Jn 4.

3. Cf. Phil 2:8.

4. What is contrasted here with life "outside" (*de fore*) is not life "inside," the cloistered life, but an interior openness to the Spirit. It may be interpreted best through the *Earlier Rule*, c. XVII, 11–12. "For the spirit of the flesh desires and is most eager to have words, but [cares] little to carry them out. And it does not seek a religion and holiness in the interior spirit, but it wishes and desires to have a religion and holiness outwardly apparent to people."

4. I beg you through great love,
   to use with discretion
   the alms which the Lord gives you.
5. Those who are weighed down by sickness
   and the others who are wearied because of them,
   all of you: bear it in peace.[5]
6. For you will sell this fatigue at a very high price[6]
   and each one [of you] will be crowned queen
   in heaven with the Virgin Mary.

---

5. Cf. *The Canticle of Brother Sun*, 10–11: "Praised be You, my Lord, through those who . . . bear infirmity and tribulation. Blessed are those who endure in peace, for by You, Most High, they shall be crowned."

6. This imagery of selling can also be found in Thomas of Celano's *Second Life*, n. 12, in which Saint Francis met his brother, Angelo, who could not understand his spiritual ways and sarcastically remarked to a companion: "Tell Francis to sell you a pennysworth of sweat." To which Francis replied: "Indeed, I will sell my sweat more dearly to my Lord."

The Exhortation to the Praise of God

The text of this prayer comes through a manuscript written by the Franciscan historian Marianus of Florence (†1537). The author claims that the prayer was written on a wooden panel that formed an antependium of an altar in the hermitage of Cesi di Terni in Umbria. Marianus and an anonymous scribe, who copied the verses in the Naples Codex V, G.33, concur that Saint Francis wrote some verses on the panel and had pictures of various creatures drawn on it. Unfortunately the panel was lost after these witnesses brought attention to it, but its description provides a tool for understanding the contents of the prayer.

At a later date, Luke Wadding described the hermitage of Cesi di Terni as a small chapel built after the model of Saint Mary of the Angels, that is, the Portiuncula, which Saint Francis loved so very much. This might explain the quotation of the greeting of the angel and the invocation of Saint Michael the Archangel.

The case for the authenticity of the Exhortation *was strengthened in 1971 when Cesare Cenci described the Naples Codex, dated late fifteenth century, in his catalog of Franciscan manuscripts in the National Library of that city. Kajetan Esser, O.F.M., studied both texts to reach his judgement on its authenticity.[1]*

1. *Fear the Lord and give Him honor* (Rev 14:7).
2. The Lord is *worthy to receive* praise and honor (Rev 4:11).
3. All you *who fear the Lord, praise Him* (cf. Ps 21:24).
4. *Hail Mary, full of grace, the Lord is with you* (Lk 1:28).
5. Heaven and earth, praise Him (cf. Ps 68:35).
6. All you rivers, praise Him (cf. Dan 3:78).
7. *All you children* of God, *bless the Lord* (cf. Dan 3:78).

---

1. For further information on this text, consult Kajetan Esser, O.F.M., " 'Exhortatio ad laudem Dei.' Ein wenig beachtetes Loblied des hl. Franziskus," *Archivum Franciscanum Historicum* 67 (1974): 3–17; also, L. Oliger, O.F.M., "Argumentum vero et stylus praedictae inscriptionis penitus sapiunt S. Franciscum. Conferantur exempla gratia Canticum solis et Regula non bullata, c. 23," *Antonianum* 2 (1927): 389–390.

8. *This is the day which the Lord has made, let us exalt and rejoice in it* (Ps 117:24)! Alleluia, alleluia, alleluia! *O King of Israel* (Jn 12:13)!

9. *Let every spirit praise the Lord* (Ps 150:6).

10. *Praise the Lord for He is good* (Ps 146:1); all you who read this, *bless the Lord* (Ps 102:21).

11. All you creatures, bless the Lord (cf. Ps 102:22).

12. *All you birds of the heavens,* praise the Lord (cf. Dan 3:80; Ps 148:10).

13. All you *children,* praise the Lord (cf. Ps 112:1).

14. *Young men and virgins,* praise the Lord (cf. Ps 148:12).

15. *The Lamb Who was slain is worthy to receive* praise, glory, and honor (cf. Rev 5:12).

16. Blessed be the holy Trinity and undivided Unity.[2]

17. Saint Michael the Archangel, defend us in battle.[3]

---

2. This verse is taken from the Introit of the Liturgy of the Feast of the Holy Trinity.

3. This verse is taken from the Liturgy of Saint Michael the Archangel, which was celebrated by the friars on May 8 and September 29. Cf. G. Abate, O.F.M. Conv., "Il primitivo Breviario Francescano (1224–1227)," *Miscellanea Francescana* 60 (1960): 174, 188.

The Form of Life Given to Saint Clare and Her Sisters

This brief text comes through the Rule of Saint Clare, Chapter VI, in which Clare reflects on the early years of her religious life. "When the Blessed Father saw that we had no fear of poverty, hard work, suffering, shame or the contempt of the world, but that, instead, we regarded such things as great delights, moved by compassion he wrote for us a form of life." The form of life she then presents is not the entire pattern of religious life given to her by Saint Francis, but it does contain the important Trinitarian foundation that the Poverello perceived in the pursuit of evangelical perfection. Confirmation of this early document can be found in a letter of Pope Gregory IX to Blessed Agnes of Prague, dated May 11, 1238: "After Clare and some other holy women in the Lord had chosen to serve the Lord in religion, the blessed Francis gave them a formula of life" (cf. Bullarium Franciscanum *I 243). Although Thomas of Celano does not explicitly mention this form of life in his* Second Life of Saint Francis *(c. 1246), many of the elements of this text are suggested. Thus it is a well-established writing that comes to us through both Saint Francis and Saint Clare.*

1. Since by divine inspiration[1] you have made yourselves daughters and servants of the most high King, the heavenly Father, and

---

1. Saint Francis uses the term *divina inspiratio*, divine inspiration, to express the dynamic principle of the call of Saint Clare and her sisters. He describes the vocation of his brothers to the Order and to the missions in the same way; cf. *Earlier Rule*, II, 1, and *Later Rule*, XII, 1. In her own Rule, Saint Clare uses the same phrase; cf. *Rule of St. Clare* II, 1. Thus both saints emphasize the work of the Holy Spirit in the embrace of the Franciscan ideal.

have taken the Holy Spirit as your spouse, choosing to live according to the perfection of the holy Gospel,[2] 2. I resolve and promise for myself and for my brothers always to have that same loving care and special solicitude for you as [I have] for them.[3]

---

2. It is helpful to see the Trinitarian pattern of life Saint Francis envisions as a result of the working of the Holy Spirit in the soul. This Trinitarian consciousness pervades many of the Saint's writings and enhances our understanding of his absorption in the life of Jesus, the Son of the heavenly Father.

3. The special bond established between Saint Francis and the Poor Ladies of San Damiano can best be interpreted through the writings of Saint Clare, particularly her Rule, and the early biographers of both saints, e.g., Thomas of Celano, *Second Life of Saint Francis*, 204–207. For further insights, consult Chiara August Lainati, O.S.C., "Una 'Lettura' di Chiara d'Assisi Attraverso Le Fonti," *Approccio Storico-Critico alle Fonti Francescane* (Rome: Antonianum, 1979), pp. 155–177.

The Last Will Written for Saint Clare and Her Sisters

The source of this writing is the Rule of Saint Clare, *Chapter VI, in which Clare tells of the Seraphic Father's eagerness to have his followers persevere in the life and poverty of the Lord Jesus Christ. The work has great significance in its witness to the basic ideals that absorbed the Poverello during the last days of his life. No doubt Saint Clare placed it in her Rule to encourage her sisters to embrace a life of poverty in a manner faithful to the teachings of the Poverello.*

1. I, brother Francis, the little one, wish to follow the life and poverty of our most high Lord Jesus Christ and of His most holy mother and to persevere in this until the end; 2. and I ask and counsel you, my ladies, to live always in this most holy life and in poverty. 3. And keep most careful watch that you never depart from this by reason of the teaching or advice of anyone.

A Letter to Brother Leo

This short letter is preserved on a small piece of parchment that Brother Leo, a close companion of Saint Francis during his last years, treasured. It is one of the two writings of the Seraphic Father that have been transmitted as they were written by his own hand. (The other is the parchment containing the Praises and Blessing that were written for Brother Leo while he and the saint were on La Verna in 1224.) The Letter is missing from any lists of the writings until 1604, when the Poor Clares gave it to the Conventual Friars in Spoleto. It then disappeared until 1895, when Father Clito Cardinali, a parish priest of Spoleto, brought it to Monsignor Faloci-Pulignani to determine its authenticty. The latter presented it to Pope Leo XIII who entrusted it to the canons of the Cathedral of Spoleto, who still care for it.[1]

It is difficult to determine the date of the letter or the circumstances that surround its composition. None of the early biographies suggest any background for the letter. Nonetheless, the Letter is a precious indication of the friendship of Saint Francis and Brother Leo. It is also a simple yet profound statement of the saint's understanding of the Gospel life to which he and his followers were called.

1. Brother Leo, [wish] your Brother Francis health and peace![2]
2. I speak to you, my son, as a mother. I place all the words which we spoke on the road in this phrase, briefly and [as] advice.

---

1. For further information, consult Michele Faloci-Pulignani, "Tre autografi di San Francesco," *Miscellanea Francescana* VI (1895): 33–39; idem, "La calligrafia di San Francesco," *Miscellanea Francescana* VII (1898): 67–71; idem, "Un autografo di San Francesco d'Assisi a Spoleto," *Miscellanea Francescana* IX (1902): 106–107. Also, Kajetan Esser, O.F.M., *Die Opuscula des Hl. Franziskus von Assisi* (Grottaferrata: Collegium S. Bonaventurae, 1976), pp. 216–224.
2. The Latin text is *F. leo f. Francissco tuo salutem et pacem.* Two points have puzzled scholars: its grammar and the misspelling of the saint's name. This sentence may be seen as example of the saint's poor grasp of Latin or it may be interpreted as a request on his part for the blessing of Brother Leo. The translation provided by the editors favors the latter interpretation. No satisfactory explanations have been offered for the misspelling of Francisco.

And afterwards, if it is necessary for you to come to me for counsel, I say this to you: 3. In whatever way it seems best to you to please the Lord God and to follow His footprints and His poverty,[3] do this with the blessing of God and my obedience. 4. And if you believe it necessary for the well-being of your soul, or to find comfort, and you wish to come to me, Leo, come!

---

3. This passage aptly summarizes the foundations of the way of life Saint Francis embraced: pleasing the Lord God through following the footprints of Christ and His poverty. Cf. *Earlier Rule* I; *Last Will Written for Saint Clare and Her Sisters.*

A Letter to the Clergy

This letter reflects the influence of the Fourth Lateran Council (1215) and the postconciliar concerns of Pope Honorius III, particularly expressed in the decree Sane cum olim *(Nov. 22, 1219), which urged reverence and respect for the Blessed Sacrament. Saint Francis took up this cause and wrote the brief letter to the members of the clergy not only within the Order but within the entire Church. It is written confirmation of an attitude of the saint that is seen in the* Legend of Perugia, *18. During his preaching tours, the* Legend *narrates, "he brought along a broom to clean the churches. He suffered a great deal, in fact, when he entered a church and saw it dirty. And so, when he finished preaching to the people, he gathered together all the priests who were there and took them aside so that the laity could not hear. He then spoke to them of the salvation of souls and especially reminded them of the solicitude they were to exercise in keeping churches, altars, and everything that is used in the celebration of the divine mysteries clean."*

The letter exists in two forms: an earlier form, which is written in a Missal of the Benedictine monastery of Subiaco, and a second form that is more commonly found in the manuscript tradition. The earlier document was copied between 1229 and 1238 and was embellished with the sign of the tau, *which the saint frequently used at the end of his letters. The other version of the letter, which dates much later, is substantially the same although the ending accentuates the prescriptions of the Church and the obligation of the clergy to observe them.*

1. All of us who are clerics should be aware of the great sin and ignorance which some people have toward the most holy Body and Blood of our Lord Jesus Christ and His most holy written words which consecrate [His] Body.[1] 2. We know that it cannot become His

---

1. The Latin phrase *nomina et verba* appears several times in the writings of Saint Francis (*Letter to the Clergy*, 1, 3, 6, 12; *First Letter to the Custodians*, 2, 5; *Testament*, 14). The translation "written words" is based on the assumption that *nomen* means noun, *verbum* means verb. Since Saint Francis places such high value on the words of the

Body without first being consecrated by [His] word. 3. For in this world we have and see nothing corporally of the Most High except [His] Body and Blood, and the words through which we have been made and have been redeemed *from death to life* (1 Jn 3:14). 4. But let all who administer such holy mysteries—especially those who administer them carelessly—consider the sad state of the chalices, the corporals, and the altar-linens upon which the Body and Blood of our Lord are sacrificed. 5. And [the Body and Blood of the Lord] is left by many in dirty places, carried about in a miserable manner, received unworthily, and administered to others without discretion.[2] 6. Even His sacred written words are sometimes left to be trampled underfoot; 7. for *the person who does not have the spirit does not perceive the things of God* (1 Cor 2:14).

8. Are we not moved by a sense of piety concerning all these things, since the good Lord offers Himself into our hands and we handle Him and receive Him daily with our mouth? 9. Or do we forget that we must come into His hands (cf. Hebr 10:31)? 10. Well then, let us quickly and firmly amend our ways in these and other matters; 11. and wherever the most holy Body of our Lord Jesus Christ has been unlawfully housed and neglected, let it be removed from that place and deposited and locked in a precious location.[3] 12. Likewise, wherever the written words of the Lord may be found in unbecoming places, they are to be collected and kept in a place that is becoming. 13. And we know that we are bound to observe all of these matters above all else according to the precepts of the Lord and the

---

Lord (e.g., *First Admonition*, 9; *Letter to the Entire Order*, 34, 37), it seems more appropriate to translate this phrase simply as "written words." For a detailed study of this, consult Ignazio Brady, O.F.M., *San Francesco Uomo dello Spirito* (Vicenza: Editrice "Esca", 1978), pp. 46–50.

2. This directive reflects the influence of the Fourth Lateran Council, Canon 19: "We command also that the aforesaid churches, vessels, corporals, and vestments be kept clean and bright. For it is absurd to tolerate in sacred things a filthiness that is unbecoming even in profane things." Quoted from *Disciplinary Decrees of the General Councils*, trans. H. J. Schroeder, O.P. (St. Louis: Herder and Herder, 1937), p. 528.

3. This injunction reflects the influence of the Fourth Lateran Council, Canon 20: "We decree that in all churches the chrism and the Eucharist are to be kept in properly protected places provided with locks and keys, so that they may not be reached by rash and indiscreet persons and used for impious and blasphemous purposes." Quoted from *Disciplinary Decrees of the General Councils*, trans. H. J. Schroeder, O. P. (St. Louis: Herder and Herder, 1937), p. 529.

constitutions of holy Mother Church. 14. And whoever has not done so, let him know that he will be bound *to give an account* before our Lord Jesus Christ *on the day of judgment* (Mt 12:36). 15. Those who make copies of this writing so that it may be better observed should know that they will be blessed by the Lord God.[4]

---

4. The earlier form of this letter contains a simpler ending: 13. All of the clergy are bound above all else to observe all of these things to the letter. 14. And those who have not carried them out should realize that they must *give an account* before our Lord Jesus Christ *on the day of judgment* (Mt 12:36). 15. Let those who make copies of this letter so that it may be better observed know that they will be blessed by the Lord God. Thus Kajetan Esser, O.F.M., included another version of the text in both editions of the *Opuscula*. Cf. *Die Opuscula des Hl. Franziskus von Assisi* (Grottaferrata: Collegium S. Bonaventurae, 1976), pp. 163–64; *Opuscula Sancti Patris Francisci Assisiensis* (Grottaferrata: Collegium S. Bonaventurae, 1978), pp. 97–99.

The First Letter to the Custodians[1]

The historical setting for this letter is similar to that of the Letter to the Clergy. It, too, flows from that postconciliar concern for reverence and respect for the Blessed Sacrament accentuated by Pope Honorius III in the decree Sane cum olim. *Saint Francis directs this encouragement to all those brothers who exercise the apostolate of ministry to their confreres in the different provinces established in 1217.*

Three new items are introduced in this text: (1) the request of preachers to exhort people to penance and to awaken within them an awareness of the need of the Eucharist; (2) an exhortation to kneel when the Blessed Sacrament is carried through the streets and elevated after the Consecration; and (3) the urging of praise at every hour and whenever the bells are rung. These points indicate the eagerness with which the Poverello encouraged his brothers to fulfill not only the letter of the conciliar decrees but the spirit that animated them.

The text of this letter is preserved in the codex 225 that Paul Sabatier discovered in the Guarnacci Library in Volterra, Italy, in 1900. Although it is found in only this one manuscript, there is little doubt that it is an authentic writing of Saint Francis, since the style and mannerisms are those of his other writings.

1. To all the custodians of the Friars Minor[2] to whom this letter is sent, Brother Francis, your servant and little one in the Lord God, sends a greeting with new signs of heaven and earth, which are great

---

1. *Custos* or *custodes* is a technical word that is not easily translated into English. Father Kajetan Esser, O.F.M., has attempted to trace the use of the word to describe an office of ministry to the needs of the friars. There is an evolution of the term that can be seen most clearly in the *Later Rule*, 4, in which the term could designate either the highest office within the entire Order, i.e., the Minister General, or the highest office within a province, i.e., the Minister Provincial. The Testament indicates a clearly defined office. This is in keeping with the subdivision of the provinces by that time (1226). Each subdivision was called "a custody" cared for by a *custos* or custodian. (Cf. Kajetan Esser, O.F.M., *Origins of the Franciscan Order* [Chicago: Franciscan Herald Press, 1970], pp. 67–68.)

2. Cf. *The Earlier Rule* VI, note 17, concerning the term "Friars Minor." The editors have decided to translate the Latin word *frater* as "brother" throughout this volume,

and extraordinary in the sight of God and yet are regarded as of little importance by many religious and other people.

2. I beg you, with all that is in me and more, that, when it is appropriate and you judge it profitable, you humbly beg the clergy to revere above everything else the most holy Body and Blood of our Lord Jesus Christ and His holy written words which consecrate [His] Body. 3. The chalices, corporals, appointments of the altar, and everything which pertains to the sacrifice must be of precious material. 4. And if the most holy Body of the Lord is very poorly reserved in any place, it should be placed in a precious location under lock and kept according to the mandate of the Church and carried about with great reverence and administered to others with discretion. 5. In a similar way the written words of the Lord, whenever they are found in an improper place, should be gathered together and kept in a becoming place.

6. And in every sermon which you give, admonish the people concerning [the need of] penance, and [tell them] that no one can be saved unless he receive the Body and Blood of the Lord (cf. Jn 6:54). 7. And when It is sacrificed upon the altar by the priest and carried to any place, let all the people, on bended knee, praise, glorify, and honor the Lord God living and true.[3] 8. And you must announce and preach His praise to all peoples in such a manner that at every hour and whenever the bells are rung, praise, glory, and honor are given to the all-powerful God throughout all the earth. 9. And my brothers [who are] custodians to whom this writing shall come and [who] have made copies to keep for themselves and to give to the brothers who have the office of preaching or the care of the brothers; and who have preached everything which is contained in this writing to the very end, should know that they have the blessing of the Lord God as well as my own. 10. And let these matters be for them [an expression of] true and holy obedience.

---

except for those instances in which the official title of the Order is given, i.e., the *Ordo Fratrum Minorum*, "the Order of Friars Minor." In these texts it would seem more desirable to maintain the commonly accepted translation—one that can be traced to the entrance of the friars into the English-speaking world. Nonetheless, "brother" seems to capture the meaning intended by Saint Francis in the remaining texts. It is a more personal and familial term than "friar."

3. This reflects the decree, *Sane cum olim:* "Every priest should frequently teach his people that they should bow in reverence whenever the life-giving Host is elevated at the celebration of the Mass and that each one should do the same thing when the priest is carrying It to the sick" (Honorius III, *Bullarium Romanum*, n. XL, tom. III, pp. 366a–366b; trans. Canisius Connors, O.F.M.).

The Second Letter to the Custodians

Luke Wadding discovered this manuscript in a Spanish translation in the archives of the friary of Saragossa, Spain. It had been preserved in this friary from the time of John Parenti, the Minister General of the Order from 1227 to 1232, who had once been the Minister Provincial of the friars in Spain. Wadding retranslated the text into Latin, which makes it difficult to identify many of the characteristics of Saint Francis that emerge in his other writings. However, the contents of the letter are sufficient evidence to establish its authenticity. Furthermore, this document refers to the other letters of this period that are concerned with the Eucharist, that is, the Letter to the Clergy, *the* First Letter to the Custodians, *and the* Letter to the Rulers of the Peoples.

1. To all the custodians of the Friars Minor whom these letters shall reach, Brother Francis, the least of the servants of God, sends greetings and holy peace in the Lord.
2. Know well that in the sight of God there are certain matters which are very lofty and sublime which are sometimes considered worthless and inferior by people; 3. while there are other things, cherished and esteemed by people, which are considered worthless and inferior by God. 4. I ask you in the sight of the Lord our God, as much as I can, to give the letters which treat of the most holy Body and Blood of our Lord to the bishops and other members of the clergy; 5. and keep in mind what we recommended to you in this regard. 6. Make many copies of the other letter containing an invitation to proclaim the praises of God among the peoples and in the piazzas which I am sending to you to give to mayors, consuls, and rulers. 7. And propagate them with great diligence among those to whom they should be given.

A Letter to the Entire Order

Of all the letters of Saint Francis, the Letter to the Entire Order *is perhaps the most liturgical in its orientation. "I implore all of you brothers to show all possible reverence and honor to the most holy Body and Blood of our Lord Jesus Christ," he writes in this work and then proceeds to encourage the friars to manifest devotion and respect for the celebration of the Eucharist and the Liturgy of the Hours.*

Ubertino da Casale, in his Arbor vitae crucifixae Iesu Christi *(1305), indicates that the Letter was written "at the end of the days" of the Seraphic Father. The promulgation of the papal bull* Quia populares tumultus, *December 3, 1224, which granted the friars permission to celebrate the Eucharist in their churches and oratories, may well have occasioned this encouragement of Saint Francis. Nonetheless, the themes of this work reflect many of the concerns of the Testament, which was written as the saint was dying.*

The prayer that concludes this Letter is an excellent example of the marvelous balance the Poverello achieved in his spiritual life. Some manuscripts place it before the Letter; Luke Wadding places it separately. But this edition, following the tradition of the Assisi Codex 338, concludes that the prayer is an appropriate ending to the Letter since it is a summary of its content.

1. In the name of the most high Trinity and the holy Unity: the Father, and the Son, and the Holy Spirit.

2. To all the reverend and much beloved brothers; to Brother A.,[1] the Minister General of the Order of Friars Minor, its lord, and

---

1. It is difficult to determine the identity of the friar referred to in this passage. The majority of the manuscripts simply leave the person unspecified, although all indications point to the Minister General. Since Peter Catani had died in March 1221, Elias, who was appointed in 1221, is most likely the recipient. This may well be confirmed by the further references to Brother *H* (Latin: [H] Elias) in lines 38, 40, and 47. A number of manuscripts indicate Elias as the name that should be inserted in these places.

to the other ministers general who will come after him; to all ministers, custodians, and priests of this same brotherhood [who are] humble in Christ; and to all the simple and obedient brothers, from first to last: 3. Brother Francis, a worthless and weak man, your very little servant, [sends] his greetings in Him Who redeemed [us] and *washed us in His* most precious *blood* (Rev. 1:5). 4. [At the mention of] His name you must adore Him with fear and reverence, prostrate on the ground (cf. 2 Esdr 8:6). [It is the name of] our Lord Jesus Christ, the name of that *Son of the Most High* (cf. Lk 1:32) *Who is blessed forever* (Rm 1:25).

5. Listen, sons of the Lord and my brothers, *pay attention to my words* (Acts 2:14). 6. *Incline the ear* (Is 55:3) of your heart and obey the voice of the Son of God.[2] 7. Observe His commands with your whole heart and fulfill His counsels with a perfect mind. 8. *Give praise* to Him *since He is good* (Ps 135:1) and *exalt* Him *by your deeds* (Tob 13:6), 9. for He has sent you into the entire world for this reason (cf. Tob 13:4): that in word and deed you may give witness to His voice and bring everyone to know that there is *no one who is all-powerful* except Him (Tob 13:4). 10. Persevere *in discipline* and holy obedience (Heb 12:7) and with a firm and good purpose fulfill what you have promised to Him. 11. The Lord *God* offers *Himself* to us *as to* [His] *children* (Heb 12:7).

12. Therefore, kissing your feet and with all that love of which I am capable, I implore all of you brothers to show all possible reverence and honor to the most holy Body and Blood of our Lord Jesus Christ 13. in Whom that which is in the heavens and on the earth is brought to peace and is reconciled to the all-powerful God (cf. Col 1:20).

14. In the Lord I also beg all my brothers who are priests, or who will be or who wish to be priests of the Most High, that, whenever they wish to celebrate Mass, being pure, they offer the true Sacrifice of the most holy Body and Blood of our Lord Jesus Christ purely. [Let them do this] with reverence [and] with a holy and pure intention, not for any mundane reason or out of fear or out of love of some person, as if they were pleasing people (cf. Eph 6:6; Col 3:22). 15. But let every wish be directed to God inasmuch as grace will help [them],

---

2. The Biblical reference Isaiah 55:3 refers to that section in which the prophet speaks of the "food of the poor," i.e., the Word of God, which gives life and strength.

desiring thereby to please only the most high Lord since He alone does these things as He pleases. 16. Therefore as He Himself says: *Do this in memory of me* (Lk 22:19; 1 Cor 11:24); if anyone acts otherwise, he becomes Judas the traitor and is *guilty of the Body and Blood of the Lord* (cf. 1 Cor 11:27).

17. Remember, my brothers who are priests, what is written of the law of Moses: that whoever committed a transgression against even the externals died *without mercy* by a decree of the Lord (cf. Heb 10:28). 18. How much greater and severer will be the punishment for the person *who tramples on the Son of God, and who treats the blood of the Covenant which sanctified him as if it were not holy, and who insults the Spirit of grace* (Heb 10:29)? 19. For a person despises, defiles, and tramples on the Lamb of God when, as the Apostle says, *he does not recognize* (1 Cor 11:29) and discern the holy bread of Christ from other foods or actions or eats it unworthily or indeed, even if he were worthy, eats it unthinkingly or without the proper dispositions, since the Lord says through the prophet: *Cursed is that person* who performs the work of God fraudulently (cf. Jer 48:10). 20. And He will surely condemn priests who do not wish to take this to heart saying: *I will curse your blessings* (Mal 2:2).

21. Listen, my brothers: If the blessed Virgin is so honored, as it is right, since she carried Him in [her] most holy womb; if the blessed Baptist trembled and did not dare to touch the holy head of God;[3] if the tomb in which He lay for some time is so venerated, 22. how holy, just, and worthy must be the person who touches [Him] with his hands, receives [Him] in his heart and mouth, and offers [Him] to others to be received. [This is] He Who is now not about to die, but Who is eternally victorious and glorified,[4] upon Whom *the angels desire to gaze* (1 Pet 1:12).

23. Look at your dignity, you brothers [who are] priests, and be holy since He is holy (cf. Lev 19:2). 24. And as the Lord God has honored you above all other persons because of this ministry, so you should love, reverence, and honor Him above all others. 25. It is a

---

3. A further influence of the Cistercian author, the Pseudo-Bernard of Cluny, cf. *Tractatus de Corpore Domini* (PL 182:1149–1150).

4. Once more a Cistercian writing emerges. While the passage parallels the work of Pseudo-Bernard of Cluny, *Instructio Sacerdotis praeparationis eius ad digne celebrandum tantum mysterium* (PL 184:787A), it also reflects a passage of Bernard of Clairvaux in *Sermo I, Epiphania Domini* (PL 183:146A).

great misery and a miserable weakness that when you have Him present with you in this way, you concern yourselves with anything else in this entire world.

26. Let the whole of mankind tremble
      the whole world shake
      and the heavens exult
when Christ, *the Son of the living God*,[5]
      is [present] on the altar
      in the hands of a priest.
27. O admirable heights and sublime lowliness!
    O sublime humility!
    O humble sublimity!
    That the Lord of the universe,
      God and the Son of God,
    so humbles Himself
    that for our salvation
    He hides Himself under the little form of bread!
28. Look, brothers, at the humility of God
    and *pour out your hearts before Him!*[6]
    Humble yourselves, as well,
      that you may be exalted by Him.[7]
29. Therefore,
      hold back nothing of yourselves for yourselves
    so that
    He Who gives Himself totally to you
      may receive you totally.

30. Therefore I admonish and urge in the Lord that only one Mass according to the form of the holy Church be celebrated each day in the places in which the brothers stay. 31. If, however, there should be more than one priest in that place, let one be content, for the sake of charity, to assist at the celebration of the other priest; 32. for our Lord Jesus Christ fills those who are present and absent who are worthy of Him.[8] 33. Although He may seem to be present in many places,

---

5. Jn 11:27.
6. Ps 61:9.
7. Cf. 1 Pet 5:6; Ja 4:10.
8. For an in-depth study of Eucharistic celebration in each fraternity consult Octave d'Angers, O.F.M. Cap., "La Messe publique et privée dans la piété de Sainte Fran-

He nonetheless remains indivisible and knows no loss. One everywhere, He works as it pleases Him with the Lord God the Father and with the Holy Spirit, the Paraclete, forever and ever. Amen.

34. And since he who is of God listens to the words of God (cf. Jn 8:47), we who have been called more particularly for the divine functions should in consequence not only listen to and do what God says, but we should also guard the [sacred] vessels and other [liturgical] appointments so that we may impress upon ourselves the loftiness of our Creator and our subjection to Him.[9] 35. Therefore, I admonish all my brothers and encourage [them] in Christ that wherever they come upon the written words of God they venerate them so far as they are able. 36. And if they are not well kept or if they lie about carelessly in some place, let them, inasmuch as it concerns them, collect them and preserve them, thus honoring the Lord in the words *which He spoke* (3 Kgs 2:4). 37. For many things are made holy by the words of God (cf. 1 Tim 4:5) and in the power of the words of Christ the Sacrament of the altar is celebrated.

38. Moreover, I confess all my sins to the Lord God, the Father and the Son and the Holy Spirit, to the Blessed Mary ever Virgin, and to all the saints in heaven and on earth, to Brother H., the Minister of our Order, as to my venerable Lord, and to the priests of our Order and to all my other blessed brothers. 39. I have offended [God] in many ways through my grievous fault especially in not having kept the Rule which I promised the Lord nor in having said the Office as the Rule prescribes, either out of negligence or on account of my sickness, or because I am ignorant and unlearned. 40. Therefore, through every means which I am capable of employing, I ask Brother H., the Minister General [and] my lord, to insist that the Rule be observed inviolably by everyone. 41. [Further, he should insist] that the

---

çois," *Etudes Franciscaines* 49 (1937); 475–486; Stephen J. P. van Dijk and J. H. Walker, *The Origins of the Modern Roman Liturgy. The Liturgy of the Papal Court and the Franciscan Order in the Thirteenth Century* (Westminister, Maryland, 1960), pp. 51ff, 237, 292ff, 297; Oktavian Schmucki, O.F.M. Cap., "La 'Lettera a Tutto l'Ordine' di San Francesco," *L'Italia Franciscana* 55 (1980): 245–286.

9. This sentence suggests the diaconate of St. Francis. Cf. A. Callebaut, O.F.M., "Saint François lévite," *Archivum Franciscanum Historicum* 20 (1927): 193–196; Alban von Hermetschwil, O.F.M. Cap., "Zur Diakonatsweiche des hl. Franziskus," *St. Fidelis* (Luzern) 28 (1941): 7–11; Stephen J. P. van Dijk, "Saint Francis' blessing of Brother Leo," *Archivum Franciscanum Historicum* 47 (1954): 199–201; Mariano D'Alatri, O.F.M. Cap., *San Francesco d'Assisi diacono nella Chiesa* (Rome: Istituto Storico dei Cappuccini, 1977), 3–5.

clerics say the Office with devotion before God, not concentrating on the melody of the voice but on the harmony of the mind, so that the voice may blend with the mind, and the mind be in harmony with God.[10] 42. [Let them do this] in such a way that they may please God through purity of heart and not charm the ears of the people with sweetness of voice.[11] 43. For I promise to observe these things strictly as God may give me grace, and I shall pass these things on to the brothers who are with me so they may be observed in the Office and in all other things established in the Rule.

44. But if any of the brothers do not wish to observe these things, I do not consider them to be Catholics nor my brothers, and I do not wish to see them or speak with them until they shall have done penance. 45. I say this also of all others who go wandering about with no regard for the discipline of the Rule, 46. for our Lord Jesus Christ gave His life that He might not lose the obedience of the most holy Father (cf. Phil 2:8).

47. I, Brother Francis, a useless man and unworthy creature of the Lord God, say through the Lord Jesus Christ to Brother H., the Minister of our entire Order, and to all the ministers general who will come after him, and to the other custodians and guardians of the brothers,[12] who are and who will be, that they should have this writing with them, put it into practice, and carefully preserve it. 48. And I beg them to guard carefully those things which are written in it and to have them observed diligently according to the pleasure of the all-powerful God, now and always, as long as the world continues to be.

49. *May you* who shall have carried out these things *be blessed by the Lord* (Ps 113:23) and may the Lord be with you forever. Amen.

---

10. The influence of the *Rule of St. Benedict,* Chapter 19: "Let us, therefore, consider in what state one must be in the sight of God and his angels; we shall, then, stand while chanting, so that our hearts will be in harmony with our voices" [translation is that of editors]. It also finds resonance with the thought of St. Augustine: "While you are praying to God during the chanting of the psalms and hymns, what you express on your lips should also be alive in your hearts" (cf. Augustine, *Rule* 3; Ep. 221:7; Ep 48:3).

11. Cf. Conrad of Eberbach, *Exordium magnum Cisterciensis,* Dist. V, c. XX (PL 185: 1174s).

12. The expression "guardian" was used initially to describe a quality of ministry to the friars rather than a specific office. The function of a minister was seen as that of a protector or guardian of his brothers, protecting them from evil and leading them toward good. Only after the friars had settled down in residences—a more common practice after the death of Saint Francis—did it appear that the local minister received the title "guardian." (Cf., Kajetan Esser, O.F.M., *Origins of the Franciscan Order,* trans. Aeden Daly, O.F.M. [Chicago: Franciscan Herald Press, 1970], pp. 172–175.

[PRAYER]

50. Almighty, eternal, just, and merciful God,
    grant us in our misery [the grace]
        to do for You alone
            what we know You want us to do,
            and always
        to desire what pleases You.

51. Thus,
        inwardly cleansed,
        interiorly enlightened,
        and inflamed by the fire of the Holy Spirit,
    may we be able to follow
        in the footprints of Your beloved Son,[13]
        our Lord Jesus Christ.

52. And,
    by Your grace alone,
    may we make our way to You,
        Most High,
        Who live and rule
            in perfect Trinity and simple Unity,
        and are glorified
            God all-powerful
        forever and ever.
    Amen.

---

13. Cf. 1 Pet 2:21.

The First Version of the Letter to the Faithful

(Exhortation to the Brothers and Sisters of Penance)

The First Life *of Thomas of Celano, n. 37, indicates the presence of a "norm of life" that Saint Francis gave to all those who came to him. The biographies of the saint tell of the primitive rule or* propositum vitae *presented to Pope Innocent III in 1209, which guided the first friars. Saint Clare presents the "form of life" the Poverello gave to her and her sisters in the early days of their religious life. But the norms that were given to those men and women who associated themselves with Saint Francis through the Third Order have never been determined.[1] The studies of Kajetan Esser, O.F.M., have given new importance to a document that has been overlooked until the present and that has primary importance for those first Brothers and Sisters of Penance.[2] It is the* recensio prior *or first version of the Letter to the Faithful and forms a written instruction directed toward men and women who have joined the penitential movement.*

The document was discovered by Paul Sabatier in the Codex 225 of the Guarnacci Library in Volterra, Italy, and was published for the first time in 1900 under the title: "These are words of life and salvation: those who read them and put them into practice will find life and draw from them the salvation of the Lord." After a few brief commentaries written by Sabatier and other Franciscan scholars such as Leonard Lemmens, Walter Goetz, and Heinrich Boehmer, the document was set aside until the present time. When all the manuscripts of the Letter to the Faithful *were collected by Kajetan Esser, it was clearly seen that the "text of Volterra held a special place among all*

---

1. For further information on the penitential movements of the early thirteenth century, consult *L'Ordine della Penitenza di San Francesco d'Assisi nel secolo XIII*, Atti del Convegno di studi francescani (Rome, 1973); *I Frati Penitenti di San Francesco nella societa del Due e Trecento*, Atti del Secondo Convegno di studi francescani (Rome, 1977). Also, G. B. Meerseeman, O.P., *Dossier de L'Order de la Penitence au XIII Siècle* (Friburg, 1961).

2. Cf. Kajetan Esser, O.F.M., "Ein Vorläufer der 'Epistola ad fideles' des hl. Franziskus von Assisi (Cod. 225 der Biblioteca Guarnacci zu Volterra)," *Collectanea Franciscana* 45 (1975): 5–37.

the materials." It was given critical attention and published among the definitive writings of Saint Francis in 1976.

In the Name of the Lord!

(CHAPTER ONE) THOSE WHO DO PENANCE

1. All those who love the Lord *with their whole heart, with their whole soul and mind, with their whole strength* (cf. Mk 12:30) and love their neighbors as themselves (cf. Mt 22:39) 2. and hate their bodies with their vices and sins, 3. and receive the Body and Blood of our Lord Jesus Christ, 4. and produce worthy fruits of penance:

5. Oh, how happy and blessed are these men and women when they do these things and persevere in doing them, 6. since *the Spirit of the Lord will rest upon them* (cf. Is 11:2) and He will make His home and *dwelling among them* (cf. Jn 14:23). 7. They are children of the heavenly Father (cf. Mt 5:45) whose works they do, and they are spouses, brothers, and mothers of our Lord Jesus Christ (cf. Mt 12:50).

8. We are spouses when the faithful soul is joined to our Lord Jesus Christ by the Holy Spirit. 9. We are brothers to Him when we *do the will of the Father Who is in heaven* (Mt 12:50). 10. [We are] mothers, when we carry Him in our heart and body (cf. 1 Cor 6:20) through divine love and a pure and sincere conscience and [when] we give birth to Him through [His] holy manner of working,[3] which should shine before others as an example (cf. Mt 5:16).

11. Oh, how glorious it is, how holy and great, to have a Father in heaven! 12. Oh, how holy, consoling, beautiful and wondrous it is to have such a Spouse! 13. Oh, how holy and how loving, pleasing, humble, peaceful, sweet, lovable, and desirable above all things to have such a Brother and such a Son: our Lord Jesus Christ, Who gave up

---

3. The phrase *sancta operatio,* holy manner of working, is used frequently in the writings of Saint Francis (cf. *The First Version of the Letter to the Faithful,* II, 21; *The Second Version of the Letter to the Faithful* 53; the *Later Rule,* X, 8; the *Testament* 39). It is used most frequently in conjunction with the Spirit of the Lord or the words of Saint Francis that echo those of Jesus and are "spirit and life" (cf. Jn 6:64). Thus, Saint Francis underscores the dynamic principle of the spiritual life, the Holy Spirit, which must be operative in the life of every Christian.

His life for His sheep (cf. Jn 10:15) and who prayed to the Father saying:[4]

14. *O Holy Father, protect those in your name* (Jn 17:11) *whom you have given to me in the world; they were yours and you have given them to me* (Jn 17:6). 15. And *the words which you gave to me, I have given to them, and they have accepted them and* have believed *truly that I have come from you and* they have known *that you sent me* (Jn 17:8). 16. I pray for them and *not for the world* (cf. Jn 17:9). 17. Bless and *sanctify* [*them*] (Jn 17:17) *and I sanctify myself for them* (Jn 17:19). 18. *Not only for these do I pray, but for those who through their words will believe in me* (Jn 17:20), *so that they may be made holy in being one* (Jn 17:23) *as we are one* (Jn 17:11). 19. And I wish, Father, that *where I am they also may be with me so that they may see my glory* (Jn 17:24) *in your kingdom* (Mt 20:21). Amen.

(CHAPTER TWO) THOSE WHO DO NOT DO PENANCE

1. All those men and women who are not [living] in penance 2. and do not receive the Body and Blood of our Lord Jesus Christ; 3. [who] practice vice and sin and follow [the ways of] *wicked concupiscence* (Col 3:5) and *the desires of the flesh* (Gal 5:16); 4. [who] do not observe what they have promised to the Lord, 5. and bodily serve the world by *the desires of the flesh* (1 Pet 2:11), the anxieties of the world and the cares of this life: 6. [such people] are held fast by the devil, whose children they are and whose works they perform (cf. Jn 8:41). 7. They are blind, since they do not see the true light, our Lord Jesus Christ. 8. They do not have spiritual wisdom, since they do not possess the Son of God, Who is the true wisdom of the Father. 9. It is said of these people: *Their wisdom has been swallowed up* (Ps 106:27), and: *Cursed are those who turn away from Your commands* (Ps 118:21). 10. They see [and] acknowledge, they know and do evil deeds, and, knowingly, they lose [their] souls.

11. See, you blind ones, you who are deceived by your enemies: by the flesh, the world, and the devil; because it is sweet to the body to commit sin and it is bitter for it to serve God;[5] 12. [and] because all

---

4. Concerning the repeated use of the Gospel of Saint John in the writings of Saint Francis, consult Optatus van Asseldonk, O.F.M. Cap., "San Giovanni Evangelista negli Scritti di San Francesco," *Laurentianum* 8 (1977): 225–255; idem, "Altri Aspetti Giovanei negli Scritti di San Francesco," *Antonianum* 54 (1979): 447–486.

5. Thomas of Celano's *Second Life of Saint Francis*, 9, describes the saint's hearing "a reply of salvation and grace" in the challenge to take the bitter for sweet in order to acknowledge God. This "bitter-sweet" theme appears in both versions of the *Letter to*

vices and sins come forth and *proceed from the heart of man*, as the Lord says in the Gospel (cf. Mk 7:21). 13. And you have nothing in this world or in [the world] to come. 14. And you think you possess the vanities of this world for a while, but you are deceived, since the day and the hour will come to which you give no thought, [of which] you have no knowledge, and [of which] you are ignorant (cf. Mt 25:13). The body becomes sick, death approaches, and this man dies a bitter death. 15. And no matter where or when or how a man dies in the guilt of sin without doing penance and satisfaction, if he is able to perform [some act of] satisfaction and does not, the devil snatches up his soul from his body with so much anguish and tribulation that no one can know it unless he has experienced it.

16. And every talent and power and *knowledge and wisdom* (2 Chron 1:12) which they think they possess will be taken away from them (cf. Lk 8:18; Mk 4:25). 17. And they leave their substance to their relatives and friends, and these have taken and divided the inheritance among themselves and afterwards they have said: "May his soul be cursed since he could have acquired more and given more to us than he did!" 18. Worms eat the body. And so they have lost body and soul in this passing world, and both will go down to hell where they will be tormented without end.

19. In the love which is God (cf. 1 Jn 4:16), we beg all those whom these letters reach to accept with kindness and a divine love the fragrant words of our Lord Jesus Christ which are written above. 20. And those who do not know how to read should have them read to them frequently. 21. And, since *they are spirit and life* (Jn 6:64), they should preserve them together with [their] holy manner of working even to the end.[6]

22. And whoever shall not have done these things *will be held accountable* on the day of judgment (cf. Mt 12:36) *before the tribunal* of our Lord Jesus *Christ* (cf. Rm 14:10).

---

the Faithful and in the Testament. It may reflect the call of Saint John the Evangelist in Revelations 10:8–11.

6. Cf. *supra*, n. 3.

The Second Version of the Letter to the Faithful

The Second Version of the Letter to the Faithful *could have had a development similar to that of the* Earlier Rule *of Saint Francis. That earlier piece of legislation, the* Regula non bullata, *as it is commonly entitled, is the result of that* propositum vitae *presented to Pope Innocent III in 1209/1210 and approved orally by him. Other precepts were added to it through papal legislation, the chapters of the friars, and personal interventions of the Seraphic Father himself. It is conceivable that the* recensio prior *of the Letter to the Faithful was adjusted and modified until its final edition.*

In this longer edition, the later experiences of the Brothers and Sisters of Penance are considered and taken into account. Corrections and stronger directives are inserted in order to guide readers to a more orthodox following of a life of penance. Furthermore, the postconciliar period of the Fourth Lateran Council can easily be seen as forming its background, as the accents on the correct understanding of Christology and the Eucharist indicate. All of these differences appear to be directed toward curbing and repelling contemporary errors that threatened the movement of the penitential groups at the beginning of the thirteenth century.[1]

Both of these letters confirm the observation that Francis was deeply concerned about the Brothers and Sisters of Penance and followed their development with greater sympathy than some historians are still inclined to admit.[2]

---

1. Further information on this text can be found in Kajetan Esser, O.F.M., "La Lettera di San Francesco ai fedeli," *Collectanea Franciscana* 43 (1973): 65–75; idem, "Ein Vorläufer der 'Epistola ad Fideles' des hl. Franziskus von Assisi (Cod. 225 der Biblioteca Guarnacci zu Volterra)," *Collectanea* Franciscana 45 (1975): 5–37; idem, "Un Documento dell'Inizio del Duecento Sui Penitenti," I *Frati Penitenti di San Francesco nella Societa del Due e Trecento,* Atti del 2 Convegno di Studi Francescani (Rome 1976), pp. 87–99. Also, Oktavian Schmucki, O.F.M. Cap., "Il Terzo Ordine Francescano nelle biografie di san Francesco," *Collectanea Franciscana* 43 (1973): 117–132.

2. The titles of this particular text suggest that it is a *commonitorium,* a letter that reminds its recipients to carry out a command. Thus the Assisi Codex 338 entitles the document: "A work of *commonitorium* and exhortation of our venerable most holy Father Saint Francis." It can be seen as a reminder and an exhortation to the Brothers and Sisters of Penance urging them to fulfill the obligation they have taken upon themselves.

THE WRITINGS

1. In the name of the Father and of the Son and of the Holy Spirit. Amen. To all Christian religious: clergy and laity, men and women, and to all who live in the whole world, Brother Francis, their servant and subject, [offers] homage and reverence, true peace from heaven and sincere love in the Lord.[3]

2. Since I am the servant of all, I am obliged to serve all and to administer to them the fragrant words of my Lord. 3. Therefore, on reflecting that, since I cannot visit each one of you in person because of the infirmity and weakness of my body, I have proposed to set before you in this present letter and message the words of our Lord Jesus Christ, Who is the Word of the Father, and the words of the Holy Spirit, which *are spirit and life* (Jn 6:64).[4]

4. Through his angel, Saint Gabriel, the most high Father in heaven announced this Word of the Father—so worthy, so holy and glorious—in the womb of the holy and glorious Virgin Mary, from which He received the flesh of humanity and our frailty.[5] 5. Though *He was rich* beyond all other things (2 Cor 8:9), in this world He, together with the most blessed Virgin, His mother, willed to choose poverty. 6. And, as the Passion drew near, He celebrated the Passover with His disciples and, taking bread, gave thanks, and blessed and broke it, saying: *Take and eat: this is My Body* (Mt 26:26). 7. *And taking*

---

3. It is difficult to determine the identity of the recipients of this *Second Version of the Letter to the Faithful*. Part of the difficulty is the interpretation of the opening words of this line: *universis christianis religiosis.* Some editions place a comma between *universis christianis* and *religiosis,* indicating that the work is addressed to "all christians, religious, . . ." The editors of this volume have followed the *editio minor,* the final edition of the critical work of Kajetan Esser, O.F.M., which omits the comma and implies that the *Second Version of the Letter to the Faithful* is directed to those who in a more or less perfect way were considered religious.

4. A special bond of union between Saint Francis and the recipients of this Letter is expressed in this paragraph. This is strengthened in line 40 when the saint writes of "the yoke of service and holy obedience," as well as the special love and responsibility that characterizes their relationships. The union is further underscored in the repeated use of the first person plural in a large section of the work, lines 19 to 47. The implication, then, is that this forms some pattern of life for the Brothers and Sisters of Penance.

5. This paragraph begins an emphatic statement concerning the Incarnation. It may well be a catechetical tool prompted by the ideas of the Cathari, members of a heretical sect who maintained that Christ was not God but even less than a man since matter was seen as impure. The Cathari saw Christ as an angel adopted by God who took on the appearance of a man. They propagated their doctrine by embracing an evangelical, poor manner of living. Thus, many aspects of their life resembled that of the Brothers and Sisters of Penance. Cf. Alfonso Pompei, O.F.M. Conv., "Il movimento penitenziale nei secoli XII–XIII," *Atti del Convegno di Studi Francescani* (Assisi, 1972), p. 22.

the cup He said: *This is My Blood of the new covenant which will be shed for you and for many for the forgiveness of sins* (Mt 26:28). 8. Then He prayed to His Father, saying: *Father, if it is possible, let this cup pass from me* (Lk 22:42). 9. *And His sweat became as drops of blood falling on the ground* (Lk 22:44). 10. Nonetheless, He placed His will at the will of the Father, saying: *Father, let Your will be done* (Mt 26:42); *not as I will, but as You will* (Mt 26:39). 11. And the will of the Father was such that His blessed and glorious Son, Whom He gave to us and [Who] was born for us, should, through His own blood, offer Himself as a sacrifice and oblation on the altar of the cross: 12. not for Himself through Whom all things were made (cf. Jn 1:3), but for our sins, 13. leaving us an example that we should follow in His footprints (cf. 1 Pet 2:21). 14. And [the Father] wills that all of us should be saved through Him and that we receive Him with our pure heart and chaste body. 15. But there are few who wish to receive Him and be saved by Him, although His *yoke is sweet* and His *burden light* (cf. Mt 11:30).

16. Those who do not wish to taste how *sweet the Lord is* (cf. Ps 33:9) and love *the darkness rather than the light* (Jn 3:19), not wishing to fulfill the commands of God, are cursed; 17. of them the prophet says: *They are cursed who stray from your commands* (Ps 118:21). 18. But Oh, how happy and blessed are those who love God and do as the Lord Himself says in the Gospel: *You shall love the Lord your God with all your heart and all your mind, and your neighbor as yourself* (Mt 22:37, 39).

19. Let us love God, therefore, and adore Him with a pure heart and a pure mind because He Who seeks this above all else has said: *The true worshipers will adore the Father in spirit and in truth* (Jn 4:23). 20. For all those *who worship Him* are to worship Him *in the spirit* of truth (cf. Jn 4:24). 21. And let us praise Him and pray to Him *day and night* (Ps 31:4), saying: *Our Father Who art in heaven* (Mt 6:9), since *we should pray always and never lose heart* (Lk 18:1).

22. We must also confess all our sins to a priest, and receive from him the Body and Blood of our Lord Jesus Christ.[6] 23. He who does

---

6. Saint Francis accentuates the sacerdotal role in the administration of the Sacraments of Penance and the Eucharist to prevent the teachings of the Waldensians from taking root. The followers of Peter Waldo embraced the principle that their system of life made them the real depositories of the Gospel and gave them the right to preach. They also maintained that the life of the clergy should be corrected and that the ministries of unworthy clergy—or those whom they considered unworthy—were invalid. Cf. Alfonso Pompei, O.F.M. Conv., "Il movimento penitenzialie nei secoli XII–XIII," *Atti del Convegno di Studi Francescani* (Assisi, 1972), p. 22.

not eat His Flesh and does not drink His Blood (cf. Jn 6:55, 57) *cannot enter the Kingdom of God* (Jn 3:5). 24. Yet let him eat and drink worthily, since he who receives *unworthily eats and drinks judgment to himself, not recognizing*—that is, not discerning—*the Body of the Lord* (1 Cor 11:29). 25. Moreover, let us perform *worthy fruits of penance* (Lk 3:8). 26. And let us love our neighbors as ourselves (cf. Mt 22:39). 27. And if there is anyone who does not wish to love them as himself, at least let him do no harm to them, but rather do good.

28. But those who have received the power to judge others should exercise judgment with mercy as they themselves desire to receive mercy from the Lord. 29. *For judgment will be without mercy* for those *who have not shown mercy* (Jas 2:13).

30. Let us then have charity and humility; let us give alms since this washes our souls from the stains of [our] sins (cf. Tob 4:11; 12:9). 31. For people lose everything they leave behind in this world; but they carry with them the rewards of charity and the alms which they gave, for which they will have a reward and a suitable remuneration from the Lord.

32. We must also fast and abstain from vices and sins (cf. Sir 3:32) and from any excess of food and drink,[7] and be Catholics. 33. We must also visit churches frequently and venerate and show respect for the clergy, not so much for them personally if they are sinners, but by reason of their office and their administration of the most holy Body and Blood of Christ which they sacrifice upon the altar and receive and administer to others. 34. And let all of us firmly realize that no one can be saved except through the holy words and Blood of our Lord Jesus Christ which the clergy pronounce, proclaim and minister. 35. And they alone must administer [them], and not others.[8] 36. But religious especially, who have left the world, are bound to do more and greater things without however leaving these undone (cf. Lk 11:42).

---

7. Once more Saint Francis addresses the erroneous teachings of the Cathari which were dualistic. In their convictions that (1) the body comes from the devil and the soul from God, and (2) that the soul is in prison in the body and must make complete satisfaction in order to be purified, the Cathari easily fell into false ascetical practices.

8. The concept of laymen's possessing the ability to minister or confect the Eucharist, as well as to preach, was firmly held by the Waldensians. Again Saint Francis uses his position to correct any erroneous thoughts of his followers and to teach the orthodox doctrine of the Church.

37. We must hate our bodies with [their] vices and sins, because the Lord says in the Gospel: All evils, vices, and sins proceed from the heart (cf. Mt 15:18–19; Mk 7:23). 38. We must love our enemies and do good to those who hate us (cf. Mt 5:44; Lk 6:27). 39. We must observe the commands and counsels of our Lord Jesus Christ. 40. We must also deny ourselves (cf. Mt 16:24) and place our bodies under the yoke of service and holy obedience, as each one has promised to the Lord. 41. And no one is to be obliged to obey another in anything by which a sin or a crime is committed.

42. The one to whom obedience has been entrusted and *who* is esteemed as *greater* should be as *the lesser* (Lk 22:26) and the servant of the other brothers. 43. And he should use and show mercy to each of his brothers as he would wish them to do to him were he in a similar position (cf. Mt. 7:12). 44. Nor should he become angry with a brother because of a fault of that brother, but with all patience and humility let him admonish him and support him.

45. We must not be wise and prudent according to the flesh; rather, we must be simple, humble, and pure. 46. And let us hold ourselves in contempt and scorn, since through our own fault all of us are miserable and contemptible, vermin and worms, as the Lord says through the prophet: *I am a worm and no man, the scorn of men and the outcast of the people* (Ps 21:7). 47. We must never desire to be over others; rather we must be servants and subject *to every human creature for God's sake* (1 Pet 2:13). 48. And upon all men and women, if they have done these things and have persevered to the end, *the Spirit of the Lord will rest* (Is 11:2) and He will make His home and *dwelling among them* (cf. Jn 14:23). 49. They will be children of the heavenly Father (cf. Mt 5:45) whose works they do. 50. And they are spouses, brothers, and mothers of our Lord Jesus Christ (cf. Mt 12:50). 51. We are spouses when the faithful soul is joined to Jesus Christ by the Holy Spirit. 52. We are brothers when we do *the will* of His *Father Who* is in heaven (cf. Mt 12:50). 53. [We are] mothers when we carry Him in our heart and body (cf. 1 Cor 6:20) through love and a pure and sincere conscience; we give birth to Him through [His] holy manner of working, which should shine before others as an example (cf. Mt 5:16).

54. Oh, how glorious it is, how holy and great, to have a Father in heaven! 55. Oh, how holy, consoling, beautiful, and wondrous it is to have a Spouse! 56. Oh, how holy and how loving, pleasing, humble, peaceful, sweet, lovable, and desirable above all things to have such a Brother and Son, Who laid down His life for His sheep (cf. Jn 10:15)

and [Who] prayed to the Father for us saying:[9] *Holy Father, protect those in your name whom you have given to me* (Jn 17:11). 57. *Father, all those whom you gave me in the world were yours and you have given them to me* (Jn 17:6). 58. And *the words which you gave to me I have given to them; and they have accepted them and truly know that I came from you and they have believed that you have sent me* (Jn 17:8). 59. I pray for them and *not for the world* (cf. Jn 17:9); bless and *sanctify them* (Jn 17:17), *and I sanctify myself for their sakes so that they may be holy* (Jn 17:19) *in being one as we are* (Jn 17:11). 60. And I wish, Father, *that where I am they also may be with me so that they may see my glory* (Jn 17:24) *in your kingdom* (Mt 20:21).

61. Let *every creature*
      in heaven, on earth,
      in the sea and in the depths,
  give praise,
      glory, honor, and blessing[10]
  to Him
      Who suffered so much for us,
      Who has given so many good things,
      and [Who] will [continue to] do so for the future.
62. For He is our power and strength,
      He Who *alone is good*[11]
        [Who] is most high,
        [Who is] all-powerful, admirable, [and] glorious;
          [Who] alone is holy, praiseworthy, and blessed
            throughout endless ages.
                  Amen.

63. All those, however, who are not [living] in penance and do not receive the Body and Blood of our Lord Jesus Christ;[12] 64. [who] practice vice and sin and walk [the paths of] *wicked concupiscence* (Col 3:5) and evil desires; 65. who do not observe what they have promised

---

9. Cf. *The First Version of the Letter to the Faithful*, n. 4.
10. Rev 5:13.
11. Lk 18:19.
12. This paragraph, lines 63 to 71, concerns the correct practice of penance. There are new elements added to the description provided in the *First Version of the Letter to the Faithful*, 1–4, which reflect the influence of the practices and teachings of the Cathari and Waldensians.

and bodily serve the world by *the desires of the flesh* (1 Pet 2:11), the cares and anxieties of this world, and the preoccupations of this life: 66. [such people] are deceived by the devil, whose children they are and whose works they perform (cf. Jn 8:41). They are blind because they do not see the true light, our Lord Jesus Christ. 67. They do not have spiritual wisdom because they do not have within them the Son of God Who is the true wisdom of the Father. Of these people it is said: *Their wisdom has been swallowed up* (Ps. 106:27). 68. They see [and] acknowledge, they know and do evil, and, knowingly, they lose (their) souls. 69. See, you blind ones, [you who] are deceived by our enemies, the flesh, the world, and the devil. For it is sweet to the body to commit sin and bitter to it to serve God, because *all evils*, vices, and sins come from and *proceed from the heart of men*, as the Lord says in the Gospel (cf. Mk 7:21, 23). 70. And you have nothing in this world or in [the world] to come. 71. You think that you possess the vanities of the world for a while, but you are deceived, since the day and the hour will come to which you give no thought, of which you have no knowledge and of which you are ignorant.

72. The body grows weak, death approaches, family and friends come, saying: "Put your affairs in order." 73. See, his wife and his children, relatives and friends pretend to cry. 74. Looking at them, he sees them weeping [and] is moved by an evil impulse. As he thinks to himself, he says: "Look, I put my soul and body, as well as everything I have, into your hands." 75. Certainly, that man is cursed who confides and entrusts his soul and body and all his possessions into such hands; 76. for, as the Lord says through the prophet, *Cursed is the man who confides in man* (Jer 17:5). 77. And immediately they summon the priest to come. The priest says to him: "Do you wish to receive pardon for all your sins?" 78. He responds: "I do." "Do you wish to make restitution as far as you can from your substance for all that you have done and for the ways [in which] you have defrauded and deceived people?" 79. He responds: "No." 80. And the priest asks: "Why not?" "Because I have placed everything in the hands of relatives and friends." 81. And he begins to lose the power of speech and thus that miserable man dies.

82. But let everyone know that whenever or however a person dies in mortal sin without making amends when he could have done so and did not, the devil snatches up his soul out of his body with so much anguish and tribulation that no one can know it unless he has experienced it. 83. And every talent and power and knowledge which

he thinks he possesses (cf. Lk 8:18) *will be taken away from him* (Mk 4:25). 84. And [whatever] he leaves his relatives and friends they will snatch up and divide among themselves. And afterwards they will say: "May his soul be cursed since he could have acquired more and given us more than he did." 85. Worms eat [his] body. And so he loses body and soul in this brief life, and will go down to hell where he will be tormented without end.

86. In the name of the Father and of the Son and of the Holy Spirit. Amen. 87. I, Brother Francis, your little servant, ask and implore you in the love which is God (cf. 1 Jn 4:16) and with the desire to kiss your feet, to receive these words and others of our Lord Jesus Christ with humility and love, and observe [them] and put [them] into practice. 88. And to all men and women who will receive them kindly [and] understand their meaning and pass them on to others by their example: If *they have persevered in them to the end* (Mt 24:13), may the Father and the Son and the Holy Spirit bless them. Amen.

A Letter to a Minister[1]

This letter contains two sections. The first concerns those attitudes that should characterize a minister in his dealings with a brother who sins; the second concerns a simplification of those chapters of the Earlier Rule that treat of sin. Most probably the letter was written prior to the Chapter of the friars in 1223 in which they considered changes in the Rule in preparation for its papal confirmation. It was sent to an unknown provincial who was having difficulty with the brothers who sin and who desired to retire to a hermitage rather than continue in such a demanding ministry. This work speaks eloquently of the Seraphic Father's compassion toward those who sin and those who are called to minister to them.

1. To Brother N., minister:[2] May the Lord bless you (cf. Num 6:24a).

2. I speak to you, as I can, concerning the state of your soul. You should accept as a grace all those things which deter you from loving the Lord God and whoever has become an impediment to you, whether [they are] brothers or others, even if they lay hands on you.

---

1. Various titles have been given to this text. (1) "A letter of Saint Francis to a certain minister." (2) "This is a letter which Saint Francis sent to the Minister General, namely, Brother Elias." (3) "A letter that [Saint Francis] sent to Brother Elias." (4) "A letter that Saint Francis sent to the Minister General about the manner of serving the brothers [who are their] subjects [and who] sin mortally or venially." With Kajetan Esser, O.F.M., the editors have chosen the simple title because of the anonymity of the minister to whom the letter is addressed.

2. Various friars have been suggested as recipients of this letter. Eduard d'Alençon, O.F.M. Cap., thought that the Minister may well have been Peter Catani (cf. Eduard d'Alençon, O.F.M. Cap., *Analecta Ordinis Minorum Capuchinorum* 15 [1899]: 83). While Paul Sabatier maintained that Elias was its recipient (cf. Paul Sabatier, *Collection d'études et de documents sur l'histoire religieuse et littéraire du Moyen Age* II [Paris, 1899], p. 119). Leonard Lemmens, O.F.M., suggested a third possibility in a minister provincial who would be present at the Chapter with his brothers (cf. 13), i.e., at the Chapter of Pentecost which was held by all the brothers until the year 1221 (cf. Leonard Lemmens, O.F.M., *Opuscula sancti patris Francisci Assisiensis*, Bibliotheca Franciscana Ascetica Medii Aevi I [Quaracchi, 1904], p. 189). Kajetan Esser, O.F.M., has maintained the anonymity of the recipient.

3. And you should desire that things be this way and not otherwise. 4. And let this be [an expression] of true obedience to the Lord God and to me, for I know full well that this is true obedience. 5. And love those who do these things to you. 6. And do not expect anything different from them, unless it is something which the Lord shall have given to you. 7. And love them in this and do not wish that they be better Christians. 8. And let this be more [valuable] to you than a hermitage.

9. And by this I wish to know if you love the Lord God and me, his servant and yours—if you have acted in this manner: that is, there should not be any brother in the world who has sinned, however much he may have possibly sinned, who, after he has looked into your eyes, would go away without having received your mercy, if he is looking for mercy. 10. And if he were not to seek mercy, you should ask him if he wants mercy. 11. And if he should sin thereafter a thousand times before your very eyes, love him more than me so that you may draw him back to the Lord. Always be merciful to [brothers] such as these. 12. And announce this to the guardians,[3] as you can, that on your part you are resolved to act in this way.[4]

13. At the Pentecost Chapter, however, with the help of God and the advice of the brothers, out of all the chapters of the Rule that treat of mortal sin[5] we shall make one chapter such as this:

14. If any one of the brothers at the instigation of the enemy should sin mortally, he is bound by obedience to have recourse to his guardian. 15. And all the brothers who might know that he has sinned are not to bring shame upon him or speak ill of him, but let them show great mercy toward him and keep most secret the sin of their brother; *because it is not the healthy who are in need of the physician, but those who are sick* (Mt 9:12). 16. Likewise let them be bound by obedience to

---

3. Cf. *A Letter to the Entire Order*, n. 15.

4. Fifteen manuscripts end with this sentence, although the majority of the early manuscripts continue with the concern for appropriate legislation concerning the friars who sin. (Cf. Kajetan Esser, O.F.M., *Opuscula sancti Francisci Assisiensis* [Grottaferrata, 1978], p. 130).

5. Saint Francis is referring to the *Earlier Rule*, Chapters V, XIII, and XX, which treat of the brothers who sin. The need to simplify the thoughts and directives of these chapters is obvious. The consequent concise statement can be seen in the *Later Rule*, Chapters VII and X.

send him to his custodian with a companion. 17. And let that custodian mercifully take care of him as he would like to be taken care of if he were in a similar position (cf. Mt 7:12). 18. And if he falls into some venial sin, let him confess this to a brother [who is a] priest. 19. And if there is no priest at hand, let him confess to his brother, until he has [contact] with a priest who will absolve him canonically, as it has been laid down. 20. And [the brothers who are not priests] should have no power to enjoin any other penance except this: *Go and sin no more* (cf. Jn 8:11).

21. Keep this writing with you until [the Chapter of] Pentecost that it may be better observed, when you will be there with your brothers.[6] 22. And you will take care to add, with the help of God, these things and all else which is lacking in the Rule.

---

6. Kajetan Esser, O.F.M., dates this work before the completion of the *Earlier Rule* (1221), but is unable to decide whether it was written before the Pentecost Chapter of 1219 or 1220 (cf. Kajetan Esser, O.F.M., *Opuscula sancti Francisci Assisiensis* [Grottaferrata, 1978], pp. 48–49). Nonetheless, the style of lines 14–20 suggests that its composition was close to the time of the composition of the Rule of 1223.

A Letter to the Rulers of the Peoples

A copy of this letter was discovered by Luke Wadding in the writings of Francisco Gonzaga, O.F.M., Minister General of the Order from 1579 to 1587. In his De Origine Seraphicae Religionis Franciscanae *(Venice, 1603, p. 806), Gonzaga mentions that John Parenti, the first Provincial Minister of Spain and later Minister General of the Order, brought a copy of the letter into Spain. However, the only edition of the letter in Latin is that published by Luke Wadding. Nonetheless, there is no reason to doubt its authenticity because (1) it shows stylistic similarities to other writings of Saint Francis; (2) its content reflects that of the other letters of this period (the* Letter to the Clergy *and the* First Letter to the Custodians*); and (3) its existence is confirmed by the* Second Letter to the Custodians 6.

The Poverello, as we learn from his early biographer, Thomas of Celano, did not hesitate to address himself directly to the rulers of the world. The First Life, *43, narrates an incident in which Emperor Otto IV passed the friars' hovel at Rivo Torto, near Assisi, on his way to Rome to be crowned by the Pope. Francis sent a friar to call out repeatedly that his glory would last only a short while. The* Second Life, *200, expressed his wish that emperors would enact laws that on Christmas Day more than the usual amount of hay be given to the birds, the oxen, and the asses. He would have no fear, then, to write such a letter as this to remind rulers of their responsibility before God.*

1. To all mayors and consuls, magistrates and rulers throughout the world, and to everyone who may receive these letters: Brother Francis, your little and despicable servant in the Lord God, sends [his] wishes of health and peace to all of you.

2. Pause and reflect, for the day of death is approaching (cf. Gen 47:29). 3. I beg you, therefore, with all possible respect, not to forget the Lord or turn away from His commandments by reason of the cares and preoccupations of this world, for all those who are oblivious of Him and *turn away from* His *commands* are cursed (cf. Ps 118:21) and *will be totally forgotten* by Him (Ez 33:13). 4. And when the day of death does come, everything which they think they have will be taken

from them (cf. Lk 8:18). 5. And the wiser and more powerful they may have been in this world, so much greater will be the punishments they will endure in hell (cf. Wis 6:7).

6. Therefore, I firmly advise you, my lords, to put aside all care and preoccupation and receive with joy the most holy Body and the most holy Blood of our Lord Jesus Christ in holy remembrance of Him.

7. And you should manifest such honor to the Lord among the people entrusted to you that every evening an announcement be made by a town crier or some other signal that praise and thanks may be given by all people to the all-powerful Lord God. 8. And if you do not do this, know that you must *render an account* before the Lord your God, Jesus Christ, *on the day of judgment* (cf. Mt 12:36).

9. Let those who keep this writing with them and observe it know that they will be blessed by the Lord God.

A Letter to Saint Anthony

According to the Chronicle of the Twenty-Four Generals, *the friars asked Brother Anthony of Padua, a former Augustinian religious who entered the Order after learning of the martyrdom of the first friars, to accept the responsibility of teaching the brothers.* "He did not presume to teach," *the* Chronicle *continues,* "no matter how urgent was the request of the friars, without first obtaining the permission of Blessed Francis."[1] *The* Chronicle *implies that the permission was requested and suggests that the favorable reply was given in writing.*

The date attributed to this letter is late 1223 or early 1224, since this date would correspond to the known activities of Saint Anthony at this time. Morcover, Saint Francis clearly refers to the text of the Later Rule, the Regula bullata, *which was approved by Pope Honorius III on November 22, 1223.*[2]

1. Brother Francis [sends his] wishes of health to Brother Anthony, my bishop. 2. It pleases me that you teach sacred theology to the brothers, as long as—in the words of the Rule—you "do not extinguish the Spirit of prayer and devotion"[3] with study of this kind.

---

1. Cf. *Chronica XXIV Generalium Ordinis Minorum, Analecta Franciscana,* III, 132.

2. For further studies of this text, consult Kajetan Esser, O.F.M., "Der Brief des hl Franziskus an de h. Antonius von Padua," *Franziskanische Studien* 31 (1949): 135–151. Also, O. Bonmann, O.F.M., "De authenticitate Epistolae s. Francisci ad s. Antonium Patavinum," *Archivum Franciscanum Historicum* 45 (1952): 474–492; Mariano d'Alatri, "Argumenta tamen, quae et qualiter ab Auctore proponuntur, propositam thesim minime probare putare," *Bibliographia Franciscana* X, n. 233.

3. Cf. *Later Rule,* V, 2; Also, *Later Rule,* n. 14.

The Office of the Passion

This work is an ensemble of seven sets of prayers or hours that corre-
spond to those of the Liturgy of the Hours. These seven collections
are arranged for five seasons of the year: (1) the last three days of
Holy Week and the weekdays throughout the year; (2) the Paschal
season; (3) Sundays and feast days throughout the year; (4) the Advent
season; and (5) Christmas and the days that follow it.

Such a devotional prayer was not something new in the history
of spirituality. At the time of Benedict of Aniane in 817, while monas-
tic religious life was undergoing reform, there was a tendency to pro-
long the Divine Office by adding personal and devotional prayers.
Saint Ulrich of Augusta (†973), for example, prayed a devotional of-
fice in honor of the Cross and another in honor of the Blessed Virgin
Mary. In this Office of the Passion, however, Saint Francis combines
a devotion to both the Cross and the Blessed Mother, but his collage
of scriptural passages and antiphons reflects many characteristics of
his unique vision.

The title of this work, Office of the Passion, is somewhat inaccu-
rate. The Poverello had other events in the history of salvation woven
into this biblical tapestry. He frequently refers to the wonders of cre-
ation, the joys of the Easter mystery, and the Fatherhood of God. The
French author J. de Schampheleer, in his study of this work, has
called it "The Office of the Paschal Mystery."[1]

[INTRODUCTION]

These are the psalms which our most holy Father Francis composed
in reverence, memory, and praise of the Passion of the Lord. They

---

1. Cf. Jacques de Schampheleer, O.F.M., *L'Office de la Pàque. Commentaire de l' "Of-*
ficium Passionis" de Saint François (Paris: Les Editiones Franciscaines, 1963). For further
studies and interpretations of the *Office of the Passion* consult: Oktavian Schmucki,
O.F.M. Cap., "Das Leiden Christi im Leben des hl. Franziskus von Assisi. Eine quel-
lenvergleichende Untersuchung im Lichte der zeitgenössischen Passionsfrömmigkeit,"
Collectanea Franciscana 30 (1960): 129–145; "L'Ufficio della Passione come Esempio per
Celebrare la Liturgia delle Ore," in *Preghiera liturgica secondo l'esempio e l'insegnamento di*
San Francesco d'Assisi: seconda editione accresciuta (Rome: Conferenza Italiana Superiori

should be said during each of the hours of the day and the one hour of the night. They begin with Compline of Holy Thursday, for on that night our Lord Jesus Christ was betrayed and taken captive. And note that Saint Francis used to recite this office in this way: First he used to say the prayer which the Lord and Master taught us: *O OUR most holy FATHER*, etc., with the Praises, that is, *HOLY, HOLY, HOLY,* etc., as they are written above. At the end of the Praises with the prayer, he used to begin this antiphon: *Holy Mary*. First he used to say the Psalms of the holy Mary; afterward he used to recite the other psalms which he had chosen, and at the end of all the psalms which he had recited, he said the psalms of the Passion. At the end of the [last] psalm he used to recite this antiphon: *Holy Virgin Mary*. At the end of the antiphon the office was finished.

PART ONE: FOR THE SACRED TRIDUUM OF HOLY WEEK AND FOR WEEKDAYS THROUGHOUT THE YEAR

At Compline[2]
Antiphon: Holy Virgin Mary
Psalm (I)

1. God, I have told you of my life †
    you have placed my tears in your sight (Ps 55:8b–9).
2. All my enemies were planning evil [things] against me (Ps 40:8a) †
    and they have taken counsel together (cf. Ps 70:10c).
3. They repaid me evil for you †
    and hatred for my love (cf. Ps 108:5).
4. In return for my love they slandered me †
    but I kept praying (Ps 108:4).
5. *My holy Father* (Jn 17:11), *King of heaven and earth*, do not leave me †
    since trouble is near and there is no one to help (Ps 21:12).
6. Let my enemies be turned back †

Provinciali Cappuccini, 1979), pp. 17–28; Laurent Gallant, O.F.M., " 'Dominus regnavit a ligno.' L'Officium Passionis de Saint François d'Assise, éditione critique et étude." (Dissertation) (Paris, Institut Catholique, 1978).

2. The opening rubric of the *Office of the Passion* indicates the reason for its beginning with Compline of Holy Thursday: "For on that night our Lord Jesus Christ was betrayed and taken captive." The psalm verses selected for this hour reflect the attitudes of the Savior on the Mount of Olives.

on whatever day I shall call upon You; for now I know that You
are my God (Ps 55:10).

7. My friends and my neighbors have drawn near and have stood
    against me †
    and those who were close to me have stayed far away (Ps 37:12).

8. You have driven my acquaintances far from me †
    they have made me an abomination to them, I have been handed
    over and I have not fled! (Ps 87:9).

9. *Holy Father* (Jn 17:11), do not remove your help from me (Ps
    21:20); †
    my God, look to my assistance (cf. Ps 70:12).

10. Come to my help †
    Lord, God of my salvation (Ps 37:23).
    Glory to the Father and to the Son and to the Holy Spirit.
    As it was in the beginning, is now, and will be forever. Amen.

Antiphon

1. Holy Virgin Mary,
    among women,
    there is no one like you born into the world:

2. you are the daughter
    and the servant of the most high and supreme King
    and Father of heaven,
    you are the mother of our most holy Lord Jesus Christ,
    you are the spouse of the Holy Spirit.

3. Pray for us
    with Saint Michael the Archangel
    and all the powers of the heavens
    and all the saints
    to your most holy beloved Son, the Lord and Master.
    Glory to the Father ... As it was in the beginning ...

[Note that the preceding antiphon is recited at all the hours and is
said in place of the antiphon, chapter, hymn, versicle, and oration;
both at Matins and likewise at all the hours. Saint Francis did not say
anything else in these hours except this antiphon with its psalms. At
the conclusion of the office, Saint Francis used to say]

THE WRITINGS

Prayer: Let us bless the Lord, the living and true God; to Him let us
always render praise, glory, honor, blessing, and every
good. Amen. Amen. So be it. So be it.

At Matins
Antiphon: Holy Virgin Mary
Psalm (II)[3]

1. Lord, God of my salvation †
   I cry to You by day and by night (Ps 87:2).
2. Let my prayer enter into Your sight †
   incline Your ear to my prayer (Ps 87:3).
3. Look to my soul and free it †
   ransom me from my enemies (Ps 68:19).
4. Since it is You Who drew me out of the womb, You, my hope
   from my mother's breasts, †
   I am cast upon You from the womb (Ps 21:10).
5. From the womb of my mother You are my God †
   do not depart from me (Ps 21:11).
6. You know my disgrace, and my confusion, †
   and my shame (Ps 68:20).
7. All those who trouble me are in Your sight †
   and my heart has expected abuse and misery (Ps 68:21a–b).
8. And I looked for someone who would grieve together [with me]
   and there was none †
   and for someone who would console me and I found none (Ps
   68:21c–d).
9. O God, the wicked have risen against me †
   and they have sought my life in the assembly of the mighty and
   they have not placed You in their sight (Ps 85:14).
10. I am numbered among those who go down into the pit; †
    I have become as a man without help, free among the dead (Ps
    87:5–6a).

---

3. The psalm for Matins cannot be related easily to a single scene of the Passion.
The reference to the "assembly of the mighty" in verse 9 may suggest Christ's presence
before the High Priest (cf. Lk 22:63ff.). Verses 4 and 5 imply Saint Francis's penetra-
tion into the central mystery of the Incarnation, i.e., Christ's uninterrupted self-giving
in obedience to the Father.

11. *You are my most holy Father* †
    my King and my God (cf. Ps 43:5a).
12. Come to my help †
    Lord, God of my salvation (Ps 37:23).

At Prime[4]
Antiphon: Holy Virgin Mary
Psalm (III)

1. Have mercy on me, O God, have mercy on me †
   since my soul places its trust in You (Ps 56:2a).
2. And I will hope [as I stay] under the shadow of Your wings †
   until wickedness passes by (Ps 56:2b).
3. I will cry to my most holy Father, the most high, †
   to the Lord, Who has done good to me (cf. Ps 56:3).
4. He has sent from heaven and delivered me †
   He has disgraced those who have trampled upon me (Ps 56:4a–b).
5. God has sent His mercy and His truth †
   He has snatched my life (Ps 56:4c–5a) from the strongest of my
   enemies and from those who hated me since they were too
   strong for me (Ps 17:18).
6. They have prepared a trap for my feet †
   and have bowed down my soul (Ps 56:7a–b).
7. They have dug a pit before my face †
   and themselves have fallen into it (Ps 56:7c–d).
8. My heart is ready, O God, my heart is ready †
   I will sing and recite a psalm (Ps 56:8).
9. Arise, my glory, arise psalter and harp, †
   I will arise at dawn (Ps 56:9).
10. I will praise You among the peoples, O Lord, †
    I will say a psalm to You among the nations (Ps 56:10).
11. Since Your Mercy is exalted even to the skies †
    and Your truth even to the clouds (Ps 56:11).

---

4. The setting of Prime suggests Christ's presence before Pilate, a common connection made by the people in the Middle Ages. This psalm is almost entirely taken
from Psalm 56. Only one verse, 5b, is taken from Psalm 17. Thus the attitudes of trust
and confidence are prominent.

12.   Be exalted above the heavens, O God, †
     and may Your glory be above all the earth! (Ps 56:12).

[Note that the preceding psalm is always said at Prime.]

At Terce[5]
Antiphon: Holy Virgin Mary
Psalm (IV)

1.   Have mercy on me, O God, for man has trampled me underfoot †
    all the day long they have afflicted me and they fight against me
    (Ps 55:2).
2.   My enemies trample upon me all the day long †
    since those who wage war against me are many (Ps 55:3).
3.   All my enemies have been thinking evil things against me †
    they set an evil plan against me (Ps 40:8b–9a).
4.   Those who guarded my life †
    have conspired together (Ps 70:10b).
5.   They went forth †
    and spoke together (Ps 40:7).
6.   All those who see me laugh at me †
    and they have spoken with [their] lips and have shaken [their]
    heads (Ps 21:8).
7.   I am a worm and no man, †
    the scorn of men and the outcast of the people (Ps 21:7).
8.   I have been made a reproach to my neighbors exceeding all of
    my enemies †
    and a fear for my acquaintances (Ps 30:12a–b).
9.   *O holy Father* (Jn 17:11), do not keep your help from me †
    but look to my defense (Ps 21:20).
10.   Come to my help, †
    Lord, God of my salvation (Ps 37:23).

---

5. Terce is clearly the hour of the scourging, the crowning with thorns, and the mockery and abuse of the crowd.

At Sext[6]
Antiphon: Holy Virgin Mary
Psalm (V)

1. I cried to the Lord with my voice †
with my voice I made supplication to the Lord (Ps 141:2).
2. I pour out my prayer in His sight †
and I speak of my trouble before Him (Ps 141:3).
3. When my spirit failed me †
You knew my ways (Ps 141:4a–b).
4. On the path on which I walked †
the proud have hidden a trap for me (Ps 141:4c–d).
5. I looked to my right and I saw †
and there was no one who knew me (Ps 141:5a–b).
6. I have no means of escape †
and there is no one who cares for my life (Ps 141:5c–d).
7. Because of You I have sustained abuse †
while confusion covers my face (Ps 68:8).
8. I have been made an outcast to my brothers †
and a stranger to the children of my mother (Ps 68:9).
9. *Holy Father* (Jn 17:11), zeal for your house has consumed me †
and the abuses of those who have attacked You have fallen upon
me (Ps 68:10).
10. And against me they have rejoiced and have united together †
and many scourges were heaped upon me and I knew not why
(Ps 34:15).
11. More numerous than the hairs of my head †
are those who hate me without cause (Ps 68:5a–b).
12. Those who persecute me unjustly, my enemies, have been
strengthened †
must I then restore what I did not steal? (Ps 68:5c–d).
13. The wicked witnesses who rise up †
have interrogated me about things of which I am ignorant (Ps
34:11).
14. They repaid me evil for good (Ps 34:12a) *and* they harassed me †
because I pursued good (Ps 37:21).

---

6. Sext: the hour of the crucifixion in which Christ seems to be totally abandoned
and "zeal for His Father's house" has consumed Him.

15. You are *my most holy Father* †
    my King and my God (Ps 43:5).
16. Come to my help, †
    Lord, God of my salvation (Ps 37:23).

At None[7]
Antiphon: Holy Virgin Mary
Psalm (VI)

1. O all of you who pass along the way †
   look and see if there is any sorrow like my sorrow (Lm 1:12a–b).
2. For many dogs have surrounded me †
   a pack of evildoers has closed in on me (Ps 21:17).
3. They have looked and stared upon me †
   they have divided my garments among them and for my tunic
   they have cast lots (Ps 21:18b–19).
4. They have pierced my hands and my feet †
   they have numbered all my bones (Ps 21:17c–18a).
5. They have opened their mouth against me †
   like a lion raging and roaring (Ps 21:14).
6. I am poured out like water †
   and all of my bones have been scattered (Ps 21:15a–b).
7. And my heart has become like melting wax †
   in the midst of my bosom (Ps 21:15c).
8. My strength is dried up liked baked clay †
   and my tongue clings to my jaws (Ps 21:16a–b).
9. And they have given gall as my food †
   and in my thirst they gave me vinegar to drink (Ps 68:22).
10. And *they have led* me into *the dust of death* (cf. Ps 21:16c) †
    and they have added grief to my wounds (Ps 68:27b).
11. I have slept and have risen (Ps 3:6) †
    and *my most holy Father* has received me with glory (cf. Ps 72:24c).
12. *Holy Father* (Jn 17:11), You have held my right hand †
    and You have led me with Your counsel (Ps 72:24).

---

7. The Synoptic Gospels see this hour as that of Christ's death. Saint Francis uses those psalm verses that most vividly portray the attitudes of Jesus. Yet even in the depths of depression, the saint perceives the hope of the Resurrection, as verse 10 suggests.

13. For what is there in heaven for me †
and besides you what do I want on earth (Ps 72:25)?

14. See, see that I am God, says the Lord †
I shall be exalted among the nations and I shall be exalted on the
earth (cf. Ps 45:11).

15. Blessed be the Lord, the God of Israel (Lk 1:68a), Who has redeemed the souls of His servants with His very own most holy
Blood †
and [Who] will not abandon all who hope in Him (Ps 33:23).

16. And we know, for He comes, †
for He will come to judge justice (cf. Ps 95:13b).

At Vespers[8]
Antiphon: Holy Virgin Mary
Psalm (VII)

1. All you nations clap your hands †
shout to God with a voice of gladness (Ps 46:2).

2. For the Lord, the Most High †
the awesome, is the great King over all the earth (Ps 46:3).

3. For *the most holy Father of heaven,* our King before all ages, †
has sent *His beloved Son from on high* and has brought salvation in
the midst of the earth (Ps 73:12).

4. Let the heavens be glad and let the earth rejoice, let the sea and
all that is in it be moved †
let the fields and all that is in them be joyful (Ps 95:11–12a).

5. Sing a new song to Him †
sing to the Lord, all the earth (cf. Ps 95:1)!

6. For the Lord is great and highly to be praised, †
and awesome is He beyond all gods (Ps 95:4)!

7. Give to the Lord, [you] families of nations, give to the Lord glory and honor, †
give to the Lord the glory due His name (Ps 95:7–8a).

8. *Offer up your bodies and take up His holy cross* †

---

8. The verses Saint Francis uses at this hour show his sense of the victory of the
Risen Lord. The psalm is redolent with expressions of wonder and his eagerness to
share his joy with all creation. Nonetheless, the saint is not satisfied with these expressions of celebration; he returns to the main theme of this paraliturgical prayer: an embrace of the cross of Jesus, which leads to victory over sin and death (cf. verse 8).

and follow His most holy commands even to the end (cf. Lk 14:27; 1 Pet 2:21).

9. Let the whole earth tremble before His face †
   say among the nations that the Lord has ruled from a tree (Ps 95:9b–10a).

[The office is recited daily to this point from Good Friday to the Feast of the Ascension. On the Feast of the Ascension, however, these versicles are added:]

10. And he ascended into heaven and is seated at the right hand of the most holy Father in heaven; O God, be exalted above the heavens †
    and above all the earth be Your glory (Ps 56:12).
11. And we know that He has come †
    that He will come to judge justice.

[And note that from the Ascension to the Advent of the Lord this Psalm is said daily in the same manner, that is: *All you nations* with the preceding versicles; the *Glory to the Father* is said at the ending of the Psalm, that is: *that He will come to judge justice.*

Note that the preceding Psalms are recited from Good Friday until Easter Sunday. They are said in the same manner from the octave of Pentecost until the Advent of the Lord and from the Octave of the Epiphany until Easter Sunday, with the exception of Sundays and the principal feasts, on which they are not said; on the other days, however, they are said daily.]

PART TWO: FOR THE EASTER SEASON
On Holy Saturday, namely at the end of Saturday

At Compline
Antiphon: Holy Virgin Mary
Psalm (VIII)

1. God, come to my assistance †
   Lord, make haste to help me.
2. Let them be put to shame and confounded †
   who seek my life.

3. Let them be put to flight and disgraced †
   who rejoice at my misfortune.
4. Let them be turned back in shame †
   who say to me: Aha! Aha!
5. May all those who seek You exult and be glad in You †
   and may those who love Your salvation ever say: "May God be
   glorified!"
6. But I am afflicted and poor: †
   help me, O God.
7. You are my help and my deliverer †
   Lord, do not delay (Ps 69:2–6).

[. . . and this is said daily at Compline up to the octave of Pentecost.]

At Matins of Easter Sunday
Antiphon: Holy Virgin Mary
Psalm (IX)

1. Sing to the Lord a new song †
   for He has done wondrous deeds (Ps 97:1a–b).
2. His right hand and His holy arm †
   have sacrificed His beloved Son (Ps 97:1c–d).
3. The Lord has made His salvation known †
   in the sight of the nations He has revealed His justice (Ps 97:2).
4. On *that* day the Lord sent His mercy, †
   and His song at night (cf. Ps 41:9a–b).
5. This is the day the Lord has made †
   let us rejoice and be glad in it (Ps 117:24).
6. Blessed is he who comes in the name of the Lord †
   the Lord is God, and He has given us light (Ps 117:26a, 27a).
7. Let the heavens be glad and the earth rejoice, let the sea and all
   that is in it be moved †
   let the fields be joyful and all that is in them (Ps 95:11–12a).
8. Give to the Lord, [you] families of nations, give to the Lord glory and praise †
   give to the Lord the glory due His name (Ps 95:7–8a).

[The office is said daily to this point from Easter to the Feast of the
Ascension at all the hours except Vespers, Compline, and Prime. On
the night of the Ascension these verses are added:]

9. Sing to the Lord, O kingdoms of the earth, †
   sing to the Lord (Ps 67:33a).

10. Chant praise to God Who ascends above the heights of the heavens †
    to the east (Ps 67:33b–34a).

11. Look, He will give His voice the voice of power; give glory to
    God! †
    Above Israel is His greatness, and His power is in the skies (Ps
    67:34b–35).

12. God is marvelous in His holy ones †
    the God of Israel Himself will give power and strength to His
    people. Blessed be God (Ps 67:36)! Glory [to the Father, and to
    the Son, and to the Holy Spirit. As it was in the beginning, is
    now and will be forever. Amen.]

[. . . and note that this psalm is recited daily from the Ascension of the
Lord until the octave of Pentecost with the preceding versicles at
Matins, Terce, Sext, and None; the *Glory to the Father* is said where
Blessed be God! (cf. v. 12) is said, and not elsewhere.

Also note that it is said in the same way only at Matins on Sundays, and the principal feasts, from the octave of Pentecost until Holy
Thursday because on that day the Lord ate the Passover meal with
His disciples; or another psalm can be said at Matins or at Vespers, as
one wishes, namely: *I will praise You, O Lord* (Ps 29), etc., as it is contained in the Psalter; and this from Easter Sunday to the feast of the
Ascension, and not beyond.]

At Prime
Antiphon: Holy Virgin Mary
Psalm: *Have mercy on me, O Lord, have mercy on me,* as it is given
above (Psalm III).

At Terce, Sext, None
Psalm: *Sing,* as it is given above, is said (Psalm IX).

At Vespers
Psalm: *All you nations,* as it is given above (Psalm VII).

PART THREE: FOR SUNDAYS AND PRINCIPAL FEASTS

[Here begin the other psalms which our most blessed Father Francis also arranged, which are to be said in place of the preceding psalms of the Passion of the Lord on Sundays and the principal feasts from the Octave of Pentecost until Advent and from the Octave of the Epiphany until Holy Thursday. You will surely understand that they are to be said on that day [Holy Thursday], since it is the Passover of the Lord.]

At Compline
Antiphon: Holy Virgin Mary
Psalm: *God, come to my assistance,* as it is given in the Psalter (Psalm VIII).

At Matins
Antiphon: Holy Virgin Mary
Psalm: *Sing to the Lord,* as it is given above (Psalm IX).

At Prime
Antiphon: Holy Virgin Mary
Psalm: *Have mercy on me, O God, have mercy on me,* as it is given above (Psalm III).

At Terce
Antiphon: Holy Virgin Mary
Psalm [X]

1. Cry out to the Lord with joy, all the earth! Speak praise to His name †
   give glory to His praise (cf. Ps 65:1–2).
2. Say to God: How terrifying are Your deeds, Lord, †
   in the vastness of Your strength Your enemies shall fawn upon You (Ps 65:3).
3. Let all the earth adore You and sing praise to You †
   let us sing praise to Your name (Ps 65:4).
4. Come, listen, and I will tell all of you who fear God †
   how much He has done for my soul (Ps 65:16).
5. To Him I cried with my mouth †
   and sounds of music were on my tongue (Ps 65:17).

6. And from His holy temple He heard my voice †
   and my cry reached His ears (Ps 17:7c–d).

7. Bless our *Lord,* you peoples †
   and make the voice of His praise be heard (cf. Ps 65:8).

8. And all the tribes of the earth shall be blessed in Him †
   all the nations shall proclaim Him (Ps 71:17c–d).

9. Blessed be the Lord, the God of Israel †
   Who alone does marvelous [and] great [deeds] (Ps 71:18).

10. And blessed forever be the name of His majesty †
    and may all the earth be filled with His majesty. Amen! Amen!
    (Ps 71:19).

At Sext
Antiphon: Holy Virgin Mary
Psalm (XI)

1. May the Lord hear you on the day of distress †
   may the name of the God of Jacob protect you (Ps 19:2)

2. May He send you help from [His] sanctuary †
   and from Zion may He sustain you (Ps 19:3).

3. May He remember all of your sacrifices †
   and may your burnt offering be fruitful (Ps 19:4).

4. May He grant you what your heart desires †
   and may He fulfill your every plan (Ps 19:5).

5. May we rejoice in your victory †
   and may we be victorious in the name of the Lord our God (Ps
   19:6).

6. May the Lord fulfill all of your requests (Ps 19:6)! Now I know
   that (Ps 19:7a–b) *the Lord sent His Son Jesus Christ* †
   and He will judge the peoples with justice (Ps 9:9b).

7. And the Lord has become the refuge of the poor, a stronghold in
   times of distress †
   and let them trust in You who know Your name (Ps 9:10–11a).

8. Blessed be the Lord my God (Ps 143:1b) since He has become my
   stronghold and my refuge †
   in the day of my distress (cf. Ps 58:17c–d).

9. My helper, I will praise You, for You, God, are my stronghold †
   and my God, my mercy! (Ps 58:18).

At None
Antiphon: Holy Virgin Mary
Psalm (XII)

1. In You, Lord, I have hoped, let me never be put to shame; †
   in Your fidelity, deliver me and rescue me (Ps 70:1b–2a).
2. Incline Your ear to me †
   save me (Ps 70:2b).
3. Be my protector, O God, and a stronghold †
   that You may save me (Ps 70:3a–b).
4. For You are my patience, Lord, †
   You are my hope, Lord, from my youth (Ps 70:5).
5. In You I have been supported from birth; from my mother's
   womb You are my protector †
   and of You my song will always be (Ps 70:6).
6. May my mouth be filled with praise that I may sing of Your glory †
   and all the day long of your greatness (Ps 70:8).
7. Answer me, Lord, for Your mercy is kind †
   look upon me out of the vastness of Your mercies (Ps 68:17).
8. And hide not Your face from Your servant ; †
   because I am in distress, make haste quickly to answer me (Ps
   68:18).
9. Blessed be the Lord my God (Ps 143:1b), for He has become my
   protector and my refuge †
   on the day of my distress.
10. O my helper, Your praises will I sing, for God is my protector, †
    my God, my mercy (Ps 58:18).

At Vespers
Antiphon: Holy Virgin Mary
Psalm: *All you nations* as it is given above (Psalm VII).

PART FOUR: FOR THE TIME OF THE ADVENT OF THE LORD

[Here begin other Psalms which our most holy Father Francis similarly arranged; these are to be recited in place of the preceding psalms
of the Passion of the Lord from the Advent of the Lord until Christmas Eve inclusive.]

THE WRITINGS

At Compline
Antiphon: Holy Virgin Mary
Psalm (XIII)

1. How long, Lord, will You eternally forget me? How long will
   You turn your face from me?
2. How long must I place doubts in my soul †
   sorrow in my heart each day?
3. How long will my enemy rejoice over me? †
   Look, and hear me, O Lord, my God.
4. Give light to my eyes that I may never sleep in death †
   that my enemy may never say: I have overcome him.
5. [Those] who trouble me would rejoice if I stumbled †
   but I have trusted in Your kindness.
6. My heart shall rejoice in Your saving help; I will sing to the Lord
   who has given good things to me †
   and I will praise the name of the Lord most high (Ps 12:1–6).

At Matins
Antiphon: Holy Virgin Mary
Psalm (XIV)

1. I will praise you, Lord, *most holy Father, King of heaven and earth,* †
   for You have consoled me (cf. Is 12:1).
2. You are God my Savior; †
   I will act confidently and not be afraid (Is 12:2a–b).
3. The Lord is my strength and my glory; †
   He has become my salvation (Is 12:2c–d).
4. Your right hand, O Lord, is magnificent in strength; Your right
   hand, O Lord, has shattered the enemy, †
   and in the vastness of Your glory You have overthrown my enemies (Ex 15:6–7a).
5. Let the poor see [this] and be glad †
   seek God and your soul shall live (Ps 68:33).
6. Let heaven and earth praise Him †
   the sea and every living thing in them (Ps 68:35).
7. For God will save Zion †
   and the cities of Judah will be rebuilt (Ps 68:36a–b).

8. And they shall dwell there †
   and they shall acquire it as [their] inheritance (Ps 68:36c).
9. And the descendants of his servants shall possess it †
   and those who love His name shall dwell in it (Ps 68:37).

At Prime
Antiphon: Holy Virgin Mary
Psalm: *Have mercy on me, God, have mercy on me,* as it is given above
(Psalm III).

At Terce
Antiphon: Holy Virgin Mary
Psalm: *Shout joyfully to God,* as it is given above (Psalm X).

At Sext
Antiphon: Holy Virgin Mary
Psalm: *May the Lord hear you,* as it is given above (Psalm XI).

At None
Antiphon: Holy Virgin Mary
Psalm: *In You, Lord, I have hoped,* as it is given above (Psalm XII).

At Vespers
Antiphon: Holy Virgin Mary
Psalm: *All you nations,* as it is given above (Psalm VII).

[Also note that this psalm is said only to the verse: *Let the whole earth tremble before His Face* (v. 9); you will clearly understand that the entire verse *Offer your bodies* is said. At the end of this verse the *Glory to the Father* is said and recited in this way each day at Vespers from Advent until Christmas Eve.]

THE WRITINGS

PART FIVE: FROM THE TIME OF THE NATIVITY OF THE LORD UNTIL THE OCTAVE OF EPHIPHANY

At Vespers of the Nativity of the Lord
Antiphon: Holy Virgin Mary
Psalm (XV)

1. Ring out your joy to God our help †
   and shout with cries of gladness to the Lord God living and true (cf. Ps 46:2b).
2. For the Lord, the most high, †
   the awesome, is the great king over all the earth (Ps 46:3).
3. *For the most holy Father of heaven,* our King before all ages (Ps 73:12a), *has sent His beloved Son from on high* †
   and He was born of the Blessed Virgin Holy Mary.
4. He called upon me: You are my Father (Ps 88:27a), †
   and I will enthrone Him as the firstborn, the highest, above the kings of the earth (Ps 88:28).
5. On that day the Lord sent His mercy †
   and at night His song was heard (Ps 41:9a–b).
6. This is the day the Lord has made †
   let us rejoice and be glad in it (Ps 117:24).
7. *For the most holy beloved child was given to us, and He was born for us* (cf. Is 9:5) *along the way and placed in a manger* †
   since there was no room in the inn (cf. Lk 2·7).
8. Glory to *the Lord* God in the highest †
   and on earth peace to men of good will (cf. Lk 2:14).
9. Let the heavens be glad and the earth rejoice, let the sea and all that is in it be moved †
   let the fields and everything that is in them be joyful (Ps 95:11–12a).
10. Sing a new song *to Him* †
    sing to the Lord, all the earth (cf. Ps 95:1).
11. For the Lord is great and worthy of all praise †
    He is awesome, beyond all gods (Ps 95:4)!
12. Give to the Lord, you families of nations, give to the Lord glory and praise †
    give to the Lord the glory due His name (Ps 95:7–8a).
13. *Offer your bodies and take up His holy cross* †

and follow His most holy commands even to the end (cf. Lk 14:27; 1 Pet 2:21).

[Note that this psalm is said from the Nativity of the Lord until the Octave of the Epiphany at all of the hours. If anyone wishes to say this office of Saint Francis, he should say it in this way: first he should say the *Our Father* with the praises, that is, *Holy, holy, holy*. At the end of the praises with the prayer, as it is written above, let him say the antiphon *Holy Virgin Mary* with the psalm which has been assigned for each hour of the day and night. And let this office be recited with great reverence.]

The Parchment Given to Brother Leo

With this brief piece written in his own hand (and now preserved in Assisi at the Basilica of Saint Francis), Francis opens his heart to us, to reveal not only his prayers and meditations on Mount La Verna after the reception of the Stigmata (mid-September 1224), but also his deep love and solicitude for Brother Leo, priest, companion, and scribe. Thomas of Celano relates the circumstances in his Second Life of Saint Francis, n. 49, using in part the annotations Leo had later added in red ink: "Blessed Francis wrote with his own hand this blessing for me, Brother Leo." Then: "In like manner he made this sign Tau [a large T] together with the head [skull] with his own hand." A third annotation, in red ink, in the upper margin, again of Brother Leo, narrates the circumstances and thus fixes the date: "Blessed Francis two years before his death kept a Lent [a forty-day retreat] in the place of Mount La Verna in honor of the Blessed Virgin Mary, the Mother of God, and of the blessed Michael the Archangel, from the Feast of the Assumption of the holy Virgin Mary until the September Feast of Saint Michael. And the hand of the Lord was laid upon him. After the vision and words of the Seraph and the impression of the Stigmata of Christ in his body he composed these praises written on the other side of this sheet and wrote them in his own hand, giving thanks to God for the kindness bestowed on him."[1]

SIDE ONE: THE PRAISES OF GOD

1. *You are* holy, Lord, the only *God, You do wonders.* (Ps 76:15)
2. You are strong, You are great, You are the most high,
   You are the almighty King.
   You, *Holy Father,* the King *of heaven and earth.* (Jn 17:11; Mt 11:25)

---

1. A thorough study of this document was done by Duane Lapsanski, O.F.M., in "The Autographs on the 'Chartula' of Saint Francis of Assisi," *Archivum Franciscanum Historicum* 67 (1974); 18–37. The critical text of Kajetan Esser, O.F.M., was based on this work (cf. Kajetan Esser, O.F.M., *Opuscula Sancti Patris Francisci Assisiensis* [Grottaferrata: Collegium S. Bonaventurae, 1978], pp. 89–93).

3. You are Three and One, Lord God of gods; (cf. Ps 135:2)
   You are good, all good, the highest good,
   Lord, God, living and true. (cf. 1 Thes 1:19)
4. You are love, charity.
   You are wisdom; You are humility; You are patience; (cf. Ps 70:5)
   You are beauty; You are meekness; You are security;
   You are inner peace; You are joy; You are our hope and joy;
   You are justice; You are moderation, You are all our riches
   [You are enough for us].
5. You are beauty, You are meekness;
   You are the protector, (cf. Ps 30:5)
   You are our guardian and defender;
   You are strength; You are refreshment. (cf. Ps 42:2)
6. You are our hope, You are our faith, You are our charity,
   You are all our sweetness,
   You are our eternal life:
   Great and wonderful Lord,
   God almighty, Merciful Savior.

SIDE TWO: A BLESSING GIVEN TO BROTHER LEO[2]

1. *May the Lord Bless you and keep you;*
   May He show His face to you and be merciful to you.
2. *May He turn His countenance to you and give you peace* (Num 6:24–26).
3. May the Lord bless you, Brother Leo (cf. Num 6:27b).

---

2. S. J. P. van Dijk has argued convincingly that Saint Francis very likely became acquainted with this formula not from his study of the Old Testament but rather from the liturgy. It is probable, the scholar states, "that Francis was so deeply impressed by this blessing, when his own confreres were ordained clerics by one of the bishops of the Central Italian dioceses" (S. J. P. van Dijk, "Saint Francis' Blessing of Brother Leo," *Archivum Franciscanum Historicum* 47 [1954]: 201). The *Ordo ad clericum faciendum*, a fragment from a twelfth-century pontifical that probably originated in Arezzo, contains precisely this formula.

The Praises To Be Said at All the Hours

There is no doubt about the authenticity of this text. It is found in many of the early manuscripts, including the Assisi Codex 338, which indicates that Saint Francis "arranged and recited [it] at every Hour of the day and night and before the Office of the Blessed Virgin Mary." The contents of this medley of Biblical praises is sufficient to characterize it as coming from the Seraphic Father, for it is filled with many texts that he uses throughout his writings. The prayer that concludes the praises is simply an echo of that prominent image of God Who is "all good, supreme good, wholly good." This, too, can be discovered throughout the writings.

Three sets of rubrics that accompany this text in the manuscript tradition suggest that Saint Francis arranged these Biblical praises so that the friars would pray them before each hour of the Office. The Mirror of Perfection, n. 82, however, suggests that it was imposed by the saint as a penance for the utterance of an idle word. In all of these instances, these Praises are associated with the Prayer Inspired by the Our Father (p. 104) and indicate the desire of the Seraphic Father that expressions of praise for a loving Father characterize the speech of the friars.[1]

1. Holy, holy, holy Lord God Almighty, Who is and Who was and Who is to come (cf. Rev 4:8):
   Let us praise and glorify Him forever.
2. O Lord our God, You are worthy to receive *praise* and glory and honor *and blessing* (cf. Rev 4:11):
   Let us praise and glorify Him forever.
3. The Lamb Who was slain is worthy to receive power and divin-

---

1. For further information on this text, consult Oktavian Schmucki, O.F.M. Cap., "Le 'Lodi per Ogni Ora'—Un Invitatorio Francescano alla Celebrazione dell' Ufficio Divino," *Preghiera Liturgica secondo l'Esempio e l'Insegnamento di San Francesco d'Assisi: seconda edizione accresciuta* (Rome: Conferenza Italiana Superiori Provinciali Cappuccini, 1979), pp. 29–34.

ity, and wisdom and strength, and honor and glory and blessing (Rev 5:12):
> Let us praise and glorify Him forever.

4. Let us bless the Father and the Son with the Holy Spirit:
> Let us praise and glorify Him forever.

5. Bless the Lord, all you works of the Lord (Dan 3:57):
> Let us praise and glorify Him forever.

6. Sing praise to our God, all you His servants and you who fear
God, the small and the great (Rev 19:5):
> Let us praise and glorify Him forever.

7. Let heaven and earth praise Him Who is glorious (cf. Ps 68:35):
> Let us praise and glorify Him forever.

8. And every creature that is in heaven and on earth and under the
earth and in the sea and those which are in them (Rev 5:13):
> Let us praise and glorify Him forever.

9. Glory to the Father and to the Son and to the Holy Spirit:
> Let us praise and glorify Him forever.

10. As it was in the beginning, is now, and will be forever. Amen.
> Let us praise and glorify Him forever.

11. Prayer:
> All-powerful, most holy,
> most high, and supreme God:
> all good,
> supreme good,
> totally good,
> You Who *alone are good;*[2]
> may we give You
> all praise, all *glory,*
> all thanks, all *honor:*
> all *blessing,*[3]
> and all good things.
> So be it.
> So be it.
> Amen.

---

2. Lk 18:19.
3. Rev 4:9,11; 5:12.

The Prayer Before the Crucifix

The biographies of Saint Francis written by Thomas of Celano and Saint Bonaventure characterize the early years of the saint's conversion as a struggle to discern God's will. Both of these authors, as well as the author of the Legend of the Three Companions, *describe the scene in the deserted church of San Damiano in Assisi during which the young Francis heard a command of the Crucified Lord while he was absorbed in prayer. "Francis," the voice told him, "go and repair my house, which, as you see, is falling completely into ruin." The remainder of his life was spent consciously or unconsciously responding to that command.*

Almost all of the manuscripts that contain this simple prayer indicate its origin at the foot of the crucifix in the church of San Damiano. It clearly reflects the struggle of the early years of the saint's life as well as his ever-present desire to fulfill the will of God. Thus it is a prayer that can be seen as characterizing the Poverello's entire life.

The form in which this prayer is presented in this volume reflects a simple version that has been transmitted through various Italian idioms. The manuscript of the Bodleian Library in Oxford, England (cod Can. Misc. 525), contains a Latin translation as well as a notation that this version would enable others throughout the world to profit from the prayer. As it became more popular, the prayer was embellished and lost some of its simplicity.

Most high,
glorious God,
enlighten the darkness of my heart
and give me, Lord,
a correct faith,
a certain hope,
a perfect charity,
sense and knowledge,
so that I may carry out Your holy and true command.

The Prayer Inspired by the Our Father

Both Thomas of Celano (First Life, n. 45) and Saint Bonaventure (Legenda Major IV, 3) write of the lessons on prayer that Saint Francis gave to his friars and that centered on the Our Father. The Second Version of the Letter to the Faithful, 21, and the Earlier Rule, XXII, 28, verify the saint's love of this simple Gospel prayer. Meditation on each phrase of the Our Father was quite common in the Middle Ages as the writings of Saint Bernard of Clairvaux and Hugh of Saint Victor indicate. The manuscript tradition calls into question the authenticity of this prayer. (Kajetan Esser, O.F.M., discovered no manuscripts from the thirteenth century and only six manuscripts from the fourteenth century.) Nonetheless, recent scholarship, including that of Kajetan Esser, has accepted the prayer as authentic, though not original because Saint Francis borrowed heavily from other writings. The scholars base their arguments on the presence of many Biblical images and passages that are present in the other writings of the saint. In many ways, this Prayer Inspired by the Our Father *is an expression of the inner life of Saint Francis.*[1]

1. O OUR most holy FATHER,
    Our Creator, Redeemer, Consoler, and Savior
2. WHO ARE IN HEAVEN:
    In the angels and in the saints,
    Enlightening them to love, because You, Lord, are light
    Inflaming them to love, because You, Lord, are love
    Dwelling [in them] and filling them with happiness,
        because You, Lord, are the Supreme Good,
            the Eternal Good
        from Whom comes all good
        without Whom there is no good.

---

1. For further information on this text, consult Kajetan Esser, O.F.M., "Die dem hl. Franziskus von Assisi zugeschriebene 'Expositio in Pater Noster,' " *Collectanea Franciscana* 40 (1970): 241–271.

3. HALLOWED BE YOUR NAME:
   May our knowledge of You become ever clearer
   That we may know the breadth of Your blessings
       the length of Your promises
       the height of Your majesty
       the depth of Your judgments[2]
4. YOUR KINGDOM COME:
   So that You may rule in us through Your grace
   and enable us to come to Your kingdom
       where there is an unclouded vision of You
           a perfect love of You
           a blessed campanionship with You
           an eternal enjoyment of You
5. YOUR WILL BE DONE ON EARTH AS IT IS IN
   HEAVEN:
   That we may love You with our whole heart by always thinking
   of You[3]
           with our whole soul by always desiring You
           with our whole mind by directing all our
               intentions to You and by seeking Your
               glory in everything
           and with our whole strength by spending all our
               energies and affections
               of soul and body
               in the service of Your love
               and of nothing else
   and may we love our neighbors as ourselves
       by drawing them all with our whole strength to Your love
       by rejoicing in the good fortunes of others as well as our
         own
       and by sympathizing with the misfortunes of others
       and by giving offense to no one[4]
6. GIVE US THIS DAY:
   in memory and understanding and reverence
       of the love which [our Lord Jesus Christ] had for us

---

2. Cf. Eph 3:18.
3. Cf. Lk 10:27.
4. Cf. 2 Cor 6:3.

and of those things which He said and did and suffered for
us
OUR DAILY BREAD:
Your own Beloved Son, our Lord Jesus Christ
7. AND FORGIVE US OUR TRESPASSES:
Through Your ineffable mercy
through the power of the Passion of Your Beloved Son
together with the merits and intercession of the Blessed Virgin
Mary and all Your chosen ones
8. AS WE FORGIVE THOSE WHO TRESPASS AGAINST
US:
And whatever we do not forgive perfectly,
do you, Lord, enable us to forgive to the full
so that we may truly love [our] enemies
and fervently intercede for them before You
returning no one evil for evil[5]
and striving to help everyone in You
9. AND LEAD US NOT INTO TEMPTATION
Hidden or obvious
Sudden or persistent
10. BUT DELIVER US FROM EVIL
Past, present and to come.
Glory to the Father and to the Son and to the Holy Spirit
As it was in the beginning, is now, and will be forever. Amen.

---

5. Cf. 1 Thes 5:15.

The Earlier Rule

The development of the Rule of the Friars Minor is one of the areas of Franciscan research that has prompted the greatest attention throughout the centuries. Entire treatises have been written concerning the evolution of the primitive legislation that received the oral approval of Pope Innocent III in 1209 or 1210 and that developed finally into the Rule of 1223, the Regula bullata *or Later Rule, having received the papal bull of approval on 29 November 1223. Three general structures are known regarding this development: (1) the "propositum vitae" or the simple pattern of life that Saint Francis presented in 1209 or 1210; (2) the Rule of 1221, the* Regula non bullata *(The Earlier Rule as it is entitled in this volume), which built on the earlier proposal; and (3) the* Regula bullata *of 1223, which, according to Saint Bonaventure, was written for a second time after the first text was lost by the saint's vicar.*

The primitive rule of 1209 or 1210, the propositum vitae, *has been lost, probably because it was gradually expanded or amplified and absorbed into the* Regula non bullata. *The Testament Saint Francis wrote shortly before his death may well provide the best insights into the contents of this primitive Rule. Profound convictions emerge in the Testament concerning the divine inspiration that guided Saint Francis, the complete autonomy of his charism, and yet the important role of the Church from the very beginning of his religious experience. There have been many attempts to reconstruct the exact text "written down simply and in a few words" (Testament, 15) that Saint Francis presented to Pope Innocent III, yet historians are generally agreed that it is impossible to determine the exact work.*

As long as the primitive fraternity was still small in number, however, the charismatic personality of Saint Francis substituted for the lack of precise regulations and specifications that would come in a longer Rule. It is difficult to determine exactly the length of time in which the primitive fraternity stayed in this condition. The early biographies and chronicles describe frequent gatherings of the first friars in which they reflected on their experiences and listened to the guidance of the Seraphic Father. After the marvelous growth of the Order—especially after 1217 and 1219 when the friars scaled the Alps and crossed the Mediterranean—it was necessary to provide new guidelines to maintain the ideals and enthusiasm of the primitive fraternity. Furthermore, the impact of the Fourth Lateran Council (1215), as well as the papal initiatives of Pope Honorious III, contributed to the development of the primitive rule.

Thus it is possible to discern in the Earlier Rule, the Regula non bullata, the presence of (1) the guiding principles of the propositum vitae; (2) the personal admonitions and exhortations of Saint Francis himself; (3) the directives of the Chapters of the friars; (4) the prescriptions of the Fourth Lateran Council; and (5) the papal decrees of Pope Honorius III. In addition, the presence of someone well versed in Scripture, particularly the Synoptic Gospels, can be seen in this text. That person, according to the Chronicle of Jordan of Giano 15, is Caesar of Speyer, whom Saint Francis asked to embellish the text of the Rule with appropriate Scriptural passages.

The Earlier Rule is one of the richest spiritual documents of the Franciscan tradition. It provides innumerable insights into the ideals of Saint Francis, as well as indications of the tensions and forces that shaped the brotherhood gathered around him.[1]

PROLOGUE

1. In the name of the Father and of the Son and of the Holy Spirit.

2. This is the life of the Gospel of Jesus Christ[2] which Brother Francis asked the Lord Pope to be granted and confirmed for him;

---

1. A thorough study of the development of the Rules of Saint Francis was done by Oktavian Schmucki, O.F.M. Cap., "Gli Scritti Legislativi di San Francesco," *Approccio Storico-Critico alle Fonti Francescane* (Rome: Ed. Antonianum, 1979), pp. 73–98. It contains an excellent bibliography of scholarship on the *propositum vitae*, the *Earlier Rule* (the *Regula non Bullata*), and the Later Rule (the *Regula Bullata*). Critical studies of the *Earlier Rule* have been undertaken by (1) Kajetan Esser, O.F.M., "Zur Textgeschichte der 'Regula non bullata' des hl. Franziskus," *Studien zu den Opuscula des hl. Franziskus von Assisi* (Rome, 1973), pp. 59–77; *Textkritische Untersuchungen sur Regula non bullata der Minderbrüder* (Grottaferrata: Collegium S. Bonaventurae, 1974). (2) David E. Flood, O.F.M., *Die Regula non bullata der Minderbrüder*, Franziskanische Forschungen, 19 (Werl/Westf., 1967).

2. The Rule begins with the tremendously important concept of life, suggesting that this document is more than a legal text. It is a description of a concrete way of living the Gospel of Jesus Christ.

and he granted and confirmed it for him and his brothers present and to come.[3] 3. Brother Francis and whoever will be the head of this Order promises obedience and reverence to the Lord Pope Innocent and to his successors. 4. And all the other brothers are bound to obey Brother Francis and his successors.

CHAPTER I THE BROTHERS MUST LIVE WITHOUT ANYTHING OF THEIR OWN AND IN CHASTITY AND IN OBEDIENCE

1. The rule and life of these brothers is this: to live in obedience, in chastity, and without anything of their own,[4] and to follow the teaching and the footprints of our Lord Jesus Christ, Who says: 2. *If you wish to be perfect, go* (Mt 19:21) and *sell* everything (cf. Lk 18:22) *you have and give it to the poor, and you will have treasure in heaven; and come, follow me* (Mt 19:21). 3. And, *If anyone wishes to come after me, let him deny himself and take up his cross and follow me* (Mt 16:24). 4. Again: *If anyone wishes to come to me and does not hate father and mother and wife and children and brothers and sisters, and even his own life, he cannot be my disciple* (Lk 14:26). 5. And: *Everyone who has left* father or mother, brothers or sisters, wife or children, houses or lands because of me, *shall receive a hundredfold and shall possess eternal life* (cf. Mt 19:29; Mk 10:29, Lk 18:30).[5]

---

3. This sentence suggests that the *propositum vitae*, or primitive form of life that Saint Francis and his first followers presented to Pope Innocent III in 1209/1210, is somehow contained in this document.

4. This formula was in use during the last part of the twelfth century. The Roman Curia imposed it on all new religious orders during the pontificate of Pope Innocent III (cf. Sr. Margaret Mary, "Evolution of the Teaching on Commitment by Monastic Vow: Cluny to the End of the 19th Century," *Cistercian Studies* 12 (1977): 41–65.

5. The Chronicler, Jordan of Giano, narrates that Saint Francis asked Brother Caesar of Speyer to adorn with words from the Gospel the Rule that he had written in simple words (cf. Jordan of Giano, *Chronicle* in *Thirteenth Century Chronicles*, trans. Placid Hermann, O.F.M., [Chicago: Franciscan Herald Press, 1961], p. 30).

CHAPTER II   THE RECEPTION AND THE CLOTHING OF THE BROTHERS[6]

1. If anyone, desiring by divine inspiration to accept this life,[7] should come to our brothers, let him be received by them with kindness. 2. And if he is determined to accept our life, the brothers should take great care not to become involved in his temporal affairs; but let them present him to their minister as quickly as possible. 3. The minister on his part should receive him with kindness and encourage him and diligently explain to him the tenor of our life. 4. When this has been done, the aforesaid person—if he wishes and is able to do so spiritually and without any impediment—should sell all his possessions and strive to give them all to the poor. 5. The brothers and the minister of the brothers should take care not to become involved in any way in his temporal affairs; 6. nor should they accept any money either themselves or through an intermediary. 7. However, if they are in need, the brothers can accept instead of money other things needed for the body like other poor people.[8] 8. And when he has returned, let the minister give him the clothes of probation for a whole year, namely, two tunics without a hood, a cord and trousers,[9] and a small cape reaching to the cord. 9. When the year and term of probation has ended, let him be received into obedience. 10. Afterward he will not be allowed to join another Order or to "wander outside obedience" according to the decree of the Lord Pope and according to the Gospel;[10]

---

6. An in-depth treatment of the material in this chapter, as well as in the *Later Rule*, II, can be found in Oktavian Schmucki, O.F.M. Cap., "De Initiatione in Vitam Franciscanum Luce Regulae Aliorumque Primaevorum Fontium," *Laurentianum* 12 (1971): 169–197, 241–264.

7. Cf. *The Form of Life Given to Saint Clare and Her Sisters*, n. 1, for an understanding of the phrase "divine inspiration."

8. For a discussion of the abuses connected with entrance into religious life at this period of history, consult Joseph H. Lynch, *Simoniacal Entry into Religious Life from 1000 to 1260: A Social, Economic, and Legal Study* (Columbus: Ohio State University, 1976).

9. The Latin word used here and in the *Later Rule*, II, is *braccas*, which designates short trousers that could be worn while traveling. The texts also speak of a *caperone* or a small cape, which was a kind of upper garment extending down to the cord.

10. This prescription fulfills the papal bull *Cum secundum consilium* of Pope Honorius III, September 22, 1220: "We forbid you to receive to profession in your Order anyone who has not been on probation for one year. After profession has been made, none of the friars should dare to leave your Order. Furthermore, it is forbidden to anyone to receive anyone who has left the Order. We also forbid anyone in the habit of your Order to wander about outside obedience and to debase the purity of your poverty" (Honorius III, *Bullarium Franciscanum* I, 6; trans. Canisius Connors, O.F.M.).

for *no one who puts his hand to the plow and looks back is fit for the king-dom of God* (Lk 9:62).

11. But if someone should come who cannot give away his posses-sions without an impediment and yet has the spiritual desire [to do so], let him leave those things behind; and this suffices for him. 12. No one should be accepted contrary to the form and the prescription of the holy Church. 13. The other brothers who have already prom-ised obedience should have one tunic with a hood and another with-out a hood, if that is necessary, and a cord and trousers. 14. And all the brothers should wear poor clothes, and they can patch them with sackcloth and other pieces with the blessing of God; for the Lord says in the Gospel: *Those who wear costly clothes and live in luxury* (Lk 7:25) and *who dress in soft garments are in the houses of kings* (Mt 11:8). 15. And although they may be called hypocrites, nonetheless they should not cease doing good nor should they seek costly clothing in this world, so that they may have a garment in the kingdom of heaven.

CHAPTER III THE DIVINE OFFICE AND FASTING

1. The Lord says: *This kind* of devil *cannot come out except* by fast-ing and *by prayer* (Mk 9:28); 2. and again, *When you fast do not become sad like the hypocrites* (Mt 6:16).

3. For this reason all the brothers, whether clerical or lay, should celebrate the Divine Office, the praises and prayers, as is required of them. 4. The clerical [brothers] should celebrate the office and say it for the living and the dead according to the custom of the clergy.[11] 5. And for the failings and negligence of the brothers, they should say daily the *Miserere mei, Deus* (Psalm 50), with the Our Father; 6. and for the deceased brothers let them say the *De Profundis* (Psalm 129) with the Our Father. 7. And they may have only the books necessary to fulfill their office. 8. And the lay [brothers] who know how to read the psalter may have it. 9. But those who do not know how to read should not have any book. 10. The lay [brothers] should say the *I Be-lieve in God* and twenty-four *Our Father*'s with the *Glory to the Father*

---

11. This prescription reflects the practice of reciting the Divine Office according to the custom of the region. The reform of the Liturgy of the Hours (the Divine Office) took place in 1213 under the direction of Pope Innocent III. Cf. Stephen J. P. Van Dijk and J. H. Walker, *The Origins of the Roman Liturgy: The Liturgy of the Papal Court and the Franciscan Order in the Thirteenth Century* (Westminster, Md.: Newman, 1960).

for Matins; for Lauds, they should say five; for Prime, the *I Believe in God* and seven *Our Father*'s with the *Glory to the Father;* for each of the hours, Terce, Sext, and None, seven; for Vespers, twelve; for Compline, the *I Believe in God* and seven *Our Father*'s with the *Glory to the Father;* for the deceased [brothers], seven *Our Father*'s with the *Eternal Rest;* and for the failings and negligence of the brothers three *Our Father*'s every day.[12]

11. Similarly, all the brothers should fast from the feast of All Saints until Christmas, and from the Epiphany, when Our Lord Jesus Christ began to fast, until Easter. 12. At other times, however, they are not obliged to fast according to this life except on Fridays. 13. And they may eat whatever food is placed before them, according to the Gospel (cf. Lk 10:8).

CHAPTER IV THE MINISTERS AND THE OTHER BROTHERS: HOW THEY ARE RELATED

1. In the name of the Lord.[13] 2. All the brothers who have been established as ministers and servants of the other brothers should assign their brothers to the provinces and to the places where they are to be, and they should visit them frequently and spiritually admonish and encourage them.[14] 3. And all my other blessed brothers should diligently obey them in those matters which concern the well-being of their soul and [which] are not contrary to our life. 4. And among themselves let them behave according to what the Lord says: *Whatever you wish that men should do to you, do that to them* (Mt 7:12); 5. and, *That which you do not wish to be done to you, do not do to another* (Tb 4:16). 6. And let the ministers and servants remember what the Lord says: I

---

12. The directives offered for those lay brothers who cannot read reflect those contained in the *Propositum Humiliatorum* 10, 13 (The Way of Life of the *Humiliati*), which received papal approbation on June 7, 1201, i.e., during the pontificate of Pope Innocent III. Cf. G. G. Meerseeman, O.P., *Dossier de L'Order de la Penitence au XIII Siècle* (Fribourg: Editions Universitaires Fribourg Suisse, 1961), p. 281.

13. This is a traditional formula used at the beginning of many legal documents in this period of history. Its presence at the beginning of this chapter has led some to believe that the following sections (Chapters IV, V, and VI) were added to the *propositum vitae* of 1209/1210, possibly after the Chapter of Pentecost, 1217. Cf. David Flood, O.F.M., and Thadée Matura, O.F.M., *The Birth of a Movement: A Study of the First Rule of Saint Francis* (Chicago: Franciscan Herald Press, 1975), pp. 29–30.

14. "Provinces" refer to geographical regions. The Chapter of 1217 divided the Order into eleven provinces. The "places" referred to in this text suggest places of work or prayer rather than friaries or convents.

have *not* come *to be served, but to serve* (Mt 20:28); and because the care of the souls of the brothers has been entrusted to them, if anyone of them should be lost because of their fault or bad example, [these ministers and servants] will have to *render an account* before the Lord Jesus Christ *on the day of judgment* (cf. Mt 12:36).

CHAPTER V   THE CORRECTION OF BROTHERS WHO ARE AT FAULT

1. Therefore, guard your soul and those of your brothers, since *it is a terrible thing to fall into the hands of the living God* (Heb 10:31). 2. But should any of the ministers command any of the brothers to do something contrary to our life or against his conscience, he is not bound to obey him, since that is not obedience in which a fault or sin is committed.[15] 3. Nonetheless, all the brothers, who are subject to the ministers and servants, should reasonably and diligently consider the actions of the ministers and servants. 4. And if they should see that any of them is living according to the flesh and not according to the Spirit—[as demanded] for the integrity of our life—if he does not amend his way, after a third admonition they should inform the minister and servant of the whole fraternity at the Chapter of Pentecost without any interference or opposition. 5. If, moreover, among the brothers anywhere there should be some brother who wishes to live according to the flesh and not according to the Spirit, the brothers with whom he is [living] should admonish, instruct, and correct him humbly and diligently. 6. But if, after the third admonition, he should refuse to change his ways, as soon as they can they should send him or report him to their minister and servant, and the minister and servant should deal with him as he considers best before God.

7. And let all the brothers, both the ministers and servants as well as the others, take care not to be disturbed or angered at the sin or the evil of another, because the devil wishes to destroy many through the fault of one; 8. but they should spiritually help [the brother] who has sinned as best they can, because *it is not the healthy who are in need of the physician, but those who are sick* (cf. Mt 9:12; Mk 2:17).

9. Similarly, all the brothers in this regard should not hold power or dominion, least of all among themselves. 10. For, as the Lord says

---

15. Cf. *Admonition* III, 7.

in the Gospel: *The rulers of the peoples have power over them, and their leaders rule over them* (Mt 20:25); *it shall not be* like this *among* the brothers (cf. Mt 20:26a). 11. And *whoever* among them *wishes to become the greater should be their minister* (cf. Mt 20:26b) and servant. 12. And *whoever is the greater* among them *should become like the lesser* (cf. Lk 22:26).

13. Nor should any brother do evil or say something evil to another; 14. on the contrary, through the charity of the Spirit, they should voluntarily serve and obey one another (cf. Gal 5:13). 15. And this is the true and holy obedience of our Lord Jesus Christ. 16. And all the brothers, as often as *they have turned away from the commands of the Lord* and wandered outside obedience, as the prophet says (Ps 118:21), should know that they are cursed outside obedience as long as they knowingly persist in such sin. 17. And when they have persevered in the commands of the Lord, which they have promised through the holy Gospel and their life, they should know that they are standing firm in true obedience and that they are blessed by the Lord.

CHAPTER VI   THE RECOURSE OF THE BROTHERS TO THE MINISTER; NO BROTHER SHOULD BE CALLED PRIOR

1. If the brothers, in whatever places they are, cannot observe our life, they should have recourse as quickly as possible to their minister and report this to him. 2. The minister, on his part, should be eager to provide for them as he would wish to be done for him were he in a similar position (cf. Mt 7:12). 3. And no one should be called Prior,[16] but all generally should be called Friars Minor.[17] 4. And the one should wash the feet of the others (cf. Jn 13:14).

---

16. In the Benedictine tradition, a "prior" was a vicar or delegate of a monastery that had no abbot. The title was also used to designate the head of a small house that was dependent on an abbey, but this developed only at a later time. At the time of Saint Francis, a prior was the superior of a small house and in this sense the word was adopted by the Friars Preacher, the Augustinians, et al.

17. Apart from this reference, the oldest acknowledgement of the title "Friars Minor" appears in the chronicle of the Premonstratensian Burchard of Ursppurg (+1230), who met the friars in 1210 and attests to a change in their name from "Poor Minors" to "Friars Minor." Cf. *Testimonia Minora Saeculi XIII de S. Francisco Assisiensis,* ed. L. Lemmens (Quaracchi: Collegium S. Bonaventurae, 1926), pp. 17–18.

THE WRITINGS

CHAPTER VII THE MANNER OF SERVING AND WORKING

1. None of the brothers should be administrators or managers in whatever places they are staying among others to serve or to work, nor should they be supervisors in the houses in which they serve; nor should they accept any office which might generate scandal or be harmful to their souls (cf. Mk 8:36); 2. instead, they should be the lesser ones and subject to all who are in the same house.

3. And the brothers who know how to work should do so and should exercise that trade which they [already] know, if it is not against the good of the soul and can be performed honestly. 4. For the prophet says: *You shall eat the fruits of your labors; you are blessed and it will be well for you* (Ps 127:2). 5. And the Apostle [says]: *Whoever does not wish to work shall not eat* (cf. 2 Thes 3:10); 6. and, *Everyone should remain* in that skill and office *in which he has been called* (1 Cor 7:24). 7. And they may receive for their work everything necessary except money. 8. And when it should be necessary, let them seek alms like other poor people. 9. And they may have the tools and instruments suitable for their trades.

10. All the brothers should always be intent on good works, for it is written: "Always do something good so that the devil will find you occupied."[18] 11. And again: "Idleness is the enemy of the soul."[19] 12. Therefore, the servants of God must always give themselves totally to prayer or to some good work.

13. The brothers should beware that, whether they are in hermitages or in other places, they do not make any place their own or contend with anyone about it. 14. And whoever comes to them, friend or foe, thief or robber, should be received with kindness. 15. And wherever the brothers are and in whatever place they meet other brothers, they must greet one another wholeheartedly and lovingly, and honor *one another without complaining* (1 Pet 4:9). 16. And they must beware not to appear outwardly sad and like gloomy hypocrites; but let them

---

18. The references here are to Saint Gregory the Great, *Homilia XIII in Evangelica* (PL 76:1123); Saint Jerome, *Epostola 125* (PL 22:1078); Ionae Aureliano, *Instituto Laicalis* 3:6 (PL 106:2450); and Saint Anselm, *Epistola 3:49* (PL 159:81A).

19. Saint Francis echoes the *Rule of Saint Benedict,* Chapter 48, which opens with "Idleness is the enemy of the soul."

show that they are *joyful in the Lord* (cf. Phil 4:4) and cheerful and truly gracious.[20]

CHAPTER VIII   THE BROTHERS ARE NOT TO RECEIVE MONEY

1. The Lord commands us in the Gospel: *Watch, be on your guard against all* malice and *greed* (cf. Lk 12:15). 2. *Guard yourselves* against the preoccupations of this world *and the cares of this life* (cf. Lk 21:34). 3. Therefore, none of the brothers, wherever he may be or wherever he goes, should in any way carry, receive, or have received [by another] either money or coins, whether for clothing or books or payment for any work—indeed, for no reason—unless it is for the evident need of the sick brothers; for we must not suppose that money or coins have any greater value than stones.[21] 4. And the devil would like to blind those who desire it or consider it better than stones. 5. Therefore, let us who have left all things behind (cf. Mt 19:27) take care that we do not lose the kingdom of heaven for so little. 6. And if we were to find coins in any place, let us give them no more thought than the dust which we crush with our feet; for all [this is] *vanity of vanities, and all is vanity* (Eccl 1:2). 7. And if by chance—which God forbid—it should happen that some brother has collected or is hoarding money or coins, with the sole exception of the needs of the sick as mentioned above, all the brothers are to consider him as a false brother and an apostate, and a thief and a robber, and as the one who held the purse (cf. Jn 12:6),[22] unless he has truly repented.

8. And in no way may the brothers receive [money] or arrange to have it received, or beg money or arrange to have it sought as alms or coins for any houses or places; and they may not go with a person who is begging money or coins for such places. 9. But the brothers may perform for these places other services which are not contrary to

---

20. This prescription was the result of a decision reached at a general chapter. Cf. Thomas of Celano, *Second Life of Saint Francis*, 128.

21. It is helpful to understand the new values of commerce and profit that form the background of this attitude toward coins and money. Cf. Lester K. Little, *Religious Poverty and the Profit Economy in Medieval Europe* (Ithaca: Cornell University Press, 1978), pp. 19–41.

22. The reference concerns Judas, who symbolizes for Saint Francis not only someone who clings to material possessions, but who also appropriates other gifts to himself. Cf. *Admonition*, IV, 3.

our life, with the blessing of God. 10. Nevertheless, at times of the evident necessity of the lepers the brothers can beg alms for them. 11. Nonetheless, they should beware of money. 12. Likewise, all the brothers should beware of running around the world for filthy gain.

CHAPTER IX   BEGGING ALMS

1. All the brothers should strive to follow the humility and the poverty of our Lord Jesus Christ and remember that we should have nothing else in the whole world except, as the Apostle says, *having something to eat and something to wear, we be content with these* (cf 1 Tim 6:8). 2. And they must rejoice when they live among people [who are considered to be] of little worth and who are looked down upon, among the poor and the powerless, the sick and the lepers, and the beggars by the wayside. 3. And when it may be necessary, let them go for alms.[23] 4. And they should not be ashamed, but rather recall that our Lord Jesus *Christ, the Son of the living and all-powerful God* (cf. Jn 11:27), *set His face* like *flint* (Is 50:7) and was not ashamed. 5. And He was a poor man and a transient and lived on alms, He and the Blessed Virgin, and His disciples. 6. And should people shame them and refuse to give them alms, let them give thanks to God for this, since from such insults they will receive great honor before the tribunal of our Lord Jesus Christ. 7. And let them know that such shame is credited not to those who suffer it but to those who caused it. 8. And alms are a legacy and a just right due to the poor, which our Lord Jesus Christ acquired for us. 9. And the brothers who labor to acquire them will receive a great reward and [at the same time] enable those who give [such alms] to gain and acquire [that reward] in return, for everything that people leave behind in the world will perish, but for the charity and the almsgiving which they have done they will receive a reward from the Lord.

10. And each one should confidently make known his need to the other, so that he might find what he needs and minister it to him. 11. And each one should love and care for his brother in all those things in which God will give him grace, as a mother loves and cares for her

---

23. For consideration of the novelty of this prescription, which encourages a practice previously forbidden to canons and monks, consult J. M. Canivez, *Statuta Capitularia Generalis Ordinis Cisterciensis*, I (Louvain, 1933), pp. 340, 385.

son (cf. 1 Thes 2:7). 12. And *he who does not eat should not judge the one who does* (Rom 14:3b).

13. And whenever necessity should come upon them, all the brothers, wherever they may be, may eat all foods which people can eat, as the Lord says of David who ate *the loaves of proposition* (cf. Mt. 12:4) *which no one was permitted to eat except the priests* (Mk 2:26). 14. And let them recall what the Lord says: *Be on your guard that your hearts do not become bloated with self-indulgence and drunkenness and the cares of this life, for that day will come upon you unexpectedly;* 15. *for like a trap it will come upon all who dwell upon the face of the earth* (Lk 21:34–35). 16. Likewise, even in times of manifest necessity, all the brothers should take care of their needs, as the Lord gives them the grace, since "necessity knows no law."[24]

CHAPTER X   THE SICK BROTHERS

1. If any of the brothers shall fall ill, wherever he may be, the other brothers should not leave him behind unless one of the brothers, or several of them if that be necessary, are assigned to serve him as they would wish to be served themselves (cf. Mt 7:12);[25] 2. but in case of grave necessity, they can entrust him to some person capable of taking care of him in his illness. 3. And I beg the sick brother to give thanks to the Creator for everything; and whatever the Lord wills for him, he should desire to be that, whether healthy or sick, since all those whom God *has predestined for everlasting life* (cf. Acts 13:48) He instructs by means of the afflictions of punishment and sickness and the spirit of repentance.[26] As the Lord says: I correct *and punish those whom I love* (Rev 3:19).

4. And if anyone should be disturbed or become angry at God or at [his] brothers, or if by chance he persistently asks for medicines

---

24. This is a canonical axiom that can be found in *Decretum Gratiani*, P. II, C.q.1 *glossa ante* c. 40. See also Saint Bernard of Clairvaux, *Liber de Praecepto*, V (PL 182:867); and William of Saint Thierry, *Commentatio ex Bernardo*, 33 (PL 184:433).

25. Willibrord Lampen, O.F.M., claims this passage was added by Brother Caesar of Speyer, who took it from a letter of Saint Augustine to Saint Jerome, *Epistola 40*, III, 3 (PL 33:155). Cf. Willibrord Lampen, O.F.M., *Archivum Franciscanum Historicum* 23 (1930): 239–240.

26. This passage comes from Saint Gregory the Great, *Homilia XVII in Evangelica*, 18 (PL 76:1148).

with a great desire to free the flesh which is soon to die and is the enemy of the soul [remember:] All this comes from the evil one. [Such a person] is totally caught up with the flesh and he does not seem to be one of the brothers, since he loves his body more than his soul.

CHAPTER XI   THE BROTHERS ARE NOT TO BLASPHEME OR DETRACT BUT SHOULD LOVE ONE ANOTHER

1. And all the brothers should beware that they do not slander or engage in disputes (cf. 2 Tim 2:14); 2. rather, they should strive to keep silence whenever God gives them [this] grace. 3. Nor should they quarrel among themselves or with others, but they should strive to respond humbly, saying: I am a useless servant (cf. Lk 17:10). 4. And they should not become angry, since *everyone who grows angry with his brother shall be liable to judgment; and he who has said to his brother "fool" shall be liable to the Council; whoever has said "idiot" shall be liable to the fires of hell* (Mt 5:22). 5. And they should love one another, as the Lord says: *This is my commandment: that you love one another as I have loved you* (Jn 15:12). 6. And let them express the love which they have for one another by their deeds (cf. Jas 2:18), as the Apostle says: *Let us not love in word or speech, but in deed and in truth* (1 Jn 3:18). 7. And *they should slander no one* (cf. Tit 3:2). 8. Let them not murmur nor detract from others, for it is written: Gossips and detractors are detestable to God (Rm 1:29, 30). 9. And let them be modest, *by showing meekness toward everyone* (cf. Tit 3:2). 10. Let them not judge or condemn. 11. And as the Lord says, they should not take notice of the little defects of others (cf. Mt 7:3; Lk 6:41). 12. Rather they should reflect much more on their own [sins] *in the bitterness of their soul* (Is 38:15). 13. And let them strive *to enter through the narrow gate* (Lk 13:24), for the Lord says: *Narrow is the gate and hard the road that leads to life; and there are few who find it* (Mt 7:14).

CHAPTER XII   IMPURE GLANCES AND FREQUENT ASSOCIATION WITH WOMEN

1. All the brothers, wherever they are or go, should avoid impure glances and association with women. 2. And no one should counsel them or travel alone [with them] or eat at table [with them] from the same plate. 3. The priests should speak honorably with them when

giving them [the sacrament of] penance or some spiritual advice.[27] 4. And absolutely no woman should be received to obedience by any brothers, but once she has been given spiritual advice, let her perform a penance where she will. 5. And all of us must keep close watch over ourselves and keep all parts of our body pure, since the Lord says: *Anyone who looks lustfully at a woman has already committed adultery with her in his heart* (Mt 5:28); 6. and the Apostle says: *Do you not know that your members are the temple of the Holy Spirit?* (cf. 1 Cor 6:19); therefore, whoever *violates God's temple, God will destroy him* (1 Cor 3:17).

CHAPTER XIII THE AVOIDANCE OF FORNICATION

1. If any brother, at the instigation of the devil, commits a sin of fornication, he should be deprived of the habit, which he has lost through his wickedness, and he should put it aside completely, and be totally expelled from our Order. 2. And afterward let him do penance for his sins (cf. 1 Cor 5:4–5).

CHAPTER XIV THE MANNER OF THE BROTHERS' CONDUCT IN THE WORLD

1. When the brothers go about through the world, they should carry *nothing* for the journey, *neither* (cf. Lk 9:3) *a knapsack* (cf. Lk 10:4), *nor a purse, nor bread, nor money* (Lk 9:3), *nor a staff* (cf. Mt 10:10). 2. And *into whatever house they enter,* let them *first say: Peace to this house* (cf. Lk 10:5). 3. And, remaining in that house, they may eat and drink *whatever* [their hosts] *have offered* (cf. Lk 10:7). 4. They should *not* offer resistance *to evil* (cf. Mt 5:39), but if someone should strike them on one cheek, let them *offer him the other* as well (cf. Mt 5:39; Lk 6:29). 5. And if someone *should take away their clothes,* they should not deny him also their tunic (cf. Lk 6:29). 6. They should give *to all who ask; and if anyone takes what is theirs,* they should not demand that it be returned (cf. Lk 6:30).

---

27. *The Legend of Perugia,* 34, offers an example of the effects that the preaching of the friars had on the laity and especially on women. The history of the Penitential movement of the thirteenth century indicates the presence of many women.

THE WRITINGS

CHAPTER XV   THE BROTHERS ARE NOT TO RIDE HORSES

1. I enjoin upon all my brothers both cleric and lay that, when they go through the world or stay in places, they should in no way have any animal either with themselves or in the care of another or in any other way. 2. Nor may they ride horses unless they are compelled by sickness or great necessity.

CHAPTER XVI   THOSE WHO ARE GOING AMONG THE SARACENS AND OTHER NONBELIEVERS

1. The Lord says: *Behold, I am sending you as lambs in the midst of wolves.* 2. Therefore, be *prudent as serpents and simple as doves* (Mt 10:16). 3. Therefore, any brother who, by divine inspiration,[28] desires to go among the Saracens and other nonbelievers[29] should go with the permission of his minister and servant. 4. And the minister should give [these brothers] permission and not oppose them, if he shall see that they are fit to be sent; for he shall be bound to give an account to the Lord (cf. Lk 16:2) if he has proceeded without discretion in this or in other matters. 5. As for the brothers who go, they can live spiritually among [the Saracens and nonbelievers] in two ways. 6. One way is not to engage in arguments or disputes, but to be subject *to every human creature for God's sake* (1 Pet 2:13) and to acknowledge that they are Christians. 7. Another way is to proclaim the word of God when they see that it pleases the Lord, so that they believe in the all-powerful God—Father, and Son, and Holy Spirit—the Creator of all, in the Son Who is the Redeemer and Savior, and that they be baptized and

---

28. Cf. *The Form of Life Given to Saint Clare and Her Sisters*, n. 1, for an understanding of the phrase "divine inspiration." In this instance, the editors deviate from the *Opuscula Sancti Patris Francisci Assisiensis* of Kajetan Esser, O.F.M., by incorporating this phrase into the text. As Esser notes, all of the manuscripts except that of Angelo Clareno contain the phrase (cf. Kajetan Esser, O.F.M., *Opuscula Sancti Patris Francisci Asisiensis* [Grottaferrata: Collegium S. Bonaventurae, 1978], p. 268, n. 2).

29. This call to missionary activity among the Saracens and other nonbelievers may have been enhanced by the opening of the Fourth Lateran Council and its canon 71, both of which speak of common action against the encroaching power of Islam. Saint Francis clearly emerges as a leader in the beginnings of the modern missionary activity of the Church. Cf. Kajetan Esser, O.F.M., "Das missionarische Anliegen des heiligen Franziskus," *Wissenschaft und Weischeit* 35 (1972): 12–18; Julien-Eymard d'Angers, "La Spiritualité missionaire de Saint François," *Les Amis de Saint Francois*, n.s. 10 (1969): 202–208.

become Christians; because *whoever has not been born again of water and the Holy Spirit cannot enter into the kingdom of God* (cf. Jn 3:5).

8. They can say to [the Saracens] and to others these and other things which will have pleased the Lord, for the Lord says in the Gospel: *Everyone who acknowledges me before men I will also acknowledge before my Father Who is in heaven* (Mt 10:32). 9. And: *Whoever is ashamed of me and my words, the Son of Man will also be ashamed of him when He comes in His majesty and that of the Father and the angels* (Lk 9:26).

10. And all the brothers, wherever they may be, should remember that they gave themselves and abandoned their bodies to the Lord Jesus Christ. 11. And for love of Him, they must make themselves vulnerable to their enemies, both visible and invisible, because the Lord says: *Whoever loses his life for my sake will save it* (cf. Lk 9:24) *in eternal life* (Mt 25:46). 12. *Blessed are those who suffer persecution for the sake of justice, for the kingdom of heaven is theirs* (Mt 5:10). 13. *If they have persecuted me, they will also persecute you* (Jn 15:20). 14. And: *If they persecute you in one city, flee to another* (cf. Mt 10:23). 15. *Blessed are you* (Mt 5:11) *when people shall hate you* (Lk 6:22) *and malign* (Mt 5:11) and persecute you and *drive you out, abuse you, denounce your name as evil* (Lk 6:22) and *utter every kind of slander against you because of me* (Mt 5:11). 16. *Rejoice on that day and be glad* (Lk 6:23) *because your reward is very great in heaven* (cf. Mt 5:12). 17. And *I say to you, my friends, do not be frightened by these things* (Lk 12:4) 18. *and do not fear those who kill the body* (Mt 10:28) *and after* that *can do no more* (Lk 12:4). 19. *Take care not to be disturbed* (Mt 24:6). 20. *For through your patience, you will* possess your souls (Lk 21:19); 21. and *whoever perseveres to the end will be saved* (Mt 10:22; 24:13).

CHAPTER XVII   PREACHERS

1. No brother should preach contrary to the form and regulations of the holy Church nor unless he has been permitted by his minister. 2. And the minister should take care not to grant [this permission] to anyone indiscriminately. 3. All the brothers, however, should preach by their deeds. 4. And no minister or preacher should appropriate to himself the ministry of the brothers or the office of preaching, but he should set it aside without any protest whenever he is told.

5. Therefore, in the love which is God (cf. 1 Jn 4:16), I beg all my brothers—those who preach, pray, work, whether cleric or lay—to

strive to humble themselves in all things 6. [and] not to take pride in themselves or to delight in themselves or be puffed up interiorly about their good works and deeds—in fact, about any good thing that God does or says or sometimes works in them and through them. [This is] in keeping with what the Lord says: *Yet do not rejoice in this: that the spirits are subject to you* (Lk 10:20). 7. And we should be firmly convinced that nothing belongs to us except [our] vices and sins. 8. Rather we must rejoice when we would fall *into various trials* (Jas 1:2) and endure every sort of anguish of soul and body or ordeals in this world for the sake of eternal life.

9. Therefore, all [of us] brothers must beware of all pride and vainglory. 10. And let us keep ourselves from the wisdom of this world and *the prudence of the flesh* (Rm 8:6). 11. For the spirit of the flesh desires and is most eager to have words, but [cares] little to carry them out. And it does not seek a religion and holiness in the interior spirit, 12. but it wishes and desires to have a religion and holiness outwardly apparent to people. 13. And these are the ones of whom the Lord says: *Truly I say to you: They have received their reward* (Mt 6:2). 14. But the Spirit of the Lord wishes the flesh to be mortified and despised, worthless and rejected. 15. And it strives for humility and patience, and the pure and simple and true peace of the spiritual person. 16. And above all things it always longs for the divine fear and the divine wisdom and the divine love of the Father, and of the Son, and of the Holy Spirit.

17. And let us refer all good
>to the most high and supreme lord God,
>and acknowledge that every good is His,
>and thank Him for everything,
>>[He] from Whom all good things come.

18. And may He,
>the Highest and Supreme,
>Who alone is true God,
>have and be given and receive
>>every honor and reverence,
>>every praise and blessing,
>>every thanks and glory,
>for every good is His,
>>*He Who alone is good.*[30]

---

30. Cf. Lk 18:19.

19. And when we see or hear an evil [person] speak or act or blaspheme God, let us speak well and act well and praise God (cf. Rm 12:21), *Who is blessed forever* (Rm 1:25).[31]

CHAPTER XVIII   HOW THE MINISTERS MEET TOGETHER

1. Once a year each minister can come together with his brothers, wherever they wish, on the feast of Saint Michael the Archangel to treat of the things which refer to God.[32] 2. All the ministers who are in those parts which are overseas and beyond the Alps may come together once every three years, and the other ministers once each year, to the Chapter of Pentecost at the church of Saint Mary of the Portiuncula, unless it has been decided otherwise by the minister and servant of the entire fraternity.

CHAPTER XIX   THE BROTHERS ARE TO LIVE AS CATHOLICS

1. All the brothers must be Catholics, [and] live and speak in a Catholic manner.[33] 2. But if any of them has strayed from the Catho-

---

31. Many manuscripts conclude this chapter with "Amen" (cf. Kajetan Esser, O.F.M., *Opuscula Sancti Patris Francisci Assisiensis* [Grottaferrata: Collegium S. Bonaventurae, 1978], p. 274, n. 23). This has led David Flood, O.F.M., and Thadée Matura, O.F.M., to suggest that the *Earlier Rule*, in one of its first forms, came to an end at this point. Cf. David Flood, O.F.M., and Thadée Matura, O.F.M., *The Birth of a Movement: A Study of the First Rule of Saint Francis* (Chicago: Franciscan Herald Press, 1975), pp. 39–40.

32. This chapter fulfills the directive of the Fourth Lateran Council, Canon 12: "In every ecclesiastical province there shall be held every three years, saving the rights of the diocesan ordinaries, a general chapter of abbots and priors having no abbots, who have not been accustomed to celebrate such chapters" (cf. H. J. Schroeder, O.P., *Disciplinary Decrees of the General Councils* [St. Louis: Herder and Herder, 1937], p. 253). In a monographic work entitled *De Capitulo Generali*, Fr. Maurinus of Neukirchen maintains that the institution of chapters began in 1212 among the friars. Kajetan Esser, O.F.M., in *Origins of the Franciscan Order*, maintains an early date and gives no specifics (cf. Kajetan Esser, O.F.M., *Origins of the Franciscan Order*, trans. Aeden Daly, O.F.M., and Irina Lynch [Chicago: Franciscan Herald Press, 1970], p. 71ff.).

33. This chapter also shows the influence of the Fourth Lateran Council, Canon 3, which addresses a concern for orthodoxy and excommunicates every heretic. (Cf. H. J. Schroeder, O.P., *Disciplinary Decrees of the General Councils* [St. Louis: Herder and Herder, 1937], p. 242).

lic faith and life, in word or in deed, and has not amended his ways, he should be completely expelled from our fraternity. 3. And we should regard all clerics and all religious as our lord in those things which pertain to the salvation of the soul and who have not deviated from our religion, and, in the Lord, we should respect their order and their office and government.

CHAPTER XX PENANCE AND THE RECEPTION OF THE BODY AND BLOOD OF OUR LORD JESUS CHRIST

1. And my blessed brothers, both the clerics as well as the lay, should confess their sins to priests of our Order.[34] 2. And if they should not be able to do so, they should confess to other prudent and Catholic priests, knowing full well that when they have received penance and absolution from any Catholic priests, they are without doubt absolved from their sins, provided they have humbly and faithfully fulfilled the penance imposed upon them. 3. But if they have not been able to find a priest, they may confess to their brother, as the apostle James says: *Confess your sins to one another* (Jas 5:16).[35] 4. Despite this let them not fail to have recourse to a priest, since the power of binding and loosing is granted only to priests. 5. And thus contrite and confessed, they should receive the Body and Blood of our Lord Jesus Christ with great humility and reverence, remembering what the Lord says: *Whoever eats my flesh and drinks my blood has eternal life* (cf. Jn 6:55); 6. and: *Do this in memory of me* (Lk 22:19).

---

34. This chapter also reflects the influence of the Fourth Lateran Council, Canon 21: "All the faithful of both sexes shall, after they have reached the age of discretion, faithfully confess all their sins at least once a year to their own [parish] priest and perform to the best of their ability the penance prescribed, receiving reverently at least at Easter the sacrament of the Eucharist" (cf. H. J. Schroeder, O.P., *Disciplinary Decrees of the General Councils* [St. Louis: Herder and Herder, 1937], p. 259).

35. The practice of confessing sins to another Christian in the absence of a priest was common in the Middle Ages. It was a means of expressing reconciliation among the community of the faithful. Cf. Damien Isabell, O.F.M., *The Practice and Meaning of Confession in the Primitive Franciscan Community according to the Writings of Saint Francis of Assisi and Thomas of Celano* (Assisi, 1973); also, Lawrence C. Landini, O.F.M., *The Causes of the Clericalization of the Order of Friars Minor, 1209–1260, in the Light of early Franciscan Sources* (Chicago: Franciscan Herald Press, 1968).

CHAPTER XXI THE PRAISE AND EXHORTATION WHICH ALL THE BROTHERS CAN OFFER

1. And whenever it may please them, all my brothers can proclaim this or a like exhortation and praise among all the people with the blessing of God:[36]

2. Fear and honor, praise and bless, give thanks[37] and adore
    the Lord God Almighty in Trinity and in Unity,
    the Father and the Son and the Holy Spirit
    the Creator of all.
3. Do penance,[38] performing worthy fruits of penance[39]
    since we will soon die.
4. *Give and it shall be given to you.*[40]
5. *Forgive* and you shall be forgiven.[41]
6. And if you do not forgive men their sins,[42]
    the Lord *will not forgive you your sins.*[43]
    Confess all your sins.[44]
7. Blessed are those who die in penance, for they shall be in the
    kingdom of heaven.
8. Woe to those who do not die in penance, for they shall be the
    children of the devil[45]
    whose works they do,[46]
    and they shall go into the eternal fire.[47]
9. Beware and abstain from every evil and persevere in good till
    the end.

---

36. This chapter may well be understood in light of the directives of the Fourth Lateran Council to promote orthodox preaching. This simple formula was easily memorized by the friars and could be used by those who had no patents or permission for preaching.
37. 1 Thes 5:18.
38. Cf. Mt 3:2.
39. Cf. Lk 3:8.
40. Cf. Lk 6:38.
41. Cf. Lk 6: 37.
42. Mt 6:14.
43. Mk 11:26.
44. Cf. Jas 5:16.
45. Cf. 1 Jn 3:10.
46. Cf. Jn 8:41.
47. Mt 18:8.

THE WRITINGS

CHAPTER XXII   AN ADMONITION TO THE BROTHERS

1. Let us pay attention, all [my] brothers, to what the Lord says: *Love your enemies* and *do good to those who hate you* (cf. Mt 5:44), 2. for our Lord Jesus Christ, Whose footprints we must follow (cf.1 Pet 2:21), called His betrayer "friend" (cf. Mt 26:50) and gave Himself willingly to those who crucified Him. 3. Our friends, then, are all those who unjustly afflict upon us trials and ordeals, shame and injuries, sorrows and torments, martyrdom and death; 4. we must love them greatly for we will possess eternal life because of what they bring upon us.[48]

5. And we must hate our body with its vices and sins; because, by living according to the flesh, the devil wishes to take from us the love of Jesus Christ and eternal life and to lose himself with everyone in hell. 6. For through our own fault we are rotten, miserable, and opposed to good, but prompt and willing to [embrace] evil, for as our Lord says in the Gospel: 7. *From the heart of man come forth and flow evil thoughts, adulteries, fornications, murders, thefts, avarice, wantonness, deceit, lewdness, evil looks, false testimonies, blasphemy, foolishness* (cf. Mk 7:21–22; Mt 15:19). 8. All *these evil things flow from within*, from the heart of a person (cf. Mk 7:23) and *these are the things that make a person unclean* (Mt 15:20).

9. And now that we have left the world, we have nothing else to do except to follow the will of the Lord and to please Him. 10. Let us take great care not to be earth along the wayside, or among the rocks, or among thorns, as the Lord says in the Gospel: 11. *The seed is the word of God* (Lk 8:11).

12. *But that which fell along the wayside and was trampled under foot* (cf. Lk 8:5) *are those who hear* (Lk 8:12) *the word and do not* understand it (cf. Mt 13:19). 13. *And immediately* (Mk 4:15) *the devil comes* (Lk 8:12) *and snatches up* (Mt 13:19) *what was planted in their hearts* (Mk 4:15) *and takes the word out of their hearts, otherwise believing they might be saved* (Lk 8:12).

14. *But that which fell upon stony ground* (cf. Mt 13:20) *are those who, once they have heard the word, at the outset receive it with joy* (Mk

---

48. David Flood, O.F.M., has suggested that this chapter was written by Saint Francis as a testament or final message prior to his departure for the Near East (c. 1219) where he hoped to obtain the prize of martyrdom (cf. David Flood, O.F.M., *Die Regula non bullata der Minderbrüder* [Werl/West, 1967]).

4:16). 15. *But when tribulation and persecution overtake them because of the word, they falter at once* (Mt 13:21) and they have no roots in them, *but last only for a time* (cf. Mk 4:17), *because they believe for a time and in time of temptation they fail* (Lk 8:13).

16. *That which fell among thorns are those* (Lk 8:14) *who hear the word of God* (cf. Mk 4:18) *yet anxiety* (Mt 13:22) *and the worries* (Mk 4:19) *of this world and the lure of riches* (Mt 13:22) *and other inordinate desires come in to choke the word and they remain without fruit* (cf. Mk 4:19).

17. *But that which is sown on good soil are those who hear the word with a good and noble heart* (Lk 8:15) and understand it and (cf. Mt 13:23) *keep it and bear fruit in patience* (Lk 8:15).

18. And so we brothers, as the Lord says, should leave *the dead to bury their own dead* (Mt 8:22).

19. And let us be very careful of the malice and the subtlety of Satan, who wishes that a man not raise his mind and heart to God. 20. And as he roams about he wishes to ensnare the heart of a person under the guise of some reward or help, and to snuff out our memory of the word and the precepts of the Lord, and wishes to blind the heart of a person through wordly affairs and concerns, and to live there, as the Lord says: 21. *When an unclean spirit has gone out of a person, it wanders through dry and waterless places* (Mt 12:43) *seeking rest; and not finding any, says:* 22. *I will return to the house which I left* (Lk 11:24). 23. *And coming to it, it finds it empty, swept, clean, and tidied* (Mt 12:44). 24. *And it goes off and brings seven other spirits more wicked than itself, and they go in and live there. And the last condition of the person is worst than the first* (cf. Lk 11:26).

25. Therefore, all [my] brothers, let us be very much on our guard so that we do not lose or turn away our mind and heart from the Lord under the guise of [achieving] some reward or [doing] some work or [providing] some help. 26. But in the holy love which is God (cf. 1 Jn 4:16), I beg all [my] brothers, both the ministers and the others, as they overcome every obstacle and put aside every care and anxiety, to strive as best they can to serve, love, honor, and adore the Lord God with a clean heart and a pure mind, for this is what He desires above all things.

27. And let us make a home and dwelling place (cf. Jn 14:23) for Him Who is the Lord God Almighty, Father and Son and Holy Spirit, Who says: *Watch, therefore, praying constantly that you may be considered worthy to escape all the evils that are to come and to stand secure before the Son of Man* (Lk 21:36). 28. *And when you stand to pray* (Mk 11:25) *say*

(Lk 11:2): *Our Father Who are in heaven* (Mt 6:9). 29. And let us adore Him with a pure heart, because *we should pray always and not* lose heart (Lk 18:1); 30. *for the Father seeks such worshipers.* 31. *God is Spirit, and those who worship Him must worship Him in spirit and in truth* (cf. Jn 4:23–24).

32. And let us have recourse to Him as *to the shepherd and guardian of our souls* (1 Pet 2:25), Who says: "I am the good shepherd who feeds my sheep and I lay down my life for my sheep."[49] 33. *All of you are brothers.* 34. *And do not call anyone on earth your father, for one is Your Father, the One in heaven.* 35. *And do not let yourselves be called teachers,* for *your teacher is the One Who is in heaven* (cf. Mt 23:8-10). 36. *If you remain in me, and my words remain in you, you may ask whatever you will and it will be done for you* (Jn 15:7). 37. *Wherever two or three are gathered together in my name, I am there in the midst of them* (Mt 18:20). 38. *Behold I am with you until the consummation of the world* (Mt 28:20). 39. *The words which I have spoken to you are spirit and life* (Jn 6:64). 40. *I am the way, the truth, and the life* (Jn 14:6).

41. Let us, therefore, hold onto the words, the life, and the teaching and the Holy Gospel of Him Who humbled Himself to ask His Father for us and to make His name known to us, saying: *Father, glorify Your name* (Jn 12:28a) *and glorify Your Son so that Your Son may glorify You* (Jn 17:1b). 42. Father, *I have made Your name known to the men whom You have given to Me* (Jn 17:6). *The words which You have given to Me I have given to them; and they have accepted them and know truly that I came from You, and have believed that You sent me* (Jn 17:8).

43. *I pray for them, not for the world,* 44. *but for those whom You have given Me, because they belong to You and all I have is Yours* (Jn 17:9–10). 45. *Holy Father, protect those in Your name whom You have given to Me, so that they may be one as We are* (Jn 17:11b). 46. *I say these things while still in the world that they may have joy within them.* 47. *I gave them Your word; and the world hated them because they do not belong to the world just as I do not belong to the world.* 48. *I am not asking that You remove them from the world, but that You protect them from the evil one* (Jn 17:14b–15).

49. *Sanctify them in the truth.*[50] 50. *Your word is truth.* 51. *As You*

---

49. This quotation is taken from the ancient Office of the Second Sunday after Easter, the Sunday of the Good Shepherd, and is based on John 10:14a, 10, 15.

50. A number of the manuscripts preserve the word *sanctifica* (sanctify) as the Latin Vulgate translates this passage of John's Gospel. However, Kajetan Esser, O.F.M., places the word *mirifica* (glorify) since it follows the majority of manuscripts.

have sent Me into the world, so I have sent them into the world. 52. And for their sake I sanctify Myself, so that they may be sanctified in truth.

53. I pray not only for these, but also for those who because of their words will believe in me (cf. Jn 17:17–20), *so that they may be completely one, and the world may know that You have sent Me and that You have loved them as You have loved Me* (Jn 17:23).[51] *54. And* I shall make *Your name known to them, so that the love with which You have loved Me* may be in them *and I may be in them* (cf. Jn 17:26). *55. Father, I wish that where I am those whom You have given Me may be with Me, so that they may see Your glory* (cf. Jn 17:24) *in Your Kingdom* (Mt 20:21). *Amen.*

CHAPTER XXIII   PRAYER AND THANKSGIVING

1. All-powerful, most holy, most high and supreme God
   Holy and just *Father*[52]
   Lord, King *of heaven and earth*[53]
   we thank You for Yourself
   for through Your holy will
   and through Your only Son
   with the Holy Spirit
   You have created all things spiritual and corporal
   and, having made us *in Your own image and likeness,*
   You placed us in paradise.[54]
2. And through our own fault we have fallen.
3. And we thank You
   for as through Your Son You created us
   so also, through Your holy love, with which You loved us[55]
   You brought about His birth
       as true God and true man
       by the glorious, ever-virgin, most blessed, holy Mary
   and You willed to redeem us captives
       through His cross and blood and death.

---

51. One family of manuscripts contains John 17:21–23a: "May they all be one as You, Father, are in me and I am in You, that they may be one in Us and the world may believe that You have sent Me. And I have given to them the glory which You have given to Me, that they may be one as We are One, I in them and You in me."
52. Jn 17:11.
53. Cf. Mt 11:25.
54. Cf. Gen 1:26; 2:15.
55. Jn 17:26.

4. And we thank You
   for Your Son Himself will come again
   in the glory of His majesty
   to send the wicked ones
   who have not done penance and who have not known You
   into the eternal fire,
   and to say to all those who have known You and have adored
   You
   and have served You in penance:
   "Come, you blessed of my Father,
   receive the kingdom,
   which has been prepared for you
   from the beginning of the world."[56]

5. And because all of us
   wretches and sinners
   are not worthy to pronounce Your name,
   we humbly ask that
   our Lord Jesus Christ
   Your *beloved Son*
   in whom You were *well* pleased[57]
   together with the Holy Spirit, the Paraclete,
   give You thanks
   as it pleases You and Him
   for everything,
   [He] Who always satisfies You in everything
   through Whom You have done such great things for us.
   Alleluia!

6. And through Your love
   we humbly beg
   the glorious Mother, most blessed Mary ever-virgin,
   Blessed Michael, Gabriel, and Raphael
   and all the blessed choirs of seraphim, cherubim, thrones,
   dominations, principalities, powers,[58]
   virtues, angels, archangels,
   blessed John the Baptist,
   John the Evangelist,

---

56. Cf. Mt 25:34.
57. Cf. Mt 17:5.
58. Cf. Col 1:15.

Peter, Paul,
and the blessed patriarchs, prophets,
the Innocents, apostles, evangelists, disciples,
    martyrs, confessors, virgins,
the blessed Elijah and Henoch,
and all the saints who were, who will be, and who are
to give You thanks for these things as it pleases You,
the supreme and true God
eternal and living
with Your most beloved Son, our Lord Jesus Christ,
and the Holy Spirit, the Paraclete,
world without end.[59]
Amen. Alleluia.[60]

7. And all of us lesser brothers, *useless servants* (Lk 17:10), humbly ask and beg all those who wish to serve the Lord God within the holy, catholic, and apostolic church, and all the following orders: priests, deacons, subdeacons, acolytes, exorcists, lectors, porters, and all clerics, all religious men and all religious women, all lay brothers and youths, the poor and the needy, kings and princes, workers and farmers, servants and masters, all virgins and continent and married women, all lay people, men and women, all children, adolescents, the young and the old, the healthy and the sick, all the small and the great, all peoples, races, tribes, and tongues, all nations and all peoples everywhere on earth who are and who will be—that all of us may persevere in the true faith and in penance, for otherwise no one will be saved.

8. Let us all love the Lord God *with all [our] heart, all [our] soul, with all [our] mind and all [our] strength* (cf. Mk 12:30) and *and with fortitude and with total understanding* (Mt 12:33), *with all of our powers* (cf. Lk 10:27), with every effort, every affection, every emotion, every desire, and every wish (Mt 12:30). He has given and gives to each one of us [our] whole body, [our] whole soul, and [our] whole life. He created us and redeemed us, and will save us by His mercy alone (cf. Tob 13:5). He did and does every good thing for us [who are] miserable and wretched, rotten and foul-smelling, ungrateful and evil.

---

59. Rev 9:13.
60. Rev 19:4.

9. Therefore
   let us desire nothing else
   let us wish for nothing else
   let nothing else please us
        and cause us delight
   except our Creator and Redeemer and Savior,
   the one true God,
   Who is the Fullness of Good
        all good, every good, the true and supreme good
   Who alone is Good[61]
        merciful and gentle
        delectable and sweet
   Who alone is holy
        just and true
        holy and right
   Who alone is kind
        innocent
        pure
   from Whom and through Whom and in Whom[62] is
        all pardon
        all grace
        all glory
            of all the penitent and the just
            of all the blessed who rejoice together in heaven.

10. Therefore
    let nothing hinder us
        nothing separate us
        or nothing come between us.

11. Let all of us
        wherever we are
        in every place
        at every hour
        at every time of day
        everyday and continually
    believe truly and humbly
    and keep in [our] heart

---

61. Cf. Lk 18:19.
62. Cf. Rm 11:36.

and love, honor, adore, serve
    praise and bless
    glorify and exalt
    magnify and give thanks to
the most high and supreme eternal God
Trinity and Unity
the Father and the Son and the Holy Spirit
Creator of all
Savior of all who believe in Him
    and hope in Him
    and love Him
Who is
    without beginning and without end
    unchangeable, invisible,
    indescribable, ineffable,
    incomprehensible, unfathomable,[63]
    blessed, worthy of praise,
    glorious, exalted on high,[64] sublime,
    most high, gentle, lovable,
    delectable and totally desirable above all else
    forever.
  Amen.

CHAPTER XXIV   CONCLUSION

1. In the name of the Lord! I ask all the brothers to learn the tenor and sense of these things which have been written in this life for the salvation of our souls, and to call them frequently to mind. 2. And I ask God that He Who is All-powerful, Three and One, bless all those who teach, learn, retain, remember, and put into practice all these things, each time they repeat and perform what has been written here for the salvation of our soul, 3. and, kissing their feet, to love deeply, to guard and cherish [them]. 4. And on behalf of Almighty God and the Lord Pope and by obedience, I, Brother Francis, firmly command and decree that no one remove anything from what has

---

63. Cf. Rm 11:33.
64. Cf. Dan 3:52.

been written in this life or make any written addition to these things (cf. Dt 4:2); nor should the brothers have any other rule.

5. Glory to the Father, and to the Son, and to the Holy Spirit. As it was in the beginning, is now, and will be forever. Amen.

The Later Rule

The fundamental charter and form of life for the Order of Frairs Minor is known as the Regula bullata, *the Later Rule, which received papal approval by means of the decree* Solet annuere, *November 29, 1223. This simple document, which Thomas of Celano in his* Second Life of Saint Francis, *208, calls "the marrow of the Gospel," has become the foundation of the three families of the First Order of Saint Francis, that is, the Friars Minor, the Friars Minor Conventual, and the Friars Minor Capuchin. Moreover, the* Later Rule *is an expression of the deep bond of unity that firmly establishes the life of the Order within that of the Church.*

Contemporary historians have attempted to achieve a fuller understanding of this document by underscoring the many legendary circumstances that have developed concerning its composition. In addition to these historical studies, Franciscan scholars have studied the text according to the methods of Biblical exegesis in order to determine the rich spiritual tradition that has been transmitted through this medieval text. [1]

When the Later Rule is studied against the background of the Earlier Rule, its marvelous vision of the Gospel life comes into focus. [2] *This is a pattern or form of life that is meant to be lived in the pursuit of the Gospel mission; that is, in the striving to witness and proclaim*

---

1. A thorough study of the development of the Rules of Saint Francis was done by Oktavian Schmucki, O.F.M. Cap., "Gli Scritti Legislativi di San Francesco," *Approccio Storico-Critico alle Fonti Francescane* (Rome: Ed. Antonianum, 1979), pp. 73–98. See also Armando Quaglia, O.F.M., *L'Originalità della Regola Francescana* (Sasoferrato, 1943); *Origine e Sviluppo della Regola Francescana* (Napoli, 1948); Kajetan Esser, O.F.M., and F. Lothar Hardik, O.F.M., *The Marrow of the Gospel*, trans. and ed. Ignatius C. Brady, O.F.M. (Chicago: Franciscan Herald Press, 1958); Kajetan Esser, O.F.M., *Rule and Testament of Saint Francis*, trans. Bruce Malina, O.F.M., Audrey Marie Rothweil, O.S.F.

2. The *Opuscula Sancti Patris Francisci Assisiensis* contains fragments of three versions of a Rule which seems to have developed between the *Earlier Rule* and the *Later Rule*. The most important of these versions is found in a fourteenth-century manuscript preserved in the library of the Worcester Cathedral, Worcester, England, cod. Q27. The other two versions are quoted by Hugh of Digne in his *Expositio Regulae Ordinis Fratrum Minorum* and by Thomas of Celano in his *Second Life of Saint Francis*, 66, 128, 143, 175.

the mystery of the Incarnate Word of God. At the very heart of this document Saint Francis articulates the dynamism or the fundamental principle of the spiritual life: "the Spirit of the Lord and His holy manner of working."[3] Thus he provides for his followers an important tool for understanding the totality of his vision.

HONORIUS, BISHOP, SERVANT OF THE SERVANTS OF GOD, TO HIS BELOVED SONS, BROTHER FRANCIS AND THE OTHER BROTHERS OF THE ORDER OF FRIARS MINOR, HEALTH AND APOSTOLIC BLESSING:

The Apostolic See is accustomed to accede to the pious requests and to be favorably disposed to grant the praiseworthy desires of its petitioners. Wherefore, beloved sons in the Lord, attentive to your pious prayers, We confirm for you with our apostolic authority, and by this document ratify the rule of your Order herein contained and approved by our predecessor, Pope Innocent of happy memory, which is as follows:[3a]

(Chapter I)
In the name of the Lord!
The Life of the Friars Minor begins:

1. The rule and life of the Friars Minor is this: to observe the holy Gospel of our Lord Jesus Christ by living in obedience, without anything of their own, and in chastity.[4] 2. Brother Francis promises obedience and reverence to the Lord Pope Honorius and his canonically elected successors and to the Roman Church. 3. And let the other brothers be bound to obey Brother Francis and his successors.

---

3. Cf. *The Later Rule*, X, 8.

3a. The definitive text and fundamental charter of the life that is binding for the three families of the First Order of the Friars Minor is known as the *Regula bullata*, for it was solemnly approved in the papal bull *Solet annuere*, which was promulgated by Pope Honorius III on November 29, 1223. The formula that introduces the actual Rule of the Friars Minor is a stereotype that had been used previously in granting privileges to the Cistercians.

4. Cf. *The Earlier Rule*, I, n. 4.

(Chapter II)
*Those who wish to embrace this life
and how they should be received*

1. If there are any who wish to accept this life and come to our brothers, let them send them to the ministers provincial, to whom and to no other is permission granted for receiving brothers.[5] 2. The ministers should diligently examine them concerning the Catholic faith and the sacraments of the Church. 3. And if they believe all these things and are willing to profess them faithfully and observe them steadfastly to the end; 4. and [if] they have no wives, or if they have wives [who] have already taken a vow of continence and are of such an age that suspicion cannot be raised about them, [and who] have already entered a monastery or have given their husbands permission by the authority of the bishop of the diocese,[6] 5. let the ministers speak to them the words of the holy Gospel (cf. Mt 19:21) that they should go and sell all that belongs to them and strive to give it to the poor. 6. If they cannot do this, their good will suffices. 7. And let the brothers and their ministers beware not to become solicitous over their temporal affairs, so that they may freely dispose of their goods as the Lord may inspire them.[7] 8. But if they stand in need of counsel, the ministers may have permission to send them to some God-fearing persons who may advise them how they should give what they have to the poor. 9. Then they may be given the clothes of probation, namely, two tunics without a hood, a cord, short trousers, and a little cape reaching to the cord,[8] 10. unless at some time it seems [proper] to these same ministers before God to make other provisions. 11. When the year of probation is ended, let them be received into obedience, whereby they promise to observe this life and rule always. 12. And in no way shall it be lawful for them to leave this Order, according to the decree of the Lord Pope,[9] 13. since, according to the Gospel: *No one having put his hand to the plow and looking back is fit for the kingdom of God* (Lk 9:62). 14. And those who have already promised obedience

---

5. Cf. *The Earlier Rule*, II, n. 5.

6. This is taken literally from the decree of Pope Innocent III in 1198 and another of Pope Honorius III, both of which were incorporated into the *Decretals of Pope Gregory IX*, III, 32, 18.

7. Cf. *The Earlier Rule*, II, n. 6.

8. Cf. *The Earlier Rule*, II, n. 7.

9. Cf. *The Earlier Rule*, II, n. 8.

may have one tunic with a hood, and, if they wish, another without a hood. 15. And those who are forced by necessity may wear shoes. 16. And let all the brothers wear poor clothes, and let them mend them with pieces of sackcloth or other material, with the blessing of God. 17. I admonish and exhort them not to look down or pass judgment on those people whom they see wearing soft and colorful clothing and enjoying the choicest food and drink; instead, each must criticize and despise himself.

(Chapter III)

The Divine Office and Fasting and
The way the Brothers should go about the world

1. The clerical [brothers] shall celebrate the Divine Office according to the rite of the holy Roman Church, except for the Psalter, 2. for which reason they may have breviaries.[10] 3. The lay [brothers], however, shall pray twenty-four Our Fathers for Matins, five for Lauds, seven for each of the hours of Prime, Terce, Sext, and None, twelve for Vespers, and seven for Compline. 4. And they shall pray for the dead. 5. And [all the brothers] shall fast from the feast of All Saints until the Nativity of the Lord. 6. May those who fast voluntarily for that holy Lent which begins at Epiphany and continues for forty days, which the Lord consecrated by His own fast (cf. Mt 4:2), be blessed by the Lord; and those who do not wish to keep it shall not be obliged. 7. But they shall fast during that other Lent which lasts until the Resurrection. 8. At other times, however, they are not bound to fast except on Fridays. 9. But in times of manifest necessity the brothers are not obliged to corporal fasting.

10. I counsel, admonish and exhort my brothers in the Lord Jesus Christ, that, when they go about the world, they do not quarrel or fight with words (cf. 2 Tim 2:14), or judge others;[11] 11. rather, let them be meek, peaceful and unassuming, gentle and humble, speaking courteously to everyone, as is becoming. 12. And they should not

---

10. Cf. *The Earlier Rule*, III, n. 4. It is important to note the change in the phrasing of this passage, which speaks of the celebration of the Office "according to the rite of the holy Roman Church." *The Earlier Rule*, III, 4 indicated its celebration "according to the custom of the clergy."

11. This sentence seems to shift the direction of the thought of the Rule from the "inner life" of the friars, i.e., the reception of brothers, the profession of obedience, and the visible expressions of prayer and asceticism, to the life of the brothers in the world.

ride horseback unless they are forced by manifest necessity or infirmity. 13. *In whatever house* they enter, let them say: *Peace to this house* (cf. Lk 10:5). 14. And, according to the holy Gospel, they are free to eat of whatever food is set before them (cf. Lk 10:8).

(Chapter IV)
The Brothers are never to receive money

1. I firmly command all the brothers that they in no way receive coins or money, either personally or through an intermediary. 2. Nonetheless let the ministers and custodians alone take special care to provide for the needs of the sick and the clothing of the other brothers through spiritual friends according to [diversity of] places and seasons and cold climates, as they may judge the demands of necessity;[12] 3. excepting always, as stated above, they do not receive coins or money.

(Chapter V)
The Manner of working

1. Those brothers to whom the Lord has given the grace of working should do their work faithfully and devotedly[13] 2. so that, avoiding idleness, the enemy of the soul, they do not extinguish the Spirit of holy prayer and devotion to which all other things of our earthly existence must contribute.[14] 3. As payment for their work they may receive whatever is necessary for their own bodily needs and [those of] their brothers, but not money in any form; 4. and they should do this humbly as is fitting for servants of God and followers of most holy poverty.

---

12. The Rule of Saint Benedict, chapter 55, also speaks of the necessity of making provisions for the needs of the sick and other brothers according to places, seasons, and cold climates.

13. The "grace of working" is seen as one among the other graces of prayer and of preaching that are mentioned in the *Earlier Rule*.

14. The medieval sense of "devotion" differs from our contemporary understanding. In order to grasp the richness of the concept as Saint Francis uses it here (and in the *Letter to Saint Anthony* 2), see Jean Chatillon, "Devotio," *Dictionnaire de Spiritualité ascétique et mystique doctrine et histoire*, tome III, pp. 702–716.

THE WRITINGS

(Chapter VI)
The Brothers shall not acquire anything as their own;
begging alms; the sick brothers

1. The brothers shall not acquire anything as their own, neither a house nor a place nor anything at all.[15] 2. Instead, as pilgrims and strangers (cf. 1 Pet 2:11) in this world who serve the Lord in poverty and humility, let them go begging for alms with full trust. 3. Nor should they feel ashamed since the Lord made Himself poor for us in this world (cf. 2 Cor 8:9). 4. This is that summit of highest poverty which has established you, my most beloved brothers, as heirs and kings of the kingdom of heaven; it has made you poor in the things [of this world] but exalted you in virtue (cf. Ja 2:5). 5. Let this be your *portion*, which leads into *the land of the living* (cf. Ps. 141:6).[16] 6. Dedicating yourselves totally to this, my most beloved brothers, do not wish to have anything else forever under heaven for the sake of our Lord Jesus Christ.

7. And wherever the brothers may be together or meet [other] brothers, let them give witness that they are members of one family. 8. And let each one confidently make known his need to the other, for, if a mother has such care and love for her son born according to the flesh (cf. 1 Thes 2:7), should not someone love and care for his brother according to the Spirit even more diligently? 9. And if any of them becomes sick, the other brothers should serve him as they would wish to be served themselves (cf. Mt. 7:12).

(Chapter VII)
The Penance to be imposed on the brothers who sin

1. If any of the brothers, at the instigation of the enemy, sin mortally in regard to those sins about which it may have been decreed among the brothers to have recourse only to the ministers provincial,

---

15. This sentence is at the very heart of Saint Francis's notion of poverty. Cf. Lazaro Iriarte de Aspurz, O.F.M. Cap., " 'Appropriatio' et 'expropriatio' in doctrina s. Francisci," *Laurentianum* 11 (1970); 3–35.

16. It was this psalm that Saint Francis recited at the hour of his death (cf. *First Life of Saint Francis*, 109, by Thomas of Celano). The reference to "portion" might be to the Portiuncula, the "Little Portion" where the saint discovered the meaning of the Gospel life.

such brothers must have recourse to them as soon as possible, without delay.[17] 2. If these ministers are priests, they shall impose a penance upon them with mercy; but if they are not priests, they shall have it imposed by other priests of the Order as it seems best to them according to God. 3. They must take care not to become angry or disturbed because of the sin of another, since anger and disturbance hinder charity in themselves and in others.

(Chapter VIII)
The Election of the Minister General of this Fraternity and the Chapter of Pentecost

1. All[18] the brothers are bound always to have one of the brothers of this Order as the minister general and servant of the entire fraternity and they are bound strictly to obey him.[19] 2. Should he die, the election of a successor should be made by the ministers provincial and the custodians at the Chapter of Pentecost, for which the ministers provincial are always bound to convene in whatever place it has been decided by the minister general; 3. and they shall do this once every three years or at a longer or shorter interval as decided by the aforesaid minister.[20] 4. And if at any time it should become evident to the body of the ministers provincial and the custodians that the aforesaid minister is not qualified for the service and general welfare of the brothers, then the same brothers, to whom the election is entrusted, are bound in the name of the Lord to elect another for themselves as custodian. 5. After the Chapter of Pentecost each minister and custodian may call his brothers to a Chapter once in the same year in their territories—if they wish and if it seems expedient to them.

---

17. This chapter reflects the attempt expressed in the *Letter to a Minister*, 13–20, to unite all of the chapters of the *Earlier Rule* that dealt with sin. It was an ancient monastic custom for a monk to confess his sins to his superior. Some statutes of various Orders required this practice for grave sins already confessed to another priest.

18. The Latin adjective *universi* used in place of *omnes* in this sentence accentuates the central position within the Order of the Minister General. Nonetheless, Thomas of Celano in his *Second Life of Saint Francis*, 193, indicates Saint Francis's vision of the Holy Spirit as the real Minister General of the Order, a point he wanted inserted into the Rule but could not have since it was already approved by papal bull.

19. For descriptions of the ideal characteristics of a Minister General and a Minister Provincial, consult Thomas of Celano's *Second Life of Saint Francis*, 184–188.

20. Cf. *The Earlier Rule*, XVIII, n. 32.

(Chapter IX)
Preachers

1. The brothers shall not preach in the diocese of any bishop when he has opposed their doing so. 2. And none of the brothers shall dare to preach to the people unless he has been examined and approved by the minister general of this fraternity and has received from him the office of preaching. 3. I also admonish and exhort these brothers that, in their preaching, their words be *well chosen* and *chaste* (cf. Ps 11:7; 17:31), for the instruction and edification of the people, speaking to them of vices and virtues, punishment and glory in a discourse that is brief, because it was in few words that the Lord preached while on earth.[21]

(Chapter X)
The Admonition and Correction
of the Brothers

1. The brothers who are the ministers and servants of the other brothers should visit and admonish their brothers and humbly and charitably correct them, not commanding them anything which might be against their conscience and our Rule. 2. On the other hand, the brothers who are subject to them should remember that they have given up their own wills for God. 3. Therefore I strictly command them to obey their ministers in all those things which they have promised the Lord to observe and which are not against [their] conscience and our Rule. 4. And wherever there are brothers who know and realize that they cannot observe the Rule spiritually,[22] it is their duty and right to go to the minister for help. 5. The ministers on their part should receive them with great kindness and love and should be so approachable that these brothers can speak and deal with [the ministers] as masters with their servants; 6. for this is the way it should be: The ministers shall be the servants of all the brothers. 7. At the

---

21. Saint Francis uses a phrase that appears frequently in medieval literature, i.e., *Verbum abbreviatum.* According to Henri de Lubac, the image comes from Saint Augustine's *De Disciplina Christiana* II (PL 40:670). Cf. Henri de Lubac, *Exégèse Medievale* (Paris, 1959), II, 1, pp. 181–197; S. de Ausejo, "Con brevedad de sermon," *Melanges M. de Pobladura* (Rome, 1964) tom I, pp. 1–33; and, E. Bihel, "Deux citations bibliques de S. François," *La France Franciscaine* 12 (1929).

22. "Spiritually," i.e., "simply and purely," cf. *Testament,* 39.

same time I admonish and exhort the brothers in the Lord Jesus Christ that they beware *of all* pride, vainglory, envy, avarice (cf. Lk 12:15), cares and worries of this world (cf. Mt. 13:22), detraction and complaint. And those who are illiterate should not be eager to learn. 8. Instead let them pursue what they must desire above all things: to have the Spirit of the Lord and His holy manner of working,[23] 9. to pray always to Him with a pure heart and to have humility, patience in persecution and weakness, 10. and to love those who persecute us, find fault with us, or rebuke us, because the Lord says: *Love your enemies, and pray for those who persecute and slander you* (Mt 5:44). 11. *Blessed are those who suffer persecution for the sake of justice for theirs is the kingdom of heaven* (Mt 5:10). 12. *But whoever perseveres to the end, he will be saved* (Mt 10:22).

(Chapter XI)

The Brothers are not to enter the monasteries of nuns

1. I firmly command all the brothers not to have any associations or meetings with women which could arouse suspicion. 2. Moreover, they should not enter the monasteries of nuns, except those [brothers] to whom special permission has been granted by the Apostolic See. 3. They should not be godfathers of men or women so that scandal not arise on this account among the brothers or concerning them.[24]

(Chapter XII)

Those who go among the Saracens and other nonbelievers

1. Those brothers who, by divine inspiration, desire to go among the Saracens and other nonbelievers should ask permission from their ministers provincial. 2. But the ministers should not grant permission except to those whom they consider fit to be sent.[25]

---

23. This passage highlights the prominent principle of the spiritual life, i.e., the Spirit of the Lord Jesus Christ and His holy manner of working within a follower of Saint Francis. Cf. *Admonition* I, n. 1; *The First Version of the Letter to the Faithful*, n. 3.

24. This was a common canonical norm for nuns, cf. *the Decretals of Gratian* III P. *De consecr.* d. 4, c. 103s; Causa 16, q. 1, c. 8. This same prescription can be found in Gregory the Great, Letters IV 42 (PL 77:717). It is also found in the Statutes of the Penitential Movement of Saint Mary Magdalene 21:12. Cf. A. Simon, *L'Ordre des Pénitentes de Ste. Madeleine en Allemagne au XII siecle* (Fribourg, 1918), pp. 165–166.

25. Cf. *The Earlier Rule*, XVI, n. 29.

3. In addition, I command the ministers through obedience to petition the Lord Pope for one of the cardinals of the holy Roman Church, who would be the governor, protector, and corrector of this fraternity,[26] 4. so that, always submissive and prostrate at the feet of the same holy Church, and steadfast in the Catholic faith, we may observe the poverty and the humility and the holy Gospel (cf. Col 1:23) of our Lord Jesus Christ which we have firmly promised.

No one, therefore, is in any way permitted to tamper with this decree of our confirmation or to oppose it rashly. If anyone, however, should presume to attempt this, let it be known that he shall incur the indignation of Almighty God and of His blessed Apostles Peter and Paul.

Given at the Lateran, the twenty-ninth day of November, in the eighth year of our Pontificate.

---

26. For information concerning the origin and development of the office of Cardinal Protector, consult: Kajetan Esser, O.F.M., *Origins of the Franciscan Order,* trans. Aedan Daly, O.F.M. (Chicago: Franciscan Herald Press 1970), pp. 178–180. Cardinal Hugolino di Segni was Cardinal Protector of the Order until he was elected to be Bishop of Rome, March 19, 1227.

The Rule for Hermitages

The importance given to the eremitical spirit in the life of Saint Francis has not escaped students of his life throughout the centuries. His biographers are in agreement concerning the Seraphic Father's zeal in cultivating the solitary life and his pleasure with those friars who gave themselves to a life of seclusion to deepen their relationship with God. The names of the hermitages are spread throughout all of the early biographies of Saint Francis: Greccio, Fonte Colombo, La Verna, Poggio Bustone, Lago Trasimene, Sant'Urbano, Monte Cassale, and so forth.

This text is found in the oldest manuscript collection, the Assisi Codex 338, a fact that witnesses to its importance in the writings of Saint Francis. The manuscript traditions of the fourteenth and fifteenth centuries strongly indicate the authenticity of the work. Yet, despite its presence among the known writings of the Poverello during these centuries, the Rule for Hermitages *was given little attention. This neglect prevailed in modern Franciscan scholarship until the recent studies of Father Kajetan Esser, O.F.M., and Father Oktavian Schmucki, O.F.M. Cap., and the recent renewed interest in the contemplative tradition of the Franciscan Order.[1]*

The Rule for Hermitages expresses a spirit of simplicity and fraternity so that the solitude of a brother is reconciled with an essential characteristic of Franciscan life, brotherhood. When this document is examined against the background of the early biographies of Saint Francis, the eremitical manner of living described in it appears to be a

---

1. Cf. Kajetan Esser, O.F.M., "Die 'Regula pro eremitoriis data' des hl. Franziskus von Assisi," *Franziskanische Studien* 44 (1962): 383–417; Oktavian Schmucki, O.F.M. Cap., "Franciscus 'Dei Laudator et Cultor.' De Orationis Vi ac Frequentia in Eius cum Scriptis tum Rebus Gestis," *Laurentianum* 10 (1969): 3–36; " 'Secretum Solitudinis.' De Circumstantiis Externis Orandi Penes Sanctum Franciscum Assisiensem," *Collectanea Franciscana* 39 (1969): 5–58; "Luogo di Preghiera, Eremo, Solitudine, Concetti e Realizzazioni in San Francésco d'Assisi," *Le Case di Preghiera nella Storia e Spiritualitá Francescana*, Studi Scelti di Francescanesimo 7 (Napoli, 1978), pp. 33–53.

symbol of his inner life. Thus it is an invaluable tool in understanding the spirit of the Poverello.[2]

1. Those who wish[3] to live religiously in hermitages should be three brothers or four at the most; two of these should be mothers and they may have two sons or at least one.[4] 2. The two who are mothers should follow the life of Martha, while the two sons should follow the life of Mary (cf. Lk 10:38–42)[5] and they may have an enclosure[6] in which each one may have his small cell[7] in which he may pray and sleep. 3. And they should always say Compline of the day immediately after sundown; and they should be eager to keep silence, and to say their hours, and to rise for Matins; and let them seek *first* of all the kingdom of God and His *justice* (Mt 6:33). 4. And let them say Prime at the proper time, and after Terce they may be free from silence, and they may speak and go to their mothers. 5. And, whenever it pleases them, they can seek alms from them as little poor ones, for the love of God. 6. And afterward they should say Sext and None and Vespers at

---

2. For further reflections on this aspect of Franciscan life, consult Thomas Merton, "Franciscan Eremiticism," *The Cord*, December 1966, pp. 356–365; reprinted in *Contemplation in a World of Action* (Garden City: Doubleday & Co. 1971), pp. 260–268.

3. "Those who wish" indicates the voluntary aspect of this expression of Franciscan life. Saint Francis did not envision the eremitical life as an imposition but as a response to a desire for an intense life of prayer.

4. It is important to underscore the fraternal aspect of this document. The life of the brothers is described by identifying positions (mothers and sons), celebrating of the Divine Office, and begging alms. Furthermore, Saint Francis suggests that the eremitical fraternity has a definite relationship with the provincial fraternity as the visit of the minister and custodian indicates.

5. The images of Martha and Mary to describe the active and contemplative lives can be found in Saint Gregory the Great, *On Morals in Job*, Book 7, c. 37 (PL 75:764); *Homilies on Ezechiel*, III 9 (PL 76:809). It can also be found in the English Cistercian, Aelred of Rievaulx, *Rule of Life for a Recluse*, *Aelredi Rievallensis Opera Omnia* I: 637–82, edited by A. Hoste and C. H. Talbot, *Corpus Christianorum, Continuatio Medievalis* I (Steenbrugge, 1971) (English translation in *Treatises, The Pastoral Prayer* [Spencer: Cistercian Publications, 1971], pp. 41–102].

6. A *claustrum*, enclosure or cloister, is not used in the monastic sense of a squared roof enclosed by the walls of a church or a monastery. It was a place enclosed by hedges or some natural barrier so that outsiders might not enter (cf. *Legend of Perugia*, 34, 101; *Omnibus*, 1011, 1077).

7. A *cellula*, cell, has the same significance as the personal hut of a hermit living in solitude. In the ancient monastic tradition this was seen as a principal support of the contemplative life.

the proper time. 7. And in the enclosure, where they live, they should not permit any person to enter, nor should they eat there. 8. Those brothers who are the mothers should be eager to stay far from every person; and because of the obedience to their minister they should protect their sons from everyone, so that no one can talk with them. 9. And the sons should not talk with any person except with their mothers and with the minister and his custodian when it pleases them to visit[8] with the blessing of the Lord God. 10. The sons, however, should sometimes assume the role of the mothers, as from time to time it may seem good to them to exchange [roles.][9] They should strive to observe conscientiously and carefully all the things mentioned above.

8. The date of this writing can be placed only between the years 1217, when the Order was divided into provinces cared for by provincials and further divided into custodies cared for by custodians, and 1222, when the papal decree *Devotionis vestrae* gave permission for oratories. Since there is no mention of an oratory in this document, it would seem that it was written before this date.

9. Concerning the exchange of positions, consult Thomas of Celano, *Second Life of Saint Francis*, n. 178; *Omnibus*, 504.

The Salutation of the Blessed Virgin Mary

In his Second Life of Saint Francis, *198, Thomas of Celano describes the love of Saint Francis for the Mother of Jesus as "inexpressible," for "it was she who made the Lord of majesty our brother." This simple litany describes Mary's role in the plan of salvation and uses many titles that were familiar to the medieval Christian to praise her unique position. Although the manuscript tradition suggests a close tie between this piece and the* Salutation of the Virtues, *it is more accurate to consider them as separate works. Nonetheless, Saint Francis clearly perceives and presents the Virgin Mary as the model for every Christian who responds to the virtuous presence of God in his life.*[1]

1. Hail, O Lady,[2]
        holy Queen,
        Mary, holy Mother of God:
        you are the virgin made church
2.   and the one chosen by the most holy Father in heaven
    whom He consecrated
        with His most holy beloved Son
        and with the Holy Spirit the Paraclete,
3.   in whom there was and is
        all the fullness of grace and every good.

---

1. Cf. Hilarius de Wingene, O.F.M. Cap., "Fuitne S. Franciscus suas duas preces mariales ad S. Mariam de Angelis ad Portiunculam," *Laurentianum* 11 (1970): 267–307, 447–458; Hilarius Pyfferoen, O.F.M. Cap., "Ave . . . Dei Genetrix Maria, Quae es Virgo Ecclesia Facta (S. Francisci)," *Laurentianum* 12 (1971): 412–434; Hilarius Pyfferoen, O.F.M. Cap., and Optatus van Asseldonk, O.F.M. Cap., "Maria Santissima e Lo Spirito Santo in San Francesco d'Assisi," *Laurentianum* 4 (1975): 446–474; Oktavian Schmucki, O.F.M. Cap., "De seraphici Patris Francisci habitudine erga beatissimam Virginem Mariam," *Regina Immaculata*, Bibliotheca Seraphica Cappucina: Sectio historico 15 (Rome, 1955), pp. 15–47.

2. The first lines of this *Salutation of the Blessed Virgin Mary* show the influence of an earlier Marian tradition to which Saint Francis was heir. However, the phrase *quae es virgo ecclesia facta*, "you are the virgin made church," sets this piece within a magnificent ecclesial perspective that is almost beyond its time. Images of Mary and the Church are linked together in medieval spiritual literature, but not in so striking a manner as in this expression of Saint Francis.

4. Hail, His Palace![3]
    Hail, His Tabernacle!
    Hail, His Home!
5. Hail, His Robe!
    Hail, His Servant!
    Hail, His Mother!
6. And, [hail] all you holy virtues[4]
        which through the grace and light of the Holy Spirit
        are poured into the hearts of the faithful
        so that from their faithless state
        you may make them faithful to God.

---

3. The prominence of *Ave*, Hail, in this line and the following suggest the litany-type prayer this forms.
4. The curious greeting of all holy virtues that broadens the scope of this prayer places the image of the Blessed Virgin Mary before the eyes of every devout Christian. This is consistent with the spirituality of Saint Francis, for whom devotion to the Blessed Mother of God was paramount.

The Salutation of the Virtues

The more one ponders this simple text, the more Saint Francis is revealed as a theologian of the workings of the Spirit and of divine grace in the soul of one who has surrendered himself entirely to God by "dying" to self to live totally for God.

Although the titles of this work differ in many early manuscripts, the authenticity of the text has been solidly established. Thomas of Celano witnesses to its existence when he quotes a section of it in the Second Life of Saint Francis, *189.*

The work can be divided into three major sections: the salutations addressed to the virtues, the dispositions necessary for their reception, and the description of each one's activity. The consideration of each of the virtues in a feminine sense is an expression of the medieval milieu from which this writing comes. What is curious, though, is the manner of linking certain virtues to one another. The combination established between wisdom and simplicity, poverty and humility, and love and obedience speak eloquently of the unique vision of Saint Francis.[1]

1. Hail, Queen Wisdom,[2] may the Lord protect you
   with your sister, holy pure Simplicity.
2. Lady, holy Poverty, may the Lord protect you
   with your sister, holy Humility.
3. Lady, holy Charity, may the Lord protect you
   with your sister, holy Obedience.

---

1. The titles found in the manuscript tradition indicate the many ways in which the friars viewed this expression of spiritual vision. The following titles are found: (1) "The virtues possessed by the holy Virgin, and which should be present in a holy soul"; (2) "The Salutation of the Virtues with which the Blessed Virgin was clothed and which should be present in a holy soul"; (3) "The Salutation of the Virtues and their efficacy in confounding vices"; (4) "The Linking of the Virtues."

2. The virtues are addressed in the feminine, particularly as *ladies*. This reflects the chivalrous and courtly mannerisms Francis seemed to have appreciated. There seem to be direct links between this piece and such medieval poems as the chansons de geste.

4.   O most holy Virtues, may the Lord protect all of you,
       from Whom you come and proceed.

5.   There is surely no one in the entire world
       who can possess any one of you
       unless he dies first.

6.   Whoever possesses one [of you]
       and does not offend the others,
       possesses all.

7.   And whoever offends one [of you]
       does not possess any
       and offends all.

8.   And each one destroys vices and sins.

9.   Holy Wisdom destroys
       Satan and all his subtlety.

10.   Pure holy Simplicity destroys
       all the wisdom of this world
       and the wisdom of the body.

11.   Holy Poverty destroys
       the desire of riches
       and avarice
       and the cares of this world.

12.   Holy Humility destroys
       pride
       and all the people who are in the world
       and all things that belong to the world.

13.   Holy Charity destroys
       every temptation of the devil and of the flesh
       and every carnal fear.

14.   Holy Obedience destroys
       every wish of the body and of the flesh

15.   and binds its mortified body
          to obedience of the Spirit
          and to obedience of one's brother

16.   and [the person who possesses her] is subject and submissive
          to all persons in the world

17.   and not to man only
          but even to all beasts and wild animals

18.   so that they may do whatever they want with him
          inasmuch as it has been given to them from above
             by the Lord.

The Testament

Shortly before his death in October 1226, Saint Francis dictated a document that he called "my testament" and declared that he was writing it "so that we may observe in a more Catholic manner the Rule which we have promised to the Lord."[1] Saint Francis expressly cautioned his followers against looking on this document as "another rule," since it was only a "remembrance" or an "admonition." Evidently he did not intend to endow the Testament with any legally binding force over and beyond the Rule of the Order. Yet the work contains statements that go beyond mere exhortation and seem to lay down commands that are binding under obedience. Thus the Testament has become one of the most controversial documents to come to us from the Seraphic Father.[2] At the same time, the Testament has always been held in great respect as an expression of the profound wisdom and vision of the Seraphic Father and of his care and concern for those who would follow him.[3]

---

1. Cf. *Testament*, 34.

2. It is difficult to determine the meaning of *testamentum* (testament) as the title of this work. The profane or legal sense of the word suggests a last will and testament about one's goods or possessions. Pope Gregory IX, in the papal bull *Quo elongati* (1230), suggests this meaning when he states: "Toward the end of his life [Saint Francis] made a command, which command is called a Testament." In 1295 Peter Olivi in a letter to Brother Conrad of Offida claims the title was given by others and calls this simply a letter. Finally, Ubertino da Casale, in the beginning of the fourteenth century, reflects a tension between the title and the text: ". . . in his Testament, as he himself calls this document . . ." (cf. Kajetan Esser, *Das Testament des hl. Franziskus* (Munster, 1949), pp. 65–69). In recent times, Auspicius von Corstanje, O.F.M., has suggested a Biblical interpretation and has interpreted the work as an expression of God's renewed covenant with the poor Francis and his brothers (cf. Auspicius von Corstanje, *The Covenant with God's Poor*, trans. Gabriel Reidy, O.F.M., ed. Stephen Anaclete Yornick, O.F.M. (Chicago: Franciscan Herald Press, 1966).

3. For further studies, consult Kajetan Esser, O.F.M., *Das Testament des heiligen Franziskus von Assisi: Eine Untersuchung uber seine Echtheit une seine Bedeutung in Vorreformationsgeschichtliche Forschugen*, vol. 15 (Munster, 1949); also, *The Rule and Testament of Saint Francis*, trans. Bruce Malina, O.F.M., and Audrey Marie Rothweil, O.S.F. (Chicago: Franciscan Herald Press, 1977); Auspicius von Corstanje, O.F.M., *The Covenant with God's Poor*, trans. Gabriel Reidy, O.F.M., ed. Stephen Anaclete Yornick, O.F.M. (Chicago: Franciscan Herald Press, 1966).

1. The Lord granted me, Brother Francis, to begin to do penance in this way: While I was in sin, it seemed very bitter to me to see lepers.[4] 2. And the Lord Himself led me among them and I had mercy upon them. 3. And when I left them that which seemed bitter to me was changed into sweetness of soul and body; and afterward I lingered a little and left the world.

4. And the Lord gave me such faith in churches that I would simply pray and speak in this way: 5. "We adore You, Lord Jesus Christ, in all Your churches throughout the world, and we bless You, for through Your holy cross You have redeemed the world."[5]

6. Afterward the Lord gave me and still gives me such faith in priests who live according to the manner of the holy Roman Church because of their order, that if they were to persecute me, I would [still] have recourse to them. 7. And if I possessed as much wisdom as Solomon had and I came upon pitiful priests of this world, I would not preach contrary to their will in the parishes in which they live. 8. And I desire to fear, love, and honor them and all others as my masters. 9. And I do not wish to consider sin in them because I discern the Son of God in them and they are my masters. 10. And I act in this way since I see nothing corporally of the Most High Son of God in this world except His Most holy Body and Blood which they receive and which they alone administer to others. 11. And these most holy mysteries I wish to have honored above all things and to be reverenced and to have them reserved in precious places. 12. Wherever I come upon His most holy written words in unbecoming places, I desire to gather them up and I ask that they be collected and placed in a suitable place.[6] 13. And we should honor and respect all theologians and those who minister the most holy divine words as those who minister spirit and life to us (cf. Jn 6:64).

14. And after the Lord gave me brothers, no one showed me what I should do, but the Most High Himself revealed to me that I should

---

4. The initial part of the *Testament* (1–13) forms an autobiographical reflection on the part of Saint Francis. This is followed by a commentary on the life of the primitive fraternity of the Order of Friars Minor (14–22). Together these two sections form the "remembrance" part of the *Testament*.

5. This prayer was inspired by the Liturgy of Holy Thursday, Saint Gregory the Great recommends its recitation in his *Liber Responsalis* (PL 78, 805), as does the monk Arnulphe, *Documenta Vitae Religiosae* (PL 184, 1177).

6. This section of the Testament echoes many themes that are present in the Eucharistic Letters, i.e., the *Letter to the Clergy*, the letters to the Custodians, and the *Letter to the Entire Order*.

live according to the form of the Holy Gospel. 15. And I had this written down simply and in a few words and the Lord Pope confirmed it for me. 16. And those who came to receive life gave to the poor everything which they were capable of possessing and they were content with one tunic, patched inside and out, with a cord and short trousers. 17. And we had no desire for anything more. 18. We [who were] clerics used to say the Office as other clerics did; the lay brothers said the Our Father; and we quite willingly stayed in churches. 19. And we were simple and subject to all.

20. And I used to work with my hands, and I [still] desire to work; and I firmly wish that all my brothers give themselves to honest work. 21. Let those who do not know how [to work] learn, not from desire of receiving wages for their work but as an example and in order to avoid idleness. 22. And when we are not paid for our work, let us have recourse to the table of the Lord, seeking alms from door to door. 23. The Lord revealed to me a greeting, as we used to say: "May the Lord give you peace."

24. Let the brothers beware that they by no means receive churches or poor dwellings or anything which is built for them, unless it is in harmony with [that] holy poverty which we have promised in the Rule, [and] let them always be guests there as pilgrims and strangers (1 Pet 2:11).[7] 25. And I firmly command all of the brothers through obedience that, wherever they are, they should not be so bold as to seek any letter from the Roman Curia either personally or through an intermediary, neither for a church or for some other place or under the guise of preaching or even for the persecution of their bodies; 26. but wherever they have not been received, let them flee into another country to do penance with the blessing of God.

27. And I firmly wish to obey the minister general of this fraternity and another guardian whom it might please him to give me. 28. And I wish to be so captive in his hands that I cannot go [anywhere] or do [anything] beyond obedience and his will, for he is my master.

29. And although I may be simple and infirm, I wish nonetheless always to have a cleric who will celebrate the Office for me as it is contained in the Rule. 30. And all the other brothers are bound to obey their guardians and to celebrate the Office according to the

---

7. This sentence as well as sentences 25 and 26 form an admonition. They have become points of discussion, legislation, and tension in the First Order of Saint Francis ever since the death of Saint Francis.

Rule. 31. And [if] any are found who do not celebrate the Office according to the Rule and [who] wish to alter it in any way or [who] are not Catholics, let all the brothers be obliged through obedience that wherever they come upon [such a brother] they must bring him to the custodian [who is] nearest to that place where they have found him.[8] 32. And the custodian is strictly bound through obedience to guard him strongly as a prisoner day and night, so that he cannot be snatched from his hands until he can personally deliver him into the hands of his minister. 33. And the minister is strictly bound through obedience to send him with brothers who shall guard him as a prisoner day and night until they deliver him before the Lord of Ostia who is the master, protector, and corrector of the entire fraternity.

34. And let the brothers not say: This is another Rule; because this is a remembrance, an admonition, an exhortation, and my testament, which I, little Brother Francis, prepare for all of you, my blessed brothers, so that we may observe in a more Catholic manner the Rule which we have promised to the Lord.

35. And the minister general and all other ministers and custodians are bound through obedience not to add to or subtract from these words. 36. And let them always have this writing with them along with the Rule. 37. And in all the chapters which they hold, when they read the Rule, let them also read these words. 38. And I through obedience strictly command all my brothers, cleric and lay, not to place glosses on the Rule or on these words, saying: They are to be understood in this way. 39. But as the Lord has granted me to speak and to write the Rule and these words simply and purely, so shall you understand them simply and without gloss, and observe them with [their] holy manner of working until the end.

40. And whoever shall have observed these [things], may he be filled in heaven with the blessing of the most high Father and on earth with the blessing of His beloved Son with the most Holy Spirit the Paraclete and with all the powers of heaven and all the saints. 41. And I, little brother Francis, your servant, inasmuch as I can, confirm for you this most holy blessing both within and without.[9]

---

8. *A Letter to the Entire Order*, 39.

9. Livarius Oliger, O.F.M., sees a parallel between this blessing and that of Saint Hugh of Cluny (†1109) (cf. Livarius Oliger, O.F.M. *Archivum Franciscanum Historicum* 42 [1949]: 314).

Francis of Assisi

DICTATED WRITINGS

The Blessing Given to Brother Bernard

In his Life of Saint Francis, *Chapter III, 3, Saint Bonaventure described Bernard of Quintavalle as the "firstborn son" of the saint. The lives of the two men are entwined from the first days at the Portiuncula, through the trips to Rome (1209) and France and Spain (1213/1215), to the moments of Francis's death. This blessing given to Brother Bernard is taken from the description of the last moments of Saint Francis found in the* Legend of Perugia, *107.*

1. Write this just as I tell you: 2. Brother Bernard was the first brother whom the Lord gave me, as well as the first to put into practice and fulfill most completely the perfection of the Holy Gospel by distributing all his goods to the poor; 3. because of this and many other prerogatives, I am bound to love him more than any other brother of the entire Order. 4. Therefore, as much as I can, I desire and command that, whoever the minister general is, he should cherish and honor him as he would me, 5. and likewise the ministers provincial and the brothers of the entire Order should esteem him in place of me.

The Blessing Sent to Saint Clare and Her Sisters

The Legend of Perugia, 109, narrates the sickness of Saint Clare during the last week of Saint Francis's life and her fear of dying without a final glimpse of the saint. Out of compassion for Clare and her sisters, Saint Francis dictated this blessing. It is contained in the Legend of Perugia *and the* Book of the Conformities *of Bartholomew of Pisa.*

To console her [Saint Francis] sent her in writing his blessing and likewise absolved her from any failure if she had committed any against his orders and wishes and the commands and wishes of the Son of God.

A Letter Written for the Citizens of Bologna

The reference to this dictated letter of Saint Francis can be found in the Chronicle of Thomas of Eccleston, De adventu fratrum Minorum in Angliam *VI (*Thirteenth Century Chronicles *[Chicago, 1961], 126). Secular chroniclers report an earthquake that occurred in Bologna on Christmas Day, 1222.*

He [Brother Martin of Barton] also said that a certain brother in Brescia who was standing in prayer on Christmas Day was found unhurt under a ruin of stones when an earthquake struck and the church collapsed. This was an earthquake which Saint Francis had foretold and had announced [by the brothers] through a letter which contained poor Latin, throughout all the schools of Bologna.

A Letter Written to Lady Jacoba

Lady Jacoba de'Settesoli became one of the prominent members of the Third Order and won the affectionate title "Brother Jacoba" by which Saint Francis made her famous in history. Saint Francis had just finished dictating this final message to her when Lady Jacoba arrived with the very items the saint had requested. The sources of this touching incident are The Tract on the Miracles *of Thomas of Celano, nn. 37–38 and the* Legend of Perugia, *n. 101.*

[... the holy woman was discovered to have brought everything for the burial of her father which the letter written just a short time before had requested.] For she brought an ashen-colored cloth with which the body of the deceased would be covered, many candles, a veil for [his] face, a little pillow for [his] head, and a certain sweetmeat which the saint had desired.

A Letter Sent to the Brothers in France

Little is known about the mission of the friars to France. Jordan of Giano narrates that the friars who went to France were asked if they were Albigensians and answered affirmatively, because they did not know what the Albigensian heresy was. The source of this letter is Thomas of Eccleston, Chronicle, *VI (Thirteenth Century Chronicles, p. 126.)*

1. . . . the blessed Francis wrote a letter with his own hand . . . to the minister and the brothers of France, 2. so that they would rejoice at the sight of his handwriting and, praising the Triune God, would say: 3. Let us bless the Father and the Son with the Holy Spirit.

The Testament Written in Siena

The First Life of Thomas of Celano, 105, describes the physical condition of Saint Francis as deteriorating so rapidly that, while he was in Siena six months before his death, it looked as though death were imminent. The friars asked him for his blessing and an expression of his last will. The three simple points Saint Francis left them reflect the three foundations of the heritage he gave his followers: fraternity, poverty, and obedience to the Church. The source of this simple testament is the Legend of Perugia, 17.

1. . . . Write that I bless all my brothers, [those] who are in the Order, and [those] who will come until the end of the world. . . . 2. Since because of my weakness and the pain of my sickness I am not strong enough to speak, I make known my will to my brothers briefly in these three phrases, namely: 3. as a sign that they remember my blessing and my testament, let them always love one another, 4. let them always love and be faithful to our Lady Holy Poverty, 5. and let them always be faithful and subject to the prelates and all clerics of Holy Mother Church.

True and Perfect Joy

This is a different type of writing, since it is transmitted through the medium of a story and through a much later witness, a fourteenth-century manuscript discovered and published by Bughetti in the Ar-chivum Franciscanum Historicum 20 (1927): 107. Father Esser published this version in his collection and supported it with parallel texts found in Admonition V, *the* Second Life of Thomas of Celano, *125 and 145. This description of perfect joy graphically portrays Saint Francis's understanding of true minority and expresses the Francis-can ideal through the medium of the human person.*

1. [Brother Leonard] related, in the same place [the Portiuncula], that one day at Saint Mary the blessed Saint Francis called Brother Leo and said: "Brother Leo, write!" 2. He answered: "I'm ready." 3. "Write," [Francis] said, "what true joy is:

4. "A messenger comes and says that all the masters in Paris have come into the Order; write: this is not true joy. 5. Or that all the prel-ates beyond the mountains [have entered the Order], as well as the archbishops and bishops; or, that the king of France and the king of England [have entered the Order]; write: this is not true joy. 6. Again, that my brothers have gone to the nonbelievers and converted all of them to the faith; again, that I have so much grace from God that I heal the sick and perform many miracles: I tell you that true joy does not consist in any of these things."

7. "What then is true joy?"

8. "I return from Perugia and arrive here in the dead of night; and it is winter time, muddy and so cold that icicles have formed on the edges of my habit and keep striking my legs, and blood flows from such wounds. 9. And all covered with mud and cold, I come to the gate and after I have knocked and called for some time, a brother comes and asks: 'Who are you?' I answer: 'Brother Francis.' 10. And he says: 'Go away; this is not a proper hour for going about; you may not come in.' 11. And when I insist, he answers: 'Go away, you are a simple and a stupid person; we are so many and we have no need of you. You are certainly not coming to us at this hour!' 12. And I stand

again at the door and say: 'For the love of God, take me in tonight.' 13. And he answers: 'I will not. 14. Go to the Crosiers' place and ask there.' 15. I tell you this: If I had patience and did not become upset, there would be true joy in this and true virtue and the salvation of the soul.''

Clare of Assisi

INTRODUCTION

Part I

Some sixty years after her birth, Pope Alexander IV proclaimed Clare of Assisi a saint of the universal Church and rhapsodized on her name:

O Clare, endowed with so many titles of clarity! Clear (*clara*) even before your conversion, clearer (*clarior*) in your manner of living, exceedingly clear (*praeclarior*) in your enclosed life, and brilliant (*clarissima*) in splendor after the course of your mortal life. In Clare, a clear mirror is given to the entire world.[1]

This papal bull of canonization, *Clara claris praeclara*, captures the unique place of the most dedicated follower of the Poor Man of Assisi by poetically expressing the symbolic dimension of her life. Clare of Assisi, one of the great women of the Christian and Franciscan tradition, is a translucent statement of the spiritual reality of life. "A clear mirror," as the Pope calls her, so that whoever gazes into her writings will discover a reflection of the glory of God and the beauty of the human person.

In the opening paragraphs of the *Legend of Saint Clare*, written shortly after her canonization in 1255, the author describes the apprehension of Ortolana, the saint's mother, as the time of her child's birth drew near. She frequently visited a nearby church, the account narrates, and one day heard a response to her prayer for the safe delivery of her child. "O lady," the voice told her, "do not be afraid, for you will joyfully bring forth a clear light which will illumine the world." Within a short time, a female child was born to Ortolana and her husband, Favarone, and was named Chiara or Clare, the clear one.[2]

Clare was the third of five children born to this somewhat well-to-do family of Assisi. The *Legend* does not hesitate in describing her

---

1. Alexander IV, *Clara claris praeclara, Bullarium Franciscanum* 2 (Rome, 1761), 81.
2. *Legend of Saint Clare*, 2, in *The Legend and Writings of Saint Clare*, trans. Ignatius Brady, O.F.M. (St. Bonaventure: New York, 1953), p. 21.

as a holy, dedicated young woman even before her "conversion." "The Spirit worked within and formed her into a most pure vessel," her biographer writes of her childhood, so that "she began to be praised by her neighbors . . . and the report of her goodness was noised about among the townspeople."[3] Docility to her parents, generosity and compassion for the poor, dedication to daily prayer: These are some of the virtues Clare's biographer lists among the qualities of her youth.

It is difficult to determine when Clare first met Francis, the popular young man who had turned his back on the military establishment and the business world, but she probably heard him proclaim his message of penance and peace in the piazzas of Assisi. It is certainly possible that Clare may have heard the young Francis preach in the cathedral of San Rufino in 1210, for her family lived directly across from it. At about this time her uncle made arrangements for her to marry Ranieri de Bernardo, but Clare refused and, with the help of her servant, Bona di Guelfuccio, made arrangements to meet Francis and receive his advice. "The Father Francis," the *Legend* narrates, "exhorted her to contempt of the world, vividly showing her how vain was earthly hope, how deceptive worldly beauty. He manifested to her the sweetness of the nuptials of Christ and persuaded her to keep the pearl of her virginal purity for that blessed Bridegroom Whom love made Man."[4] On Palm Sunday, March 18, 1212, Clare followed the advice of the Poverello, accepted a palm branch (the symbol of martyrdom) from the bishop of Assisi, and on the following evening went to the Portiuncula, where Francis received her commitment to follow him in the pursuit of Gospel perfection.

Saint Francis and the friars escorted Clare to the Benedictine nuns in the monastery of San Paolo in Bastia, a short distance from Santa Maria degli Angeli (the Portiuncula) until more definite provisions could be provided. Then, after her relatives attempted to persuade her to return to her former way of life, the Seraphic Father moved her to the monastery of San Angelo di Panzo and, finally, to San Damiano, the first of the little churches the young Francis had repaired. Clare remained in that same dwelling for forty-two years, that is, until her death in 1253. Within a short period of time the young woman was joined by others, including her younger sister Ag-

---

3. Ibid., 3, 4.
4. Ibid., 5.

nes, and the "Poor Ladies" of Assisi became recognized as followers of the Poor Man of Assisi.

In her Rule, Clare provides a short "form of life" that the Seraphic Father gave to her and her sisters.[5] It is a simple statement, which describes the Trinitarian foundations of the life at San Damiano, as well as the close ties that Saint Francis saw binding the Poor Ladies and the friars. Although there are no other documents of either Francis or Clare that provide more details concerning the daily life of the sisters, Thomas of Celano, in his *First Life of Saint Francis* (c. 1228), presents a beautiful description of the community at San Damiano. The opening sentence of these paragraphs suggests the reticence of later authors in examining in detail the manner of living followed by the Poor Ladies:

> Over her [Clare] arose a noble structure of most precious pearls, whose *praise is not from men but from God* (Rom 2:29), since neither is our limited understanding sufficient to imagine it, nor our scanty vocabulary to utter it.[6]

Yet Celano proceeds to praise Clare and her sisters for the steadfast practice of charity, humility, virginity and chastity, poverty, abstinence and silence, patience, and contemplation. What is remarkable about these paragraphs is their composition during the lifetime of Clare herself, who would have heard them read with each celebration of the feast of Saint Francis.

The development of the Poor Ladies, however, must be seen against the background of the Fourth Lateran Council (1215) and its legislation forbidding the establishment of any new religious orders. By the time of the council, Clare and her sisters had become recognized as a religious community, but there is no evidence indicating papal approbation for their way of life. Thus the prescription of the council directly affected the form of life followed by the Poor Ladies of San Damiano.

As the fame of the San Damiano foundation began to spread and new monasteries were established, the Cardinal Deacon, Hugolino, was appointed their protector from 1218 to 1219. In order to provide a more stable form of living for Clare and her sisters, Hugolino provid-

---

5. Cf. supra, *The Form of Life Given to St. Clare and Her Sisters*, p. 44.
6. Thomas of Celano, *First Life of St. Francis*, 19, in *Omnibus of Sources*, p. 244.

ed a new, detailed, and austere Rule that was based on the Benedictine Rule. Two most important points, however, were clearly missing from this Rule: the pursuit of radical poverty and dependence on the Order of Friars Minor. Thus a struggle began for Clare that was to continue throughout her entire life. The saint desired to write her own Rule based on that of the Friars Minor in which the pursuit of evangelical perfection and poverty would form a firm foundation.

Within a year of Hugolino's election as the Bishop of Rome, the new Pope Gregory IX followed the example of his predecessor, Pope Innocent III, and acceded to the wishes of Clare for a special privilege to practice poverty. The papal document, *Sicut manifestum est*, September 17, 1228, permitted the sisters to live in perfect poverty and to reject the possession of any goods.

On August 6, 1247, Pope Innocent IV provided a new Rule for all the monasteries of the Poor Ladies and in a papal bull, *Quoties a nobis*, August 23, 1247, bound them to its observance. This second Rule was a milder form of that given by Hugolino and even allowed common ownership of movable and immovable goods. The Pope declared in another papal bull, *Inter Personas*, July 6, 1250, that no sister could be forced to accept this Rule and so it lost its binding force. At about this time, Clare began to write her own Rule based on that of Saint Francis and accepted the minor details of the Rules of Hugolino and Innocent IV.

Throughout all these years of struggle, Clare was ill and confined to bed. The *Legend* speaks of her continual illness during a span of twenty-eight years, yet it does not provide any clues as to the nature of her malady. The Process of Canonization indicates that the extreme mortification and rigorous penance of Clare's life took a severe toll on her health. Nonetheless, Clare appears as a strong, determined woman who was convinced of the charism of poverty that she had received through the Seraphic Father and was insistent on obtaining papal approval in order to protect it for ages to come.

In September 1252, Cardinal Raynaldus, the Cardinal Archbishop of Ostia and Velletri and, therefore, the Protector of the Poor Ladies, visited the sickbed of Clare and approved her Rule with the following words:

> Beloved daughters in Christ, because you have rejected the splendors and pleasures of the world and, *following the footprints* (1 Pt 2:21) of Christ Himself and of His most holy

Mother, you have chosen to live in the cloister and to serve the Lord in highest poverty so that, in freedom of soul, you may be the Lord's servants, We approve your holy way of life in the Lord and with fatherly affection we desire to freely impart our benign favor to your wishes and holy desires.[7]

But this approval did not satisfy Clare, who continued to seek the approval of Pope Innocent IV. She had to wait for almost eleven more months before the papal bull *Solet annuere*, August 9, 1253, put her at ease.

Two days later, August 11, 1253, Clare died, and was buried in the church of San Giorgio where Saint Francis had been placed before his body was transferred to the basilica built in his honor. The body of Clare still remains there, although it is now honored by another basilica of Assisi, which is dedicated to her memory.

A frequent representation of Clare of Assisi depicts her holding a monstrance containing the Eucharist and, through her devotion, putting to flight the Saracens who threatened San Damiano. That image may well symbolize Clare's entire life, for it epitomizes her strong, courageous faith, which struggled against and overcame the prudence of the world. Thirty-four of the forty-one years of Clare's life at San Damiano were spent in a determined effort to preserve the purity of the Franciscan ideal of poverty. From this perspective Clare is a vital part of the Franciscan heritage and the transmission of the spirit of the Poverello was achieved through her determination. Indeed, when this "little plant of the most blessed Father Francis," as she calls herself,[8] is seen against the background of the history of the Franciscan Family between 1226, the year of the death of Saint Francis, and 1253, the year of Saint Clare's own death, it is not difficult to envision the loss of the great ideal of radical, evangelical poverty. While the friars were accepting papal indults that relaxed their practice of poverty, Clare was courageously clinging to the primitive ideals and challenging the Holy See to allow her and her sisters to maintain the charism of poverty, which she had received from Francis himself.

Through this woman, then, the Spirit of the Lord expressed the Franciscan ideal in a pure, brilliant way and confronted and challenged her contemporaries to a serious consideration of its value. Her

---

7. Cf. infra, *Rule of St. Clare*, Prologue, p. 210.
8. *The Rule of Saint Clare*, Chapter I, 3, p. 211.

very name, Clare, expresses her position as a clear and clarifying expression of the spirituality of the Poor Man of Assisi.

THE WRITINGS OF SAINT CLARE

A remarkable testimony to Saint Clare is the small number of writings she left to the literature of Christian spirituality. She has given only five known writings: her Rule and four letters to Blessed Agnes of Prague. The authenticity of the other writings—the Testament, Blessing, and the Letter to Ermentrude of Bruges—has been contested; they may be the conceptions of authors in the fourteenth or fifteenth centuries. This poverty of sources, however, is very much in keeping with the life of Clare, for it reflects her total absorption in the mystery of Christ and her desire to imitate Him in poverty and humility. Thus the few writings of Saint Clare are eloquent reminders to everyone who is curious about her place in the Franciscan heritage of her total commitment to its ideals.

The Rule alone is a marvelous expression of Clare's dedication to the vision of Saint Francis. It becomes more precious when it is examined in the context of its development, for, although the Rules of Hugolino and Pope Innocent IV can be discovered in it, the Rule of Saint Clare is clearly based on the teaching and example of the Seraphic Father. He is proposed three times as the motivation prompting obedience to the Church, the Pope, and the Minister General, an authentic life of poverty, and the spiritual ministry of the friars. In many passages of her Rule, Clare quotes directly from the Rule of the Friars Minor approved by the papal bull *Solet annuere*. Many secondary and minor prescriptions, more or less "technical points" such as the portress, the parlor, the chaplain, and so forth, are taken from the earlier Rules of Hugolino and Innocent IV, but the foundation is obviously the Rule of the Seraphic Father.

The major difference between the Rule of Saint Clare and that of Saint Francis lies in the enclosure. From the third chapter of his *Later Rule*, the Poverello envisioned a life pursued "in the world" and characterized by those virtues of "pilgrims and strangers" who proclaim the Gospel in a myriad of places and circumstances. Clare, on the other hand, describes a life integrally tied to a monastery and caught up in the struggle to preserve "unity of mutual love, which is the bond of perfection." The life of the Poor Ladies was developed through an essential preoccupation with the interior life, that is, the spiritual life of each sister, and its external manifestation in the community of love that was formed by the sisters. What is extraordinary about this manner of life, as Clare describes it, is the audacious character of its poverty, which is totally dependent on the simple work of the sisters and on the alms that are given to them. Thus the expression of Franciscan life depicted in the Rule of Saint Clare is more demanding in many respects than the life of the Friars Minor. Consequently, the need of a strong spiritual life is paramount in the acceptance of such a manner of life.

The Four Letters of Clare to Blessed Agnes of Prague provide a perception of her understanding of the spiritual life that forms the basis of a vocation to this Franciscan tradition. They were written to a woman whose embrace of a religious vocation demanded great sacrifices, since Agnes of Prague was a child of royalty and was a much sought-after young woman. Since these letters were written over a span of nineteen years, a definite maturation in Clare's teaching on religious life can be seen. The many contrasts between secular and spiritual lives presented in the First Letter give way to a profound treatment of poverty and contemplation in the Second Letter. Clare builds on these foundations in the Third Letter to strengthen Agnes in her struggle to maintain the austerities and hardships that the intensity of the Franciscan spirit demands. No doubt the joy and peace that filled Clare were released as she drew closer to death, for these sentiments are revealed in the Fourth Letter. After an interruption of possibly fifteen years, Clare resumes her correspondence with Agnes of Prague and writes one of the most beautiful pieces of spiritual literature.

Discussions concerning the authenticity of the Testament of Saint Clare still arise because the manuscript tradition is not strong. However, this document reflects the profound vision of Saint Clare and remains a most beautiful expression of her spirit. The opening paragraph sets the theme of the text as Clare bursts into an expression of gratitude for her vocation and for the gifts God has given to her. The remainder of the Testament must be read from this perspective of thanksgiving. The exhortations and encouragements contained in this writing flow quite naturally from a woman who has experienced the goodness, care, and love of God and who is eager that her sisters do the same.

Once more, the similarities between the two saints, Francis and Clare, emerge. The Testament, however, could only have been written by a woman, for it is expressive of a woman's sensitivity, intuition, and resilience. When it is accepted as a document written at the end of Clare's life—before the final papal approbation of the Rule—the strength of Clare is obvious. She writes as a woman of conviction and deep faith.

Part II

THE SPIRITUALITY OF SAINT CLARE

Within seven years of Saint Clare's death another great follower of the Poor Man of Assisi, the Seraphic Doctor Saint Bonaventure, was wrestling with the articulation of the unique vision of the Franciscan tradition. After two years as Minister General of the Friars and Protector of the Poor Ladies of Saint Clare, he went to La Verna in order to discover peace and from that place of the profound mystical experience of Saint Francis, Saint Bonaventure wrote to the Poor Ladies of Assisi asking them for their prayers. A sentence in that letter expresses perfectly the relationship and the position of Francis and Clare in the tradition of Christian spirituality: "May you walk earnestly in the footprints of your holy Mother (Clare) who, through the instrumentality of the little poor man Saint Francis, was schooled by the Holy Spirit."[9]

It is only through an understanding of the divine power of the Holy Spirit that the total unanimity of these great saints of Assisi can be brought into proper perspective. Moved by divine inspiration, they became perfect symbols of the presence of that Spirit which leads us to the Inner Life of the Father and the Son and challenges us to a profound love of one another and of the gifts of creation.

It cannot be denied, however, that Clare as a woman and as a dedicated student of the Seraphic Father Francis expressed his spiritual vision in a unique way. Her femininity expressed the universal validity of the charism of Saint Francis and accentuated its rich and enduring qualities. As a most eager and attentive student, Clare learned from her teacher, Francis, and brought his teachings to new audiences. Her great contribution to the Franciscan tradition consists in her untiring defense of the charism of poverty, which she had received from the Poverello and which was challenged by the prudent of the world. Clare of Assisi became a most important means of the transmission of the Franciscan spirit at a time when the powerful presence of the Seraphic Father was missed by all of his followers.

---

9. St. Bonaventure, *Epistola II, Opera Omnia* VIII (Quaracchi, 1945), p. 452.

In order to best determine the unique gifts of Clare to the Franciscan tradition, a comparison of her Rule with the *Later Rule* of Saint Francis should be studied in detail. Three prominent differences are immediately noticed: (1) the practice of a material separation from the world, that is, the enclosure; (2) the total permeation of daily life with the pursuit of radical poverty; and (3) the struggle to preserve "the unity of mutual love and peace" as a means of achieving sanctification. It cannot be denied that all of these elements can be discovered in the writings of the Seraphic Father, but they are prominent in that document of Clare which was challenged by the Holy See. Thus they provide an opportunity of examining Clare's vision of the Franciscan tradition as she acquired it from Saint Francis and passed it on to her own followers.

THE MATERIAL SEPARATION FROM THE WORLD

It is difficult to determine when the legislation obliging the Poor Ladies of San Damiano to live an enclosed life was actually given to them. At the beginning of the thirteenth century, women who embraced the religious life were generally obliged to live separated from the world. Clare was no exception to this. A careful examination of the documents indicates that from the earliest days San Damiano was a place of strict enclosure where Clare, on entering, enclosed herself and where there were nuns who lived in the same cloister and did not leave it during the forty-two years of Clare's life. No doubt the first prescriptions were promulgated in the Rule of Cardinal Hugolino di Segni in 1218 or 1219. But it is important to consider that Clare, who was strong enough to challenge the Pope when he proposed a way of life in contrast with her profound convictions and her ideal of gospel perfection, accepted a Rule that embraced a strict enclosure. In fact, Clare introduced into her own Rule of 1253 the practice of the enclosure, which she had observed from the beginning of her religious life, as well as the same norms of the Rule of Hugolino. This point was underscored by Cardinal Raynaldus, the Cardinal Protector of the Poor Ladies, in his letter of introduction to the Rule of Clare as he recognized her resolution "to live in the cloister and to serve the Lord in highest poverty."

Throughout the history of religious life a theology of the enclosure had gradually developed. Those early men and women of the desert discovered that the undoing of the sin of Adam was best achieved by the embrace of a life of obedience, that is, by the submission of the will to that of another person who represented God. The cenobitic life, which valued this virtue of obedience so highly, gradually conceived the monastery as a microcosm of the world in which a "new paradise" could be developed and in which the contemplative state of the first human being could be restored. Thus the monks and nuns of the monastic world developed art, architecture, music, and the literature of the Greek and Roman worlds as part of their spiritual environment. Yet such a view of the religious world that was eager to develop an atmosphere through objects of beauty and transcendence frequently overlooked the spiritual realities that were at the heart of such a perspective.

Clare was heir to this theology of the monastic world and, as a woman of the early thirteenth century, knew of many of the struggles of the religious of the previous century to return to the purity of the vision of their founders. She no doubt took the enclosure as a matter of course and in so doing she purified the monastic tradition of this most enervating force: the acceptance of movable and immovable goods. For the cloistered world of the Poor Ladies was characterized by the renunciation of every illusion, of every attraction and expectation, that was not rooted in God from Whom every good comes. The new paradise of Clare was a return to the poverty of the Garden of Eden as the anonymous author of the *Sacrum Commercium sancti Francisci cum Domina Paupertate*, written in 1227, had described it through the words of Lady Poverty:

> I was at one time *in the paradise of my God* (Rev 2:7), where man went naked; in fact I walked in man and with man in his nakedness through the whole of that most splendid paradise, fearing nothing, doubting nothing, and suspecting no evil. It was in my thoughts that I would be with him forever, for he was created just, good, and wise by the Most High and placed in that most pleasant and most beautiful place. I was rejoicing exceedingly and *playing before him all the while* (Prov 8:30), for, possessing nothing, he belonged entirely to God.[10]

---

10. Anonymous, *Sacrum Commercium Sancti Francisci cum Domina Paupertate* 25, in *Omnibus of Sources*, p. 1566.

History placed Clare in the very first place in the struggle for the defense of that Franciscan poverty and gave to her words a vibrant and passionate resonance that the norms prescribing the enclosure do not have. But this does not mean that she did not value the cloister as a necessary element of her religious life and that of her sisters. Quite the contrary; the life of the "poor enclosed nuns of the Order of Saint Mary of San Damiano," as Hugolino referred to them in his Rule, injected into the theology of the enclosure a new element: the embrace of a life of radical poverty.

THE TOTAL PERMEATION OF LIFE WITH POVERTY

From this perspective, it is understandable that Clare could so easily write to Blessed Agnes of Prague and encourage her to leave the pleasures of an earthly kingdom and to embrace a religious life that was separated materially from the world. The monastic enclosure of the Poor Ladies, as it was seen by Clare, provided the setting for the building of the kingdom of heaven in which eternal riches, glory, and honor were lavishly given by God. The *First Letter to Blessed Agnes of Prague* clearly reveals Clare's indefatigable faith in the words of Jesus: "Blessed are the poor in spirit, for the kingdom of heaven is theirs" (Mt 5:3). She writes:

O blessed poverty
  who bestows eternal riches on those who love and
  embrace her!
O holy poverty
  to those who possess and desire you
  God promises *the kingdom of heaven*[11]
  and offers indeed eternal glory and blessed life![12]

And again:

Contempt of the world has pleased You more than [its] honors, poverty more than earthly riches, and You have stored up greater *treasures in heaven* rather than on earth, *where rust*

---

11. Mt 5:3.
12. *First Letter to Blessed Agnes of Prague,* 15–16.

does not consume nor moth destroy nor thieves break in and steal
(Mt 6:20). Your reward, then, is very great in heaven (Mt
5:12)![13]

This conviction is even more emphatically stated as Clare reminds
Agnes: "You know, I am sure, that the Kingdom of heaven is promised and given by the Lord only to the poor" (cf. Mt 5:3).[14]

A curious difference between the writings of Francis and those
of Clare is the emphasis given to poverty. For Francis, the total obedience of Christ to the will of His Father prompted Him not to cling to
what was rightfully His but to empty Himself (cf. Phil 2:6–11; *Second
Letter to the Faithful*, 4–15). Thus Saint Francis wrote more on the
practice of obedience than on that of poverty. On the other hand,
Clare insisted on the importance of poverty so strongly because she
always kept her attention fixed on the "poor" Christ. Since mankind
was "spiritually" poor and deprived of eternal values, Christ made
Himself "physically" poor and helpless, in order to bring spiritual
riches and to enable man to gain possession of the kingdom of heaven.
The spiritual life, then, consists of conforming oneself to the poor
Christ by the observance of the most perfect poverty. By living in
poverty, Clare maintains, she and her sisters chose to enter upon the
"narrow" way that leads to the kingdom of heaven.[15]

Throughout her Rule, Clare repeatedly accentuates the poverty
of Christ. It is a basic prerequisite for entrance into the Order, expressed in the manner of dress; forms the foundation for the life described by Saint Francis for them; and is the means by which union
with God and with one another is achieved and maintained. Even a
superficial examination of the Rule of Saint Clare reveals how thor-
oughly poverty permeates the entire life of the community of San Damiano. Clare certainly manifests a profound appreciation of the
charism of Saint Francis and its importance for his followers' way to
God.

This dedication to poverty is beautifully expressed in the papal
Privilege of Poverty, which Pope Gregory IX gave to Clare on 17
September 1228:

---

13. Ibid., 22–23.
14. Ibid., 25.
15. Ibid., 29.

As is manifest, in the desire to dedicate yourselves to the Lord alone you have renounced all desire for temporal things; wherefore you have sold all things and given them to the poor and propose to have no possessions whatever, that in all things you may cleave to the footprints of Him Who became for us the Way, the Truth and the Life. (Jn 14:6)

Nor does the lack of possessions deter you from such a proposal; for the left hand of the heavenly Bridegroom is under your head (cf. Cant 2:6; 8:3) to support what is weak in your body which you have subordinated to the law of your mind and brought into subjection.

Finally, He who feeds the birds of the air and the lilies of the field will not fail you in both food and vesture, until He Himself comes and serves you (Lk 12:37) in eternity, when namely His right hand will embrace you in the fullness of His vision.

As you have thus petitioned us, so we confirm by Apostolic favor your proposal of highest poverty.[16]

THE STRUGGLE TO PRESERVE THE UNITY OF MUTUAL LOVE

This poverty, so highly praised by Pope Gregory IX, provides for Clare a capacity for God and an openness to His Presence. It takes on a "sacramental" quality in that it is an outward expression of a much deeper reality, a poverty in which the human person comes to know his only real possessions: his vices and sins. Thus this pursuit of radical poverty is integrally tied to the contemplative ideal as well as to the community life embraced by Clare and her sisters in the enclosure of San Damiano. The repetition of the concepts "holy unity" and "highest poverty" that are expressed in the introductions of Pope Innocent IV and Cardinal Raynaldus to the *Rule of Saint Clare* underscores the connection between these aspects of religious life.

At the heart of these concepts is the presence of the Spirit of the Lord, Who establishes the basic relationships of the spiritual life. In his *First Letter to the Faithful,* Francis states that the Spirit of the Lord rests on those who embrace a life of penance and makes them "chil-

---

16. Pope Gregory IX, *Bullarium Franciscanum,* I, 178.

dren of the heavenly Father . . . spouses, brothers, and mothers of our Lord Jesus Christ."[17] Clare echoes this theme in her *First Letter to Agnes of Prague,* but perceives poverty as the tool that opens the human person to these divine relationships. In a beautiful way, Clare gently leads Agnes to cherish her new familial and marital status, which the choice of religious life had intensified for her, and encourages her to a deeper poverty because of it. Thus the *Second Letter to Agnes of Prague* becomes a medley of the two themes of poverty and contemplation, of clinging *"to the footprints* (1 Pt 2:21) of Him to Whom you have merited to be joined as a Spouse."[18]

More than any other follower of the Poor Man of Assisi, Clare emerges as a poor, contemplative woman. Her letters definitely reveal these elements of her life and provide insights into the means she chose to intensify them. "Believing nothing, agreeing with nothing which would dissuade you from this resolution," she writes to Agnes, ". . . so that you may offer your vows to the Most High in the pursuit of that perfection to which the Spirit of the Lord has called you."[19] "As a poor virgin embrace the Poor Christ. Look upon Him . . . gaze upon [Him], consider [Him], contemplate Him, as you desire to imitate Him."[20] The result of these efforts is a magnificent Christology that focuses on the revelation of God that is found in Jesus and takes the Trinitarian spirituality of Francis a step further. Whereas Francis seems to be struggling always with that broken relationship with Pietro Bernardone, his earthly father, by accentuating the spiritual relationship with his heavenly Father, Clare appears to embrace God Who has revealed Himself as a loving Son and Spouse and chose poverty in order to make us rich.

There is a continual struggle or desire in the writings of Clare to preserve that bond of unity which the Spirit of the Lord has established in her life with God. If poverty emerges as the prerequisite for establishing her relationships with God, Father, Son, and Holy Spirit, then contemplation is the peace-filled enjoyment of them as well as the means to live more intensely the charism of that way which Francis shows.

Yet there is a further dimension that appears in the *Rule of Saint*

---

17. Saint Francis, *First Letter to the Faithful,* I, 7.
18. *Second Letter to Blessed Agnes of Prague,* 7.
19. Ibid., 14.
20. Ibid., 18–19.

Clare. It is also the overflow of the poverty and spiritual life articulated in the letters to Blessed Agnes of Prague. This is the intense life of community that the Spirit brings to Clare and her sisters and that is accentuated more strenuously than in the *Later Rule of Saint Francis.* "Let them be ever zealous to preserve among themselves the unity of mutual love," Clare writes in Chapter X, "which is the bond of perfection."

Once more the gift of brotherhood and sisterhood is brought before the followers of the Poor Man of Assisi. More than a community of support, the sisters are seen as a means of salvation in manifesting the profound relationships that exist in the Inner Life of God. No more beautiful expression of this aspect of the spiritual life of Clare can be discovered than in the *Fourth Letter to Blessed Agnes of Prague:*

> Let the tongue of the flesh be silent when I seek to express my love for you; and let the tongue of the Spirit speak because the love I have for you, O blessed daughter, can never be fully expressed by the tongue of the flesh, and even what I have written is an inadequate expression.[21]

The genius of Clare's perception of the spiritual life can be seen in this aspect of her *Rule,* for she penetrated, as Francis did, the marvelous mystery of the Revelation of God Who reveals Himself as a Community of Love. There can be little doubt that the enclosed life of San Damiano struggled on a daily basis to express that Unity of God.

CONCLUSION

Many contemporary biographers of Saint Francis imaginatively romanticized his relationship with a woman who became one of his most devoted followers: Clare of Assisi. These authors, building on the meager facts of the early biographical tradition, tend to overshadow her important role in the Franciscan tradition. Through this woman the Spirit of the Lord expressed the Franciscan ideal in a pure, brilliant manner and challenged her contemporaries to a serious consideration of its value in the history of the Church.

It is impossible to imagine the reason for Clare's birth in the ear-

---

21. *Fourth Letter to Blessed Agnes of Prague,* 35.

ly part of the thirteenth century when women were obliged to live religious life in the enclosure. If Clare had lived a few centuries later, she might well have been a dynamic woman who proclaimed the Gospel through an active, apostolic life. Yet the mystery of God's Providence has placed her in the annals of history as a stable, translucent symbol of the vision of Saint Francis of Assisi. Her long life at San Damiano expresses in a unique way the heart of the dynamism of Saint Francis, who heard the call to rebuild the church as he knelt in prayer before the crucifix of that small chapel.

The followers of Saint Clare, living in poor, enclosed communities throughout the world, have continued that tradition. While the friars have been moving throughout the world witnessing, proclaiming, and suffering for the Gospel, these noble women have remained stable, unassuming beacons of the poverty and contemplation that are at the heart of the Franciscan Ideal. The person of Clare epitomizes their call: to be clear and clarifying expressions of the Spirit of the Lord, Who works in the hearts of all men and women in hidden and mysterious ways.

Clare of Assisi

THE WRITINGS

The Letters of Saint Clare to Blessed Agnes of Prague

The letters to Blessed Agnes of Prague are invaluable expressions of the spiritual wisdom of Saint Clare as well as of her desire to guide another in the pursuit of evangelical perfection and profound poverty. These short pieces of literature are characterized by a beautiful, sensitive style and have become rich sources of the Franciscan spiritual heritage.

The oldest manuscript witness to these letters is dated between 1280 and 1330. This early collection was discovered in 1896 by Monsignor Archille Ratti, the Prefect of the Ambrosian Library in Milano, Italy, (Monsignor Ratti was elected Bishop of Rome in 1922 and took the name Pope Pius XI.) Twenty-eight years later, Walter Seton published a critical text of the Letters in the Archivum Franciscanum Historicum.[1]

Agnes of Prague was born in 1203, the daughter of King Ottakar of Bohemia and Queen Constance of Hungary. In 1206, when she was only three years old, Agnes was betrothed to Boleslaus, son of Henry, duke of Silesia, and Hedwig of Bavaria, who was later canonized. A short time afterward, Boleslaus died and the young girl was sought after by the Emperor Frederick II, who desired to have her as a bride for his son and, some years later, for himself.

In 1232, however, Agnes came to know the Friars Minor, who had come to Prague on a preaching tour. Within a short time she built a church, a friary, and a hospital dedicated to Saint Francis and became enamored of the spiritual life the friars revealed to her. On June 11, 1234, Pentecost Sunday, Agnes entered the monastery that was attached to the hospital and began to correspond with Saint Clare, whose life and spirit she desired to emulate. Agnes remained in this monastery for fifty-four years, during which time she struggled to maintain many of the same expressions of the religious life as Clare did. She died on March 2, 1282, and was beatified by Pope Pius IX in 1874.

---

1. Walter Seton, "The Letters from Saint Clare to blessed Agnes of Bohemia," *Archivum Franciscanum Historicum* 17 (1924); 509–519.

The First Letter to Blessed Agnes of Prague

This letter was written before Agnes's entrance into religious life. This embrace of such a difficult way of life must have attracted a great deal of attention, as a letter written to Agnes by Pope Gregory IX, August 30, 1234, indicates. The echo of the phrase of Saint Clare, "known not only to me but to the entire world as well," is found in the papal bull sent to Beatice of Castille, June 5, 1235, in which the same Pope presents an enthusiastic praise of the princess of Bohemia. Thus, this is a letter of respect and reverence, as well as an encouraging set of contrasts between the life of earthly royalty and the life of the kingdom of heaven.

1. To the esteemed and most holy virgin, the Lady Agnes, daughter of the most excellent and illustrious King of Bohemia: 2. Clare, an unworthy servant of Jesus Christ and *useless* handmaid (cf. Lk 17:10) of the Cloistered Ladies of the Monastery of San Damiano, her subject and servant in all things, presents herself totally with a special reverent [prayer] that she *attain the glory* of everlasting happiness (cf. Sir 50:5).

3. As I hear of the fame of Your[1] holy conduct and irreproachable life, which is known not only to me but to the entire world as well, *I greatly rejoice and exult in the Lord* (Hab 3:18). 4. I am not alone in rejoicing at such great news, but [I am joined by] all who serve and seek to serve Jesus Christ. 5. For, though You, more than others, could have enjoyed the magnificence and honor and dignity of the world, and could have been married to the illustrious Caesar[2] with

---

1. In this first letter, Saint Clare continually uses the polite (or noble) form of address: You (*Vos*), Your (*Vester*), etc., with the plural verb. In the other three letters she adopts the familiar forms.

2. Historians do not agree on the identity of the emperor (*Caesar,* the Latin word employed by Saint Clare). Most probably he was Emperor Frederick II, widower from May 1228, since a contemporary historian, Albert of Stade, states plainly that, for love of Christ, Blessed Agnes of Prague refused his offer of marriage. In his Chronicle, he states: "The same year, on the feast of Pentecost, the sister of the King of Bohemia, the Lady Agnes, at the prompting of the Friars Minor, entered the Order of the Poor La-

splendor befitting You and His Excellency, 6. You have rejected all these things and have chosen with Your whole heart and soul a life of holy poverty and destitution. 7. Thus You took a spouse of a more noble lineage, Who will keep Your virginity ever unspotted and unsullied, the Lord Jesus Christ:

8. When You have loved [Him], You shall be chaste; when You have touched [Him], You shall become pure; when you have accepted [Him], You shall be a virgin."[3]
9. Whose power is stronger,
   Whose generosity is more abundant,
   Whose appearance more beautiful,
   Whose love more tender,
   Whose courtesy more gracious.
10. In Whose embrace You are already caught up;
    Who has adorned Your breast with precious stones
        And has placed priceless pearls in Your ears[4]
11. and has surrounded You with sparkling gems
    as though blossoms of springtime
    and placed on Your head *a golden crown*
    as a sign [to all] of Your holiness.[5]

12. Therefore, most beloved sister, or should I say, Lady worthy of great respect: because You are *the spouse and the mother and the sister* of my Lord Jesus Christ (2 Cor 11:2; Mt 12:50),[6] 13. and have been adorned resplendently with the sign of inviolable virginity and most holy poverty: Be strengthened in the holy service which You have undertaken out of an ardent desire for the Poor Crucified, 14. Who for the sake of all of us *took upon Himself* the Passion *of the Cross* (Heb 12:2)

---

dies of the Rule of Blessed Francis at Prague, rejecting for Christ's sake the Emperor Frederick who had earlier asked for her in marriage."

3. This line is taken from the Divine Office of the feast of Saint Agnes, Virgin and Martyr, which was celebrated on January 21. It is from Matins, I Nocturn, III responsory.

4. This is also from the Divine Office of the feast of Saint Agnes, Matins, I Nocturn, II antiphon.

5. This, too, is from the Divine Office of the feast of Saint Agnes, Matins, I Nocturn, II responsory, and III Nocturn, II antiphon.

6. Saint Clare refers to the same biblical relationships that Saint Francis saw as consequences of the activity of the Spirit of the Lord (cf. *The First Version of the Letter to the Faithful,* I, 7; *The Second Version of Letter to the Faithful,* 50).

and delivered us from the power of the Prince *of Darkness* (Col 1:13) to whom we were enslaved because of the disobedience of our first parent, and so *reconciled us* to God the Father (2 Cor 5:18).

15. O blessed poverty,
> who bestows eternal riches on those who love and embrace her!
16. O holy poverty,
> to those who possess and desire you
> God promises *the kingdom of heaven*[7]
> and offers, indeed, eternal glory and blessed life!
17. O God-centered poverty,[8]
> whom the Lord Jesus Christ
> Who ruled and now rules heaven and earth,[9]
> *Who spoke and things were made,*[10]
> condescended to embrace before all else!

18. *The foxes have dens,* He says, *and the birds of the air have nests, but the Son of Man,* Christ, *has nowhere to lay His head* (Mt 8:20), but *bowing His head gave up His spirit* (Jn 19:30).

19. If so great and good a Lord, then, on coming into the Virgin's womb, chose to appear despised, needy, and *poor* in this world, 20. so that people who were in utter poverty and want and in absolute need of heavenly nourishment might become *rich* (cf. 2 Cor 8:9) in Him by possessing the kingdom of heaven,[11] 21. then *rejoice and be glad* (Hab 3:18)! Be filled with a remarkable happiness and a spiritual joy! 22. Contempt of the world has pleased You more than [its] honors, poverty more than earthly riches, and You have sought to store up greater

---

7. Cf. Mt 5:3.

8. The Latin word *pia* is best translated "God centered," since Saint Clare builds the foundation of a life of poverty by deepening the motives for its embrace. In the previous statements, poverty is embraced because of the bestowal of eternal riches and the promise of the kingdom of heaven. Therefore, Saint Clare calls it blessed and holy. In this sentence, however, poverty is embraced because of the example of the Lord Jesus Christ, the King and Creator. Thus, Saint Clare centers her poverty on God alone.

9. This passage is taken from the Introit of the Common of the Blessed Virgin Mary.

10. Cf. Ps 32:9; 148:5.

11. A reflection of the *Later Rule* of Saint Francis, Chapter VI, 3, in which the image of the Lord Who became poor for us (cf. 2 Cor 8:9) is presented as the motivation for poverty.

treasures in heaven rather than on earth, 23. *where rust does not consume nor moth destroy nor thieves break in and steal* (Mt 6:20). *Your reward,* then, *is very great in heaven* (Mt 5:12)! 24. And You have truly merited to be called *a sister, spouse, and mother* (2 Cor 11:2; Mt 12:50) of the Son of the Father of the Most High and of the glorious Virgin.

25. You know, I am sure, that the kingdom of heaven is promised and given by the Lord only to the poor (cf. Mt 5:3): for he who loves temporal things loses the fruit of love. 26. Such a person *cannot serve God and Mammon,* for *either the one is loved and the other hated,* or *the one is served and the other despised* (Mt 6:24).

27. You also know that one who is clothed cannot fight with another who is naked, because he is more quickly thrown who gives his adversary a chance to get hold of him;[12] and that one who lives in the glory of earth cannot rule with Christ in heaven.

28. Again, [you know] that it is easier for *a camel to pass through the eye of a needle than for a rich man to enter the kingdom of heaven* (Mt 19:24). 29. Therefore, you have cast aside Your garments, that is, earthly riches, so that You might not be overcome by the one fighting against You, [and] that You might enter the kingdom of heaven *through the straight path and the narrow gate* (Mt 7:13–14).

30.　What a great laudable exchange:[13]
　　　　　　to leave the things of time for those of eternity,
　　　　　　to choose the things of heaven for the goods of earth,
　　　　　　to receive the hundred-fold in place on one,
　　　　　　and *to possess* a blessed and eternal *life.*[14]

31. Because of this I have resolved, as best I can, to beg Your excellency and Your holiness by my humble prayers in the mercy of Christ, to be strengthened in His holy service, 32. and to progress from good to better, *from virtue to virtue* (Ps 83:8), so that He Whom You serve with the total desire of Your soul may bestow on You the reward for which You long.

---

12. Cf. Gregory the Great, *Homilia in Evangelia,* II, 32, 2 (PL 76, 1233b). It is used in the Divine Office, Common of a Martyr outside of Paschal Time, III nocturn.

13. The theme of the "exchange," or *commercium,* forms the basis of the theological reflection on Franciscan poverty, the *Sacrum Commercium S. Francisci cum Domina Paupertate* (Florence: Ad Claras Aquas, 1929). It was written in 1227 by an anonymous author.

14. Cf. Mt 19:29.

33. I also beg You in the Lord, as much as I can, to include in Your holy prayers me, Your servant, though unworthy, and the other sisters with me in the monastery, who are all devoted to You, 34. so that by their help we may merit the mercy of Jesus Christ, and together with You may merit to enjoy the everlasting vision.

35. Farewell in the Lord. And pray for me.

The Second Letter to Blessed Agnes of Prague

An early edition of this letter, which was discovered in a convent in Prague, contains the heading: "Concerning the Strong Perseverance in a Good Proposal." The text of the letter suggests its composition during the early years of Agnes's religious life, definitely between the years 1235 and 1239, when Brother Elias was Minister General of the friars. Most authors place this letter between the years 1235 and 1236. It delicately provides Agnes of Prague with the principle means of perseverance in her commitment to poverty: a life of loving contemplation on the Poor Christ.

1. To the daughter *of the King of kings*, the servant *of the Lord of lords* (Rev 19:16), the most worthy Spouse of Jesus Christ, and, therefore, the most noble Queen, Lady Agnes: 2. Clare, the *useless* and unworthy servant (Lk 17:10) of the Poor Ladies: greetings and [a wish for your] perseverance in a life of the highest poverty.

3. I give thanks to the Giver of grace from Whom, we believe, *every good and perfect gift* proceeds (Jas 1:17), because He has adorned you with such splendors of virtue and signed you with such marks of perfection, 4. that, since you have become such a diligent imitator *of the Father of all perfection* (Mt 5:48), His eyes do not see any imperfection in you.

5. This is the perfection which will prompt the King Himself to take you to Himself in the heavenly bridal chamber where He is seated in glory on a starry throne[1] 6. because you have despised the splendors of an earthly kingdom and considered of little value the offers of an imperial marriage. 7. Instead, as someone zealous for the holiest poverty, in the spirit of great humility and the most ardent charity, you have held fast *to the footprints* (1 Pt 2:21) of Him to Whom you have merited to be joined as a Spouse.

8. But since I know that you are adorned with many virtues, I will spare my words and not weary you with needless speech, 9. even

---

1. This passage is taken from the Divine Office of the feast of the Assumption of the Blessed Virgin Mary, August 15, Lauds, II antiphon.

though nothing seems superfluous to you if you can draw from it some consolation. 10. But because *one thing alone is necessary* (Lk 10:42),[2] I bear witness to that one thing and encourage you, for love of Him to Whom you have offered yourself as *a holy* and pleasing sacrifice (Rm 12:1), 11. that, like another Rachel[3] (cf. Gen 29:16), you always remember your resolution and be conscious of how you began.

What you hold, may you [always] hold.
What you do, may you [always] do and never abandon.
12. But with swift pace, light step,
    [and] unswerving feet,
    so that even your steps stir up no dust,[4]
13. go forward
    securely, joyfully, and swiftly,
on the path of prudent happiness,
14.   believing nothing,
    agreeing with nothing
    which would dissuade you from this resolution
    or which *would place a stumbling block* for you on the way,[5]
    so that you may offer *your vows to the Most High*[6]
    in the pursuit of that perfection
    to which the Spirit of the Lord has called you.[7]

---

2. This reference to Luke's Gospel appears frequently in Western mystical writers, who had no hesitancy in affirming the superiority of the contemplative life over the active. Consult Cuthbert Butler, O.S.B., *Western Mysticism* (New York, 1966), pp. 157–188.

3. Rachel, as Mary, was a favorite image of the contemplative person. She represented the clear-sighted, patient, beautiful woman who is contrasted with the near-sighted, busy, yet fruitful Leah. These two wives of Jacob symbolized the contemplative and active lives for the spiritual writers of the Middle Ages. Consult Cuthbert Butler, O.S.B., *Western Mysticism* (New York, 1966), pp. 157–188; also, Richard of St. Victor, *Benjamin Minor* (The Twelve Patriarchs), trans. Grover Zinn (New York, 1979), pp. 51–147.

4. Cf. Gregory the Great, *Dialogues*, Prologue (PL 77:152A). This exhortation was also used by Thomas of Celano, *First Life* of Saint Francis, n. 71 (Omnibus, p. 288): "[Francis's] greatest concern was to be free from everything of this world lest the serenity of his mind be disturbed even for an hour by the taint of anything which was mere dust."

5. Cf. Rm 14:13.

6. Cf. Ps 49:14.

7. Saint Clare articulates the dynamic principle of the spiritual life, the Spirit of the Lord, and echoes the teaching of Saint Francis, Cf. The *Admonitions*, p. 26, n. 1; *The Form of Life Given to Saint Clare and Her Sisters*, p. 44, n. 1; and *The First Version of the Letter to the Faithful*, p. 63, n. 3.

15. In all of this, follow the counsel of our venerable Father, our Brother Elias, the Minister General,[8] so that you may walk more securely in *the way of the commands of the Lord* (Ps 118:32). 16. Prize it beyond the advice of the others and cherish it as dearer to you than any gift. 17. If anyone would tell you something else or suggest something which would hinder your perfection or seem contrary to your divine vocation, even though you must respect him, do not follow his counsel. 18. But as a poor virgin, embrace the poor Christ.

19. Look upon Him Who became contemptible for you, and follow Him, making yourself contemptible in the world for Him. 20. Your Spouse, though *more beautiful than the children of men* (Ps 44:3), became, for your salvation, the lowest of men, despised, struck, scourged untold times throughout His whole body, and then died amid the sufferings of the Cross. O most noble Queen, gaze upon [Him], consider [Him], contemplate [Him], as you desire to imitate [Him].[9]

21. If you suffer with Him, *you shall reign with Him,*[10]
    [if you] weep [with Him], you shall rejoice with Him;
    [if you] die [with Him] on the cross of tribulation,
        you shall possess heavenly mansions *in the splendor of the saints*[11]
22.   and, *in the Book of Life*, your *name* shall be called
        glorious among men.[12]

23. Because of this you shall share always and forever the glory of the kingdom of heaven in place of earthly and passing things, and everlasting treasures instead of those that perish, and you shall live forever.

24. Farewell, most dear Sister, yes, and Lady, because of the

---

8. Brother Elias of Assisi was Minister General of the Friars in the years 1232 to 1239.

9. These may well be considered steps of prayer: gazing upon (*intuere*) the poor crucified Christ, considering (*considera*), and contemplating (*contemplare*) Him. Throughout all of these expressions of prayer, the desire to imitate the poverty of Christ is present. This may be seen as a perfect expression of affective spirituality, which characterizes the Franciscan tradition.

10. Cf. 2 Tim 2:12.

11. Ps 109:3.

12. Rev 3:5.

Lord, your Spouse. 25. Commend me and my sisters to the Lord in your fervent prayers, for we rejoice in the good things of the Lord that He works in you through His grace.

26. Commend us truly to your sisters as well.

The Third Letter to Blessed Agnes of Prague

The immediate cause of this letter was a clarification requested of Clare by Agnes concerning fast and abstinence. In a papal bull of February 9, 1237, Pope Gregory IX had mandated "total abstinence from meat in imitation of the Cistercians." Furthermore, in January 1238 Agnes had petitioned the Pope for a new Rule similar to that followed by the Poor Ladies of San Damiano in Assisi. This request was denied on May 11, 1238. Thus this response of Saint Clare may be an encouragement to Agnes to persevere in her life of prayer, poverty, and austerity, which plays an important role in the Church.

1. To the lady [who is] most respected in Christ and the sister loved more than all [other] human beings, Agnes, sister of the illustrious king of Bohemia, but now the sister and spouse of the Most High King of heaven:[1] 2. Clare, the most lowly and unworthy handmaid of Christ and servant of the Poor Ladies: the joys of redemption in *the Author of salvation* (Heb 2:10) and every good thing that can be desired.

3. I am filled with such joys at your well-being, happiness, and marvelous progress through which, I understand, you have advanced in the course you have undertaken to win the prize of heaven (cf. Phil 3:14). 4. And I sigh with such happiness in the Lord because I know you see that you make up most wonderfully what is lacking both in me and in the other sisters in following the footprints of the poor and humble Jesus Christ.

5. I can rejoice truly—and no one can rob me of such joy—6. because I now possess what under heaven I have desired. For I see that, helped by a special gift of wisdom from the mouth of God Himself and in an awe-inspiring and unexpected way, you have brought to

---

1. In the First Letter, Agnes is greeted as the daughter of the King of Bohemia, Ottakar I, also known as Premislaus II, who died some years earlier (December 15, 1230). The reference to her illustrious brother, Wenceslaus III, king from December 1230 to September 1253, accentuates the greater dignity Agnes possesses as "sister and spouse" of the Most High Lord.

ruin the subtleties of our crafty enemy and the pride that destroys human nature and the vanity that infatuates human hearts.

7. I see, too, that by humility, the virtue of faith, and the strong arms of poverty, you have taken hold of that *incomparable treasure hidden in the field* of the world and in the hearts of men (cf. Mt 13:44), with which you have purchased that field of Him by Whom all things have been made from nothing. 8. And, to use the words of the Apostle himself in their proper sense, I consider you *a co-worker of God* Himself (cf. 1 Cor 3:9; Rm 16:3) and a support of the weak members of His ineffable Body.[2] 9. Who is there, then, who would not encourage me to rejoice over such marvelous joys?

10. Therefore, dearly beloved, may you too *always rejoice in the Lord* (Phil 4:4). 11. And may neither bitterness nor a cloud [of sadness] overwhelm you, O dearly beloved Lady in Christ, joy of the angels and crown of your sisters!

12. Place your mind before the mirror of eternity!
    Place your soul in *the brilliance of glory!*[3]
13. Place your heart in *the figure of the* divine *substance!*[4]
    And *transform* your whole being *into the image* of the Godhead
        Itself
        through contemplation![5]
14. So that you too may feel what His friends feel
    as they taste *the hidden sweetness*[6]
    which God Himself has reserved
    from the beginning
    for those who love Him.

15. Since you have cast aside all [those] things which, in this deceitful and turbulent world, ensnare their blind lovers, love Him totally Who gave Himself totally for Your love. 16. His beauty the sun

---

2. This concept of the life of the enclosure is based on the writings of Saint Paul (1 Cor 3:9) and an understanding of the role of the contemplative life in the mission of the Church.

3. Cf. Heb 1:3.

4. Cf. Heb 1:3.

5. Cf. 2 Cor 3:18. Clare refers to a prominent theme of Christian spirituality: The contemplation of God in Christ gives the Christian a likeness to God.

6. Cf. Ps 30:20.

and moon admire;[7] and of His gifts there is no limit in abundance, preciousness, and magnitude. 17. I am speaking of Him Who is the Son of the Most High, Whom the Virgin brought to birth and remained a virgin after His birth.[8] 18. Cling to His most sweet Mother who carried a Son Whom the heavens could not contain;[9] 19. and yet she carried Him in the little enclosure of her holy womb and held Him on her virginal lap.

20. Who would not dread the treacheries of the enemy of mankind, who, through the arrogance of momentary and deceptive glories, attempts to reduce to nothing that which is greater than heaven itself? 21. Indeed, is it not clear that the soul of the faithful person, the most worthy of all creatures because of the grace of God, is greater than heaven itself? 22. For the heavens with the rest of creation cannot contain their Creator. Only the faithful soul is His dwelling place and [His] throne, and this [is possible] only through the charity which the wicked do not have. 23. [He Who is] the Truth has said: *Whoever loves me will be loved by My Father, and I too shall love him, and We shall come to him and make our dwelling place with Him* (Jn 14:21).

24. Therefore, as the glorious Virgin of virgins carried [Christ] materially in her body, 25. you, too, by *following in His footprints* (cf. 1 Pet 2:21), especially [those] of poverty and humility, can, without any doubt, always carry Him spiritually in your chaste and virginal body. 26. And you will hold Him by Whom you and *all things are held together* (cf. Wis 1:7; Col 1:17), [thus] possessing that which, in comparison with the other transitory possessions of this world, you will possess more securely.[10] 27. How many kings and queens of this world let themselves be deceived! 28. For, even though their pride may reach the skies and their heads through the clouds, in the end they are as forgotten as a dung-heap!

29. Now concerning those matters which you have asked me to

---

7. Taken from the Divine Office of the feast of Saint Agnes, Virgin and Martyr: Matins, III Nocturn, III antiphon, II responsory.

8. Taken from the Divine Office of the Feast of the Annunciation of the Blessed Virgin: Matins, III Nocturn, II responsory.

9. Taken from the Divine Office of the Feast of the Annunciation of the Blessed Virgin: Matins, II Nocturn, III responsory.

10. The repeated use of the word "possess" forms a literary play on words in which Clare accentuates the great value of poverty as a means of spiritual growth.

clarify for you:[11] 30. Which are the specific feasts our most glorious Father Saint Francis urged us to celebrate in a special way by a change of food, feasts of which, I believe, you already have some knowledge—I propose to respond to your love.

31. Your prudence should know then that, except for the weak and the sick, for whom [Saint Francis] advised and admonished us to show every possible care in matters of food, 32. none of us who are healthy and strong should eat anything other than Lenten fare, either on ferial days or on feast days. 33. Thus, we must fast every day except Sundays and the Nativity of the Lord, on which days we may have two meals. 34. And on ordinary Thursdays everyone may do as she wishes, so that she who does not wish to fast is not obliged. 35. However, we who are well should fast every day except on Sundays and on Christmas.

36. During the entire Easter week, as the writing of Saint Francis tells us, and on the feasts of the Blessed Mary and of the holy Apostles, we are not obliged to fast, unless these feasts occur on a Friday. 37. And, as I have already said, we who are well and strong always eat Lenten fare.

38. But *our flesh is not bronze nor is our strength that of stone* (Jb 6:12). 39. No, we are frail and inclined to every bodily weakness! 40. I beg you, therefore, dearly beloved, to refrain wisely and prudently from an indiscreet and impossible austerity in the fasting that I know you have undertaken. 41. And I beg you in the Lord to praise the Lord by your very life, to offer to the Lord your *reasonable service* (Rm 12:1), and your *sacrifice* always *seasoned with salt* (Lev 2:13).

42. May you do well in the Lord, as I hope I myself do. And remember me and my sisters in your prayers.

---

11. This section of the letter expresses the custom of the Ladies of San Damiano. A papal decree of Pope Gregory IX, February 9, 1237, imposed on all the monasteries of the "Order of San Damiano" total abstinence from meat "in imitation of the Cistercians" (cf. Gregory IX, *Bullarium Franciscanum*, I, 209).

The Fourth Letter to Blessed Agnes of Prague

It is difficult to determine the date of the composition of this letter. Certainly a long time has elapsed since the sending of the previous letter, for Clare herself suggests an infrequent exchange of letters due to a scarcity of messengers and the dangers of travel. An indication of the date, however, is given at the conclusion as Clare writes that her blood-sister, Agnes, who had been in a convent in Montecelli, had returned to San Damiano. (Agnes had returned to be with her sister in 1253, the year of Clare's death.) Thus this letter was written during the last months of Clare's life and reflects the brilliant spirit of love that permeated all of her religious life.

1. To her who is the half of her soul and the special shrine of her heart's deepest love, to the illustrious Queen and Bride of the Lamb, the eternal King: to the Lady Agnes, her most dear mother, and, of all the others, her favorite daughter: 2. Clare, an unworthy servant of Christ and a *useless* handmaid (Lk 17:10) of His handmaids in the monastery of San Damiano of Assisi: health 3. and [a prayer] that she may sing *a new song* with the other most holy virgins before the throne of God and of the Lamb and *follow the Lamb wherever He may go* (cf. Rev 14:3–4).[1]

4. O mother and daughter, spouse of the King of all ages, if I have not written to you as often as your soul and mine as well desire and long for, 5. do not wonder or think that the fire of love for you glows less sweetly in the heart of your mother. 6. No, this is the difficulty: the lack of messengers and the obvious dangers of the roads. 7. Now, however, as I write to your love, I rejoice and exult with you in *the joy of the Spirit* (1 Thes 1:6), O bride of Christ, 8. because, since you have totally abandoned the vanities of this world, like another most holy virgin, Saint Agnes, you have been marvelously espoused to *the spotless Lamb Who takes away the sins of the world* (1 Pt 1:19; Jn 1:29).

---

1. The Latin text indicates a play on the Latin word *agnus*, lamb, suggesting the close relationship between the Lamb of God, Christ, and Agnes.

203

9. Happy, indeed, is she to whom it is given to share this sacred banquet,
10. to cling with all her heart to Him
        Whose beauty all the heavenly hosts admire unceasingly,
11.   Whose love inflames our love,
        Whose contemplation is our refreshment,
        Whose graciousness is our joy,
12.   Whose gentleness fills us to overflowing,
        Whose remembrance brings a gentle light,
13.   Whose fragrance will revive the dead,
        Whose glorious vision will be the happiness
            of all the citizens of the heavenly Jerusalem;

14. Inasmuch as this vision is *the splendor of eternal glory* (Heb 1:3), *the brilliance of eternal light and the mirror without blemish* (Wis 7:26), 15. look upon that mirror each day,[2] O queen and spouse of Jesus Christ, and continually study your face within it, 16. so that you may adorn yourself within and without with beautiful robes 17. and cover yourself with the flowers and garments of all the virtues, as becomes the daughter and most chaste bride of the Most High King. 18. Indeed, blessed poverty, holy humility, and ineffable charity are reflected in that mirror, as, with the grace of God, you can contemplate them throughout the entire mirror.[3]

19. Look at the parameters of this mirror,[4] that is, the poverty of Him Who was placed in a manger and wrapped in swaddling clothes. 20. O marvelous humility, O astonishing poverty! 21. The King of the

---

2. The image of the mirror holds a prominent place in the monastic contemplative tradition, particularly that of the Cistercian school of the twelfth century, e.g., William of Saint Thierry, *Mirror of Faith*; Aelred of Rievaulx, *Mirror of Charity*. Within seven years of the composition of this letter, Saint Bonaventure used the same image in *The Soul's Journey into God*.

3. From the contemplation of the heavenly Jerusalem, Clare turns to the contemplation of the humanity of Christ, Who reveals Himself as poor, humble, and filled with love.

4. The three dimensions of the medieval mirror that Clare mentions in this passage are difficult to translate. This is particularly so since Clare uses these images to refer to three periods in the life of Christ. The medieval mirror was a thin disk of bronze that was slightly convex on one side. The parameters, therefore, reflected an image in an obscure way. Parts of the surface would do the same. Only certain in-depth parts of the mirror reflected an image clearly.

angels, the Lord of heaven and earth, is laid in a manger! 22. Then, at the surface of the mirror, dwell on the holy humility, the blessed poverty, the untold labors and burdens which He endured for the redemption of all mankind. 23. Then, in the depths of this same mirror, contemplate the ineffable charity which led Him to suffer on the wood of the Cross and die thereon the most shameful kind of death. 24. Therefore, that Mirror, suspended on the wood of the Cross, urged those who passed by to consider, saying: 25. *"All you who pass by the way, look and see if there is any suffering like My suffering!"* (Lam 1:12). 26. Let us answer Him with one voice and spirit, as He said: *Remembering this over and over leaves my soul downcast within me* (Lam 3:20)! 27. From this moment, then, O queen of our heavenly King, let yourself be inflamed more strongly with the fervor of charity![5]

28. [As you] contemplate further His ineffable delights, eternal riches and honors, 29. and sigh for them in the great desire and love of your heart, may you cry out:

30.   *Draw me after You!*
      We will run in the fragrance of Your perfumes,[6]
         O heavenly Spouse!
31.   I will run and not tire,
         until *You bring me into the wine-cellar,*[7]
32.   until Your *left hand is under my head*
         and Your *right hand will embrace me* happily[8]
         [and] *You will kiss me with the happiest kiss of Your mouth.*[9]

33. In this contemplation, may you remember your poor little mother, 34. knowing that I have inscribed the happy memory of you indelibly on the tablets of my heart, holding you dearer than all the others.

35. What more can I say? Let the tongue of the flesh be silent when I seek to express my love for you; and let the tongue of the Spir-

---

5. The inspiration for this passage may well have been a letter of Pope Gregory IX to Agnes of Prague, 15 April 1238 (cf. Gregory IX, *Bullarium Franciscanum*, 1, 236).

6. Cant 1:3.

7. Cant 2:4.

8. Cant 2:6. This passage also appears in the *Privilegium Paupertatis* given to Saint Clare by Gregory IX, September 17, 1228 (cf. *Seraphicae legislationis textus originales* [Quaracchi: Ad Aquas Claras, 1897], pp. 22–24).

9. Cant 1:1.

it speak, 36. because the love that I have for you, O blessed daughter, can never be fully expressed by the tongue of the flesh, and even what I have written is an inadequate expression.

37. I beg you to receive my words with kindness and devotion, seeing in them at least the motherly affection which in the fire of charity I feel daily toward you and your daughters, to whom I warmly commend myself and my daughters in Christ. 38. On their part, these very daughters of mine, especially the most prudent virgin Agnes, our sister, recommend themselves in the Lord to you and your daughters.

39. Farewell, may dearest daughter, to you and to your daughters until we meet at the throne *of the glory of the great God* (Tit 2:13), and desire [this] for us.

40. Inasmuch as I can, I recommend to your charity the bearers of this letter, our dearly beloved Brother Amatus, *beloved of God and men* (Sir 45:1), and Brother Bonagura. Amen.[10]

---

10. Nothing is known of the identity of these friars. Once more Clare plays with the meaning of the Latin words: Amatus, beloved, and Bonagura, good wishes.

The Letter to Ermentrude of Bruges

Luke Wadding writes in the Annales, 1257, n. 20, that Saint Clare wrote two letters to Ermentrude of Bruges, who had founded several monasteries in Flanders that sought to live after the manner of the Poor Ladies of San Damiano in Assisi.[1] However, Wadding presents only one text, which appears to be a summary of both letters. The chronicler does not indicate what manuscript or text he had at hand. This letter is much more simple and impersonal than the other writings of Clare, which has caused scholars to doubt its authenticity.[2]

A LETTER TO ERMENTRUDE OF BRUGES

1. To her dearest Sister Ermentrude: Clare of Assisi, a lowly servant of Jesus Christ: health and peace.

2. I have learned, O most dear sister, that, with the help of God's grace, you have fled in joy the corruptions of the world. 3. I rejoice and congratulate you because of this and, again, I rejoice that you are walking courageously the paths of virtue with your daughters. 4. Remain faithful until death, dearly beloved, to Him to Whom you have promised yourself, for you shall be crowned by Him with the garland of life.

5. Our labor here is brief, but the reward is eternal. Do not be disturbed by the clamor of the world, which passes like a shadow. 6. Do not let the false delights of a deceptive world deceive you. Close your ears to the whisperings of hell and bravely oppose its onslaughts. 7. Gladly endure whatever goes against you and do not let good fortune lift you up: for these things destroy faith, while these others demand it. 8. Offer faithfully what you have vowed to God, and He shall reward you.

---

1. L. Wadding, *Annales*, a. 1257, nn. 8–27. Cf. D. DeKok, O.F.M., "De origine Ordinis S. Clarae in Flandris," *Archivum Franciscanum Historicum* 7 (1914): 234–246; A. Heyesse, "Origo et progressus Ordinis S. Clarae in Flandria," *Archivum Franciscanum Historicum* (1944): 165–201.

2. M. Fassbinder, "Untersuchungen uber du Quellen zum Leben der hl. Klara von Assisi," *Franziskanische Studien* 23 (1936): 296–335; E. Grau, O.F.M., and L. Hardick, O.F.M., *Leben und Schriften der hl. Klara von Assisi*, 3rd ed. (Werl-West, 1960), p. 24.

9. O dearest one, look up to heaven, which calls us on, and take up the Cross and follow Christ Who has gone on before us: 10. for through Him we shall enter into His glory after many and diverse tribulations. 11. Love God from the depths of your heart and Jesus, His Son, Who was crucified for us sinners. Never let the thought of Him leave your mind 12. but meditate constantly on the mysteries of the Cross and the anguish of His mother as she stood beneath the Cross.

13. Pray and watch at all times! 14. Carry out steadfastly the work you have begun and fulfill the ministry you have undertaken in true humility and holy poverty. 15. Fear not, daughter! God, Who is faithful in all His words and holy in all His deeds, will pour His blessings upon you and your daughters. 16. He will be your help and best comforter for He is our Redeemer and our eternal reward.

17. Let us pray to God together for each other for, by sharing each other's burden of charity in this way, we shall easily fulfill the law of Christ.

Amen.

The Rule of Saint Clare

At the very beginning of her religious life, Clare received a pattern of life from the Seraphic Father Francis, whom she considered her mentor and guide. It is not evident that this form of life contained any detailed prescriptions for the life professed by Clare and her sisters; the only knowledge we have of its content is the small fragment that Clare herself presented in the sixth chapter of her Rule. From the Legend of Saint Clare, 12, we know that, three years after her conversion, she declined the name and office of Abbess and chose to be a subject. Nonetheless, at the urging of Saint Francis, Clare took on the responsibility but considered it a service rather than an honor.

The Fourth Lateran Council (1215) demanded that any new religious communities follow some established Rule. As a result, Cardinal Hugolino di Segni, the Cardinal Archbishop of Ostia and Velletri, a former Camaldolese abbot of the monastery of San Silvestro on Monte Subasio, was eager to provide a canonical form for the communities that followed the example of the Poor Ladies of Assisi. In 1217 Hugolino gave the Poor Ladies of San Damiano the Rule of Saint Benedict, the Constitutions of Saint Peter Damian, which were followed by the hermits of the Fonte Avalana Congregation of the Camaldolese, and, somewhat later, the Constitutions of the Benedictine Monastery of San Paolo on Monte Subasio. From these documents he formed a Rule that the Poor Ladies observed for the next three decades. In 1247 Pope Innocent IV wrote a second Rule for the Poor Ladies, which modified that of Hugolino. Neither Rule, however, contained the practice of intense poverty that Clare considered the heart of her religious commitment.

Clare began to write her own Rule, which was officially approved by Cardinal Rainaldo di Segni, the Protector of the Poor Ladies, on September 16, 1252. One year later, August 9, 1253, two days before her death, Clare received word of the papal bull Solet annuere, *which gave final approval to her Rule. The original document was brought to her deathbed and, according to an annotation added to the parchment at a later date, she kissed it many times.*[1]

---

1. For further information on the *Rule of Saint Clare*, consult Lazaro Iriarte, O.F.M. Cap, *Letra y Espiritu de la Regla de Santa Clara* (Rome, 1974); Paschal Robinson,

CLARE OF ASSISI

1. INNOCENT, BISHOP, SERVANT OF THE SERVANTS OF GOD, TO THE BELOVED DAUGHTERS IN CHRIST THE ABBESS CLARE AND THE OTHER SISTERS OF THE MONASTERY OF SAN DAMIANO IN ASSISI: OUR BEST WISHES AND APOSTOLIC BLESSING.

The Apostolic See is accustomed to accede to the pious requests and to be favorably disposed to grant the praiseworthy desires of its petitioners. Thus, we have before Us your humble request that We confirm by [our] Apostolic authority the form of life which Blessed Francis gave you and which you have freely accepted. According to [this form of life] you are to live together in unity of mind and heart and in the profession of highest poverty. Our venerable Brother, the Bishop of Ostia and Velletri, has seen fit to approve this way of life, as the Bishop's own letters on this matter define more fully, and We have taken care to strengthen it with our Apostolic protection. Attentive, therefore, to your devout prayers, We approve and ratify what the Bishop has done in this matter and confirm it by Apostolic authority and support it by this document. To this end We include herein the text of the Bishop, which is the following:

2. RAYNALDUS, BY DIVINE MERCY BISHOP OF OSTIA AND VELLETRI, TO HIS MOST DEAR MOTHER AND DAUGHTER IN CHRIST, THE LADY CLARE, ABBESS OF SAN DAMIANO IN ASSISI, AND TO HER SISTERS, BOTH PRESENT AND TO COME, GREETINGS AND FATHERLY BLESSINGS.

Beloved daughters in Christ, because you have rejected the splendors and pleasures of the world and, *following the footprints* (1 Pt 2:21) of Christ Himself and His most holy Mother, you have chosen to live in the cloister and to serve the Lord in highest poverty so that, in freedom of soul, you may be the Lord's servants, We approve your holy way of life in the Lord and with fatherly affection we desire freely to impart our benign favor to your wishes and holy desires. Therefore, moved by your pious prayers and by the authority of the Lord Pope as well as our own, to all of you who are now in your monastery and to all those who will succeed you we confirm forever this form of life and the manner of holy unity and highest poverty which

---

O.F.M., *The Rule of Saint Clare: Its Observance in the Light of the Early Documents* (Philadelphia: The Dolphin Press, 1912); Livarius Oliger, O.F.M., "De Origine Regularum Ordinis Sanctae Clare," *Archivum Franciscanum Historicum* 5 (1912).

your blessed Father Saint Francis gave you for your observance in word and writing. Furthermore, by the protection of this writing, we fortify this way of life which is the following:

CHAPTER I: IN THE NAME OF THE LORD BEGINS THE FORM OF LIFE OF THE POOR SISTERS[2]

1. The form of life of the Order of the Poor Sisters which the Blessed Francis established,[3] is this: 2. to observe the holy Gospel of our Lord Jesus Christ, by living in obedience, without anything of one's own, and in chastity.

3. Clare, the unworthy handmaid of Christ and the little plant of the most blessed Father Francis, promises obedience and reverence to the Lord Pope Innocent and to his canonically elected successors, and to the Roman Church. 4. And, just as at the beginning of her conversion, together with her sisters she promised obedience to the Blessed Francis, so now she promises his successors to observe the same [obedience] inviolably.[4] 5. And the other sisters shall always be obliged to obey the successors of the blessed Francis and [to obey] Sister Clare and the other canonically elected Abbesses who shall succeed her.

CHAPTER II: THOSE WHO WISH TO ACCEPT THIS LIFE AND HOW THEY ARE TO BE RECEIVED

1. If, by divine inspiration, anyone should come to us with the desire to embrace this life, the Abbess is required to seek the consent of all the sisters; and if the majority shall have agreed, having had the

---

2. The division into chapters and the titles affixed to these are of later origin. The original text of the Rule that was discovered in 1893 does not contain them. They are retained in this edition to facilitate a reading of the text.

3. Saint Clare affirms that the form of life professed by the Poor Ladies of San Damiano was given to them by Saint Francis. The Rule of Cardinal Hugolino in 1218–1219 imposed on the Sisters the observance of the Rule of Saint Benedict. This was done in order to conform to Canon 13 of the Fourth Lateran Council, which required any new religious community to follow a previously existing religious rule. Cf. Livarius Oliger, O.F.M., "De Origine Regularum Ordinis Sanctae Clarae," *Archivum Franciscanum Historicum* (1912): 181–209, 413–447.

4. Saint Clare follows the example of Saint Francis in promising obedience to the Pope and to the Roman Church. However, she expands her promise by including obedience to the successors of Saint Francis, i.e., the Ministers General, in order to accentuate the unity of the Franciscan family.

permission of our Lord Cardinal Protector, she can receive her.[5] 2. And if she judges [the candidate] acceptable, let [the Abbess] carefully examine her, or have her examined, concerning the Catholic faith and the sacraments of the Church. 3. And if she believes all these things and is willing to profess them faithfully and to observe them steadfastly to the end; and if she has no husband, or if she has [a husband] who has already entered religious life with the authority of the Bishop of the diocese and has already made a vow of continence; and if there is no impediment to the observance of this life, such as advanced age or some mental or physical weakness, let the tenor of our life be clearly explained to her.

4. And if she is suitable, let the words of the holy Gospel be addressed to her: that she should *go and sell* all that she has and take care to distribute the proceeds *to the poor* (cf. Mt 19:21). If she cannot do this, her good will suffices. 5. And let the Abbess and her sisters take care not to be concerned about her temporal affairs, so that she may freely dispose of her possessions as the Lord may inspire her. If, however, some counsel is required, let them send her to some prudent and God-fearing men, according to whose advice her goods may be distributed to the poor.

6. Afterward, once her hair has been cut off round her head and her secular dress set aside, she is to be allowed three tunics and a mantle. 7. Thereafter, she may not go outside the monastery except for some useful, reasonable, evident, and approved purpose.[6] 8. When the

---

5. There is a development in the reception procedures. The *Earlier Rule*, II, 1–3, envisions the brothers' receiving a candidate and then presenting him to the minister. The *Later Rule*, II, 1, refines the process by requiring the brothers to send a candidate immediately to the minister provincial "to whom and to no other is permission granted for receiving brothers." In this passage of the Rule of Saint Clare, the Abbess is required to seek the consent of all the sisters and the permission of the Cardinal Protector before she can receive a candidate.

6. The Rule of Cardinal Hugolino, 4, imposed this prescription on the Poor Ladies of San Damiano: "[The sisters] must live enclosed throughout their lifetime, and after they have entered in the enclosure of this Order, taking the regular habit, the permission or faculty to go out may no longer be given to them, unless to plant or build that same Order." The Rule of Pope Innocent IV (1247), 2, contains the same basic prescription but adds: "or for the reforming of some monastery, or for the sake of governing, or correction, or to avoid some grave expense, through the permission of the Minister General of the Order of Friars Minor, or the Provincial of that Province in which the Monastery is located." Thus, this prescription of the Rule of Saint Clare

year of probation is ended, let her be received into obedience, promising to observe always our life and form of poverty.[7]

9. During the period of probation no one is to receive the veil. 10. The sisters may also have small cloaks for convenience and propriety in serving and working. 11. Indeed, the Abbess should provide them with clothing prudently, according to the needs of each person and place, and seasons and cold climates, as it shall seem expedient to her by necessity.

12. Young girls who are received into the monastery before the age established by law should have their hair cut round [their heads]; and, laying aside their secular dress, should be clothed in religious garb as the Abbess has seen [fit]. 13. When, however, they reach the age required by law, in the same way as the others, they may make their profession. 14. The Abbess shall carefully provide a Mistress from among the more prudent sisters of the monastery both for these and the other novices. She shall form them diligently in a holy manner of living and proper behavior according to the form of our profession.[8]

15. In the examination and reception of the sisters who serve outside the monastery, the same form as above is to be observed. 16. These sisters may wear shoes. 17. No one is to live with us in the monastery unless she has been received according to the form of our profession.

18. And for the love of the most holy and beloved Child Who *was wrapped in* the poorest of *swaddling clothes and laid in a manger* (cf. Lk 2:7–12), and of His most holy Mother, I admonish, entreat, and exhort my sisters that they always wear the poorest of garments.

---

does not eradicate the earlier legislation but is not as rigid and absolute. Cf. Livarius Oliger, O.F.M., "De Origine Regularum Ordinis Sanctae Clarae," *Archivum Franciscanum Historicum* 15 (1912): 206; Chiara Augusta Lainati, O.S.C., "La Clôture de Sainte Claire et des Premières Clarisses dans la législation canonique et dans la pratique," *Laurentianum* 14 (1973): 223–250.

7. Once more a development can be discerned. The *Earlier Rule*, II, 9, states: "When the year and term of probation has ended, let him be received into obedience." The Later Rule, II, 11, states: "When the year of probation is ended, let them be received into obedience, whereby they promise to observe this life and rule always." The Rule of Saint Clare, II, 8, prescribes: "When the year of probation is ended, let her be received into obedience, promising to observe always our life and form of poverty."

8. The formation of the novices was entrusted to a Novice Mistress in the Rule of Pope Innocent IV, 3, and incorporated into the Rule of Saint Clare.

CHAPTER III: THE DIVINE OFFICE AND FASTING, CONFESSION AND COMMUNION

1. The Sisters who can read shall celebrate the Divine Office according to the custom of the Friars Minor; for this they may have breviaries, but they are to read it without singing.[9] 2. And those who, for some reasonable cause, sometimes are not able to read and pray the Hours, may, like the other sisters, say the Our Father's.

3. Those who do not know how to read shall say twenty-four Our Father's for Matins; five for Lauds; for each of the hours of Prime, Terce, Sext, and None, seven; for Vespers, however, twelve; for Compline, seven. 4. For the dead, let them also say seven Our Father's with the *Requiem aeternam* in Vespers; for Matins, twelve: 5. because the sisters who can read are obliged to recite the Office of the Dead. 6. However, when a sister of our monastery shall have departed this life, they are to say fifty Our Father's.

7. The sisters are to fast at all times. 8. On Christmas, however, no matter on what day it happens to fall, they may eat twice. 9. The younger sisters, those who are weak, and those who are serving outside the monastery may be dispensed mercifully as the Abbess sees fit. 10. But in a time of evident necessity the sisters are not bound to corporal fasting.[10]

11. At least twelve times a year they shall go to confession, with the permission of the Abbess. 12. And they shall take care not to introduce other talk unless it pertains to confession and the salvation of souls. 13. They should receive Communion seven times [a year], namely, on Christmas, and Thursday of Holy Week, Easter, Pentecost, the Assumption of the Blessed Virgin, the Feast of Saint Fran-

---

9. Saint Clare specifies the recitation of the Divine Office according to the practice of the Friars Minor in contrast to the Rule of Hugolino, 4. The Rule of Innocent IV, 5, permitted the Poor Ladies to celebrate the Office as the Friars did, elaborated on the recitation of the Lord's Prayer for those who could not read, commented on the Little Office of the Blessed Virgin, and encouraged prayers for the dead. Thus, this later piece of legislation echoed the Rules of Saint Francis and anticipated that of Saint Clare.

10. *The Third Letter to Blessed Agnes of Prague*, 29–41, indicates the difficulties the followers of Saint Clare found in following the legislation imposed by the Rule of Hugolino as well as his subsequent prescription when as Pope he mandated "total abstinence from meat in imitation of the Cistercians." The Rule of Innocent IV, 5, attempted to clarify the previous legislation. But the Rule of Saint Clare expresses quite simply the spirit of fasting and, at the same time, discretion.

cis, and the Feast of All Saints. 14. [In order] to give Communion to the sisters who are in good health or to those who are ill, the Chaplain may celebrate inside [the enclosure].

CHAPTER IV: THE ELECTION AND OFFICE OF THE ABBESS; THE CHAPTER. THOSE WHO HOLD OFFICE AND THE DISCREETS

1. In the election of the Abbess the sisters are bound to observe the canonical form. 2. However, they should arrange with haste to have present the Minister General or the Minister Provincial of the Order of Friars Minor. Through the Word of God he will dispose them to perfect harmony and to the common good in the choice they are to make.[11] 3. And no one is to be elected who is not professed. And if a nonprofessed should be elected or otherwise given them, she is not to be obeyed unless she first professes our form of poverty.[12]

4. At her death the election of another Abbess is to take place. 5. Likewise, if at any time it should appear to the entire body of the sisters that she is not competent for their service and common welfare, the sisters are bound to elect another as Abbess and mother as soon as possible according to the form given above.

6. The one who is elected should reflect upon the kind of burden she has undertaken, and to Whom she is *to render an account* (Mt 12:36) of the flock committed to her. 7. She should strive as well to preside over the others more by her virtues and holy behavior than by her office, so that, moved by her example, the sisters might obey her more out of love than out of fear. 8. She should avoid particular friendships, lest by loving some more than others she cause scandal among all. 9. She should console those who are afflicted, and be, likewise, the last refuge for those who are disturbed; for, if they fail to find in her the means of health, the sickness of despair might overcome the weak.[13]

---

11. The Rule of Innocent IV, 11, mandated that the election of the Abbess be conducted freely and without any outside interference. Yet the same directive demanded that the election be confirmed by the Minister General of the Friars or, in his absence, the Minister Provincial. The need for this confirmation is absent in this text of Saint Clare.

12. Once more the "form of poverty" is accentuated as integral to the life of the sisters. In this instance, it is seen as a prerequiste of the elected abbess.

13. This paragraph marvelously articulates the qualities of a model abbess: (1) pastorally responsible; (2) possessing the power of personal example; (3) free from personal

10. She should preserve the common life in everything, especially regarding all in the church, dormitory, refectory, infirmary, and in clothing. Her vicar is bound to do likewise.[14]

11. At least once a week the Abbess is required to call her sisters together in Chapter. 12. There both she and her sisters must confess their common and public offenses and negligences humbly. 13. There, too, she should consult with all her sisters on whatever concerns the welfare and good of the monastery; for the Lord often reveals what is best to the lesser [among us].[15]

14. No heavy debt is to be incurred except with the common consent of the sisters and by reason of an evident need. This should be done through a procurator. 15. The Abbess and her sisters, however, should be careful that nothing is deposited in the monastery for safekeeping; often such practices give rise to troubles and scandals.

16. To preserve the unity of mutual love and peace, all who hold offices in the monastery should be chosen by the common consent of all the sisters. 17. And in the same way at least eight sisters are to be elected from among the more prudent, whose counsel the Abbess is always bound to heed in those things which our form of life requires. 18. Moreover, if it seems useful and expedient, the sisters can and must sometimes depose the officials and discreets, and elect others in their place.

CHAPTER V: SILENCE, THE PARLOR, AND THE GRILLE

1. The sisters are to keep silence from the hour of Compline until Terce, except those who are serving outside the monastery. 2. They

---

preferences; (4) possessing maternal care; and (5) fidelity and concern for common life. The description echoes that of Saint Francis as narrated by Thomas of Celano in the *Second Life*, 185.

14. A common interpretation of this phrase favors the demand of "observing" everything that pertains to common life; that is, the necessity of the abbess and her vicar to govern correctly for the sake of the community and to live as all others in the community, without any privileges. But the Latin verb *servare* does not signify *observare* (observe) as much as *conservare* or *custodire*. Thus Saint Clare indicates a spirit of vigilance or attentiveness to the spirit of life of the community. Cf. Santa Chiara, *Regola, Fonti Francescane*, IV, 2253–2254, no. 13.

15. This prescription takes on full significance when it is seen that neither the Rule of Hugolino nor that of Innocent IV mention the Chapter. Neither the *Earlier Rule* nor the *Later Rule* of Saint Francis describes it in the same manner as Saint Clare does in this document. It may have been the result of her long years of ministry to the sisters of San Damiano. Cf. Lazaro Iriarte, O.F.M. Cap., *La Regola di Santa Chiara*, trans. Fiorenza Fiore (Milano: Biblioteca Francescana Provinciale, 1976), pp. 103–115.

should also keep silence continually in the church, in the dormitory, and, only while they are eating, in the refectory. 3. In the infirmary, however, they may speak discreetly at all times for the recreation and service of those who are sick. 4. However, they may briefly and quietly communicate what is really necessary always and everywhere.[16]

5. The sisters may not speak in the parlor or at the grille without the permission of the Abbess or her Vicar.[17] 6. And those who have permission should not dare to speak in the parlor unless they are in the presence and hearing of two sisters. 7. Moreover, they should not presume to go to the grille unless there are at least three sisters present [who have been] appointed by the Abbess or her Vicar from the eight discreets who were elected by all the sisters as the council of the Abbess. 8. The Abbess and her vicar are themselves bound to observe this custom in speaking. 9. [The sisters should speak] very rarely at the grille and, by all means, never at the door.

10. At the grille a curtain is to be hung inside which is not to be removed except when the Word of God is being preached, or when a sister is speaking to someone. 11. The grille should also have a wooden door which is well provided with two distinct iron locks, bolts, and bars, so that, especially at night, it can be locked by two keys, one of which the Abbess is to keep and the other the sacristan; it is to be locked always except when the Divine Office is being celebrated and for reasons given above. 12. Under no circumstances whatever is any sister to speak to any one at the grille before sunrise or after sunset. 13. Moreover, in the parlor there is always to be a curtain on the inside, which is never to be removed.[18]

14. During the Lent of Saint Martin and the Greater Lent, no

---

16. The Rule of Hugolino, 6, demanded that the sisters maintain silence continually and permitted them only official periods of conversation. In this prescription, Saint Clare deals with the silence that must prevail between Compline and Terce and in certain places. Thus she wisely prescribes a silence that enhances the spirit of prayer associated with sacred places and times.

17. The Rule of Saint Clare maintains the previous legislation of Hugolino (Rule, 6) and Pope Innocent IV (Rule, 6) concerning communication with outsiders. "Parlor" (*locutio*) is used in its original sense of a room primarily for communication. The grille was in the chapel and was that part which separated the choir of the sisters from the main body of the church.

18. Sr. Chiara Augustua Lainati, O.S.C., indicates the stricter interpretation of these points of the grille found in the Rule of Saint Clare than in those of Hugolino and Pope Innocent IV. Cf. Chiara Augusta Lainati, O.S.C., "La Clôture de Sainte Claire et des Premières Clarisses dans la législation canonique et dans la pratique," *Laurentianum* 14 (1973): 223–250.

one is to speak in the parlor, except to the priest for Confession or for some other evident necessity; judgment on this is left to the prudence of the Abbess or her vicar.

CHAPTER VI: NOT HAVING POSSESSIONS

1. After the Most High Celestial Father saw fit to enlighten my heart by His grace to do penance according to the example and teaching of our most blessed Father Saint Francis, shortly after his own conversion, I, together with my sisters, voluntarily promised him obedience.[19]

2. When the Blessed Father saw that we had no fear of poverty, hard work, suffering, shame, or the contempt of the world, but that, instead, we regarded such things as great delights, moved by compassion he wrote for us a form of life as follows: "Since by divine inspiration you have made yourselves daughters and servants of the most high King, the heavenly Father, and have taken the Holy Spirit as your spouse, choosing to live according to the perfection of the holy Gospel, I resolve and promise for myself and for my brothers always to have that same loving care and special solicitude for you as [I have] for them."[20]

3. And that we might never turn aside from the most holy poverty we had embraced [nor those, either, who would come after us], shortly before his death he wrote his last will for us once more, saying: "I, brother Francis, the little one, wish to follow the life and poverty of our most high Lord Jesus Christ and of His most holy mother and to persevere in this until the end; and I ask and counsel you, my ladies, to live always in this most holy life and in poverty. And keep most careful watch that you never depart from this by reason of the teaching or advice of anyone."

4. And just as I, together with my sisters, have been ever solici-

---

19. The treatment of the enclosure is suspended so that Saint Clare can introduce her thoughts on poverty. This is the central Chapter of the Rule because it contains the keystone of this new form of religious life. While the other chapters reflect the presence of jurists, advisers, and, above all, the *Later Rule* of Saint Francis, this Chapter comes directly from Saint Clare.

20. In order to lay a solid foundation for her total embrace of poverty, Saint Clare quotes the *Form of Life* and the *Last Will* given to her and the Sisters of San Damiano by Saint Francis. In this, she also reiterates the close ties existing between the First and Second Orders.

tous to safeguard the holy poverty which we have promised the Lord God and the Blessed Francis, so, too, the Abbesses who shall succeed me in office and all the sisters are bound to observe it inviolably to the end: 5. that is to say, they are not to receive or hold onto any possessions or property [acquired] through an intermediary, or even anything that might reasonably be called property, 6. except as much land as necessity requires for the integrity and the proper seclusion of the monastery; and this land is not to be cultivated except as a garden for the needs of the sisters.

CHAPTER VII: THE MANNER OF WORKING

1. The sisters to whom the Lord has given the grace of working are to work faithfully and devotedly, [beginning] after the Hour of Terce, at work which pertains to a virtuous life and to the common good.[21] 2. They must do this in such a way that, while they banish idleness, the enemy of the soul, they do not extinguish the Spirit of holy prayer and devotion to which all other things of our earthly existence must contribute.[22]

3. And the Abbess or her vicar is bound to assign at the Chapter, in the presence of all, the manual work each is to perform.[23] 4. The same is to be done if alms have been sent by anyone for the needs of the sisters, so that the donors may be remembered by all in prayer together. 5. And all such things are to be distributed for the common good by the Abbess or her vicar with the advice of the discreets.

CHAPTER VIII: THE SISTERS SHALL NOT ACQUIRE ANYTHING AS THEIR OWN; BEGGING ALMS; THE SICK SISTERS

1. The sisters shall not acquire anything as their own, neither a house nor a place nor anything at all; instead, as pilgrims and strangers in this world who serve the Lord in poverty and humility, let

---

21. Both the *Later Rule* of Saint Francis and this Rule of Saint Clare manifest the belief that work is not considered the punishment for original sin, or the means of livelihood. It is a grace of God, a very important factor of the spiritual life.

22. Cf. *Later Rule*, c. V, n. 14.

23. Both the grace of working and that of alms should be highlighted in the daily lives of the Sisters so that fitting gratitude may be expressed.

them send confidently for alms. 2. Nor should they feel ashamed, since the Lord made Himself poor for us in this world. This is that summit of highest poverty which has established you, my dearest sisters, as heirs and queens of the kingdom of heaven; it has made you poor in the things [of this world] but has exalted you in virtue. Let this be your portion, which leads into the land of the living (cf. Ps 141:6). Dedicating yourselves totally to this, my most beloved sisters, do not wish to have anything else forever under heaven for the name of Our Lord Jesus Christ and His most holy Mother.

3. No sister is permitted to send letters or to receive anything or give away anything outside the monastery without the permission of the Abbess. 4. Nor is it allowed to have anything which the Abbess has not given or permitted. 5. Should anything be sent to a sister by her relatives or others, the Abbess should have it given to the sister. 6. If she needs it, the sister may use it; otherwise, let her in all charity give it to a sister who does need it. If, however, money is sent to her, the Abbess, with the advice of the discreets, may provide for the sister what she needs.

7. Regarding the sisters who are ill,[24] the Abbess is strictly bound to inquire with all solicitude by herself and through other sisters what [these sick sisters] may need both by way of counsel and of food and other necessities and, according to the resources of the place, she is to provide for them charitably and kindly. 8. [This is to be done] because all are obliged to serve and provide for their sisters who are ill just as they would wish to be served themselves if they were suffering from any infirmity. 9. Each should make known her needs to the other with confidence. For if a mother loves and nourishes her daughter according to the flesh, how much more lovingly must a sister love and nourish her sister according to the Spirit!

10. Those who are ill may lie on sackcloth filled with straw and may use feather pillows for their head; and those who need woolen stockings and quilts may use them.

11. When the sick sisters are visited by those who enter the monastery, they may answer them briefly, each responding with some good words to those who speak to them. 12. But the other sisters who

---

24. Saint Clare follows the development of thought found in the *Later Rule* of Saint Francis, c. VI, by considering care for the sick within the context of poverty. There is no conflict between poverty and charity in the care of the sick; rather, there is a great resource found in the love that each sister shows to those who are sick.

have permission [to speak] may not dare to speak to those who enter the monastery unless [they are] in the presence and hearing of two sister-discreets assigned by the Abbess or her vicar. 13. The Abbess and her vicar, too, are obliged themselves to observe this manner of speaking.

CHAPTER IX: THE PENANCE TO BE IMPOSED ON THE SISTERS WHO SIN; THE SISTERS WHO SERVE OUTSIDE THE MONASTERY

1. If any sister,[25] at the instigation of the enemy, shall have sinned mortally against the form of our profession, and if, after having been admonished two or three times by the Abbess or other sisters, she will not amend, she shall eat bread and water on the floor before all the sisters in the refectory for as many days as she has been obstinate; and if it seems advisable to the Abbess she shall undergo even greater punishment. 2. Meanwhile, as long as she remains obstinate, let her pray that the Lord will enlighten her heart to do penance. 3. The Abbess and her sisters, however, must beware not to become angry or disturbed on account of anyone's sin: for anger and disturbance prevent charity in oneself and in others.

4. If it should happen—God forbid—that through [some] word or gesture an occasion of trouble or scandal should ever arise between sister and sister, let she who was the cause of the trouble, at once, before offering the gift of her prayer to the Lord, not only prostrate herself humbly at the feet of the other and ask pardon, but also beg her earnestly to intercede for her to the Lord that He might forgive her. 5. The other sister, mindful of that word of the Lord: *If you do not forgive from the heart, neither will your* heavenly *Father forgive you* (Mt 6:15; 18:35), should generously pardon her sister every wrong she has done her.

6. The sisters who serve outside the monastery should not delay long outside unless some evident necessity demands it. 7. They should conduct themselves virtuously and speak little, so that those who see them may always be edified. 8. And let them zealously avoid all meetings or dealings that could be called into question. 9. They

---

25. As in the Later Rule, c. VI, VII, the Rule of Saint Clare moves from those who are physically sick to those who are suffering from spiritual maladies.

may not be godmothers of men or women lest gossip or trouble arise because of this. 10. They may not dare to repeat the rumors of the world inside the monastery. 11. And they are strictly bound not to repeat outside the monastery anything that was said or done within which could cause scandal.

12. If any one should on occasion openly offend in these two things, it shall be left to the prudence of the Abbess to impose a penance on her with mercy. But if a sister does this through vicious habit, the Abbess, with the advice of the discreets, should impose a penance on her according to the seriousness of her guilt.

CHAPTER X: THE ADMONITION AND CORRECTION OF THE SISTERS

1. The Abbess should admonish and visit her sisters, and humbly and charitably correct them, not commanding them anything which would be against their soul and the form of our profession. 2. the sisters, however, who are subjects, should remember that for God's sake they have renounced their own wills. Hence, they are firmly bound to obey their Abbess in all things which they promised the Lord to observe and which are not against their soul and our profession.

3. On her part, the Abbess is to be so familiar with them that they can speak and act toward her as ladies do with their servant. For that is the way it should be, that the Abbess be the servant of all the sisters.

4. Indeed, I admonish and exhort in the Lord Jesus Christ that the sisters be on their guard against all pride, vainglory, envy, greed, worldly care and anxiety, detraction and murmuring, dissension and division. 5. Let them be ever zealous to preserve among themselves the unity of mutual love, which is the bond of perfection.[26]

6. And those who do not know how to read should not be eager to learn. 7. Rather, let them devote themselves to what they must desire to have above all else: the Spirit of the Lord and His holy manner of working,[27] to pray always to Him with a pure heart, and to have

---

26. This section follows closely the *Later Rule*, c. X. But Saint Clare reiterates her concern for the preservation of "the unity of mutual love and peace" (cf. *Rule*, c. IV, 16). Thus, Saint Clare accentuates not only poverty, but also mutual love. These form the foundation of the life and calling of the Poor Ladies.

27. Cf. *Later Rule*, C.X, n. 23.

humility, patience in difficulty and weakness, and to love those who persecute, blame, and accuse us; for the Lord says: *Blessed are they who suffer persecution for justice's sake, for theirs is the kingdom of heaven* (Mt 5:10). But *he who shall have persevered to the end will be saved* (Mt 10:22).

CHAPTER XI: THE CUSTODY OF THE ENCLOSURE[28]

1. The portress[29] is to be mature in her manners and prudent, and of suitable age. During the day she should remain in an open cell without a door. 2. A suitable companion should be assigned to her who may, whenever necessary, take her place in all things.

3. The door is to be well secured by two different iron locks, with bars and bolts, 4. so that, especially at night, it may be locked with two keys, one of which the portress is to have, the other the Abbess. 5. And during the day the door must not be left unguarded on any account, but should be firmly locked with one key.

6. They should take utmost care to make sure that the door is never left open, except when this can hardly be avoided gracefully. 7. And by no means shall it be opened to anyone who wishes to enter, except to those who have been granted permission by the Supreme Pontiff or by our Lord Cardinal. 8. The sisters shall not allow anyone to enter the monastery before sunrise or to remain within after sunset, unless an evident, reasonable, and unavoidable cause demands otherwise.[30]

9. If a bishop has permission to offer mass within the enclosure, either for the blessing of an Abbess or for the consecration of one of the sisters as a nun or for any other reason, he should be satisfied with as few and virtuous companions and assistants as possible.

10. Whenever it is necessary for other men to enter the monas-

---

28. The discussion of the enclosure, interrupted at the end of Chapter V, resumes, thus providing a framework for the pursuit of poverty and mutual love, which are the foundations for the way of life of the Poor Ladies.

29. The office of portress was established for the Poor Ladies by the Rule of Hugolino, 13. Saint Clare retains this position, as well as the description of the sister who may assume it.

30. The Rule of Hugolino, 10, established a strict obligation on the Abbess and her Sisters concerning entrance of outsiders into the enclosure. This mandate did not permit anyone, religious or secular, of whatever dignity, to enter the monastery without explicit permission of the Holy See. The Rule of Pope Innocent IV retained this prescription, although it added that such permission may be granted by the Minister General or the Minister Provincial.

tery to do some work, the Abbess shall carefully post a suitable person at the door who is to open it only to those assigned for the work, and to no one else. 11. At such times all the sisters should be extremely careful not to be seen by those who enter.

CHAPTER XII: THE VISITATOR, THE CHAPLAIN, AND THE CARDINAL PROTECTOR

1. Our Visitator, according to the will and command of our Cardinal, should always be taken from the Order of Friars Minor.[31] 2. He should be the kind of person who is well known for his virtue and good life. 3. It shall be his duty to correct any excesses against the form of our profession, whether these be in the leadership or among the members. 4. Taking his stand in a public place, so that he can be seen by others, he may speak with several in a group and with individuals about the things that pertain to the duty of visitation, as it may seem best to him.

5. With respect for the love of God and of Blessed Francis we ask as a favor from the Order of Friars Minor a chaplain and a clerical companion of good character and reputation and prudent discretion, and two lay brothers who are lovers of holiness of life and virtue, to support us in our [life of] poverty, just as we have always had [them] through the kindness of the Order.

6. The chaplain may not be permitted to enter the monastery without his companion. 7. And when they enter, they are to remain in an open place, in such a way that they can see each other always and be seen by others. 8. For the confession of the sick who cannot go to the parlor, for their Communion, for the Last Anointing and the Prayers for the Dying, they are allowed to enter the enclosure.

9. Moreover, for funeral services and on the solemnity of Masses for the Dead, for digging or opening a grave, or also for making arrangements for it, suitable and sufficient outsiders may enter according to the prudence of the Abbess.

---

31. The first Visitator of the Poor Ladies was a Cistercian, Ambrose, who held that position from 1218 to 1219. He was followed by Brother Philip the Tall (1219–1220), a friar, and then by a secular, Brunetus, in 1224. No doubt the prescription to have a friar as Visitator came from Saint Clare's personal experience of a Visitator who did not understand the Franciscan ideal (cf. Livarius Oliger, O.F.M., "De Origine Regularum Ordinis Sanctae Clarae," *Archivum Franciscanum Historicum* (1912): 181–209, 413–447.

10. To see to all these things above, the sisters are firmly obliged to have always that Cardinal of the Holy Church of Rome as our Governor, Protector, and Corrector, who has been delegated by the Lord Pope for the Friars Minor,[32] 11. so that, always submissive and subject at the feet of that holy Church, and steadfast in the Catholic Faith, we may observe forever the poverty and humility of our Lord Jesus Christ and of His most holy Mother and the holy Gospel which we have firmly promised. Amen.

Given at Perugia, the sixteenth day of September, in the tenth year of the Pontificate of the Lord Pope Innocent IV.[33]

Therefore, no one is permitted to destroy this page of our confirmation or to oppose it recklessly. If anyone shall have presumed to attempt this, let him know that he will incur the wrath of Almighty God and of His holy Apostles Peter and Paul.

Given at Assisi, the ninth day of August, in the eleventh year of our Pontificate.[34]

---

32. Cf. *Later Rule*, XII, n. 26. Hugolino was the Cardinal Protector of the Poor Ladies until his election as Bishop of Rome, March 19, 1227. He was succeeded by Cardinal Rainaldo, who later became the Bishop of Rome, December 12, 1254.

33. The first date given is September 16, 1252, that is, the day of the approval by the Cardinal Protector, Rainaldo dei Conti di Segni. Cf. Rule of Saint Clare, Prologue 2.

34. The second date is August 9, 1253, on which day the Pope, Innocent IV, gave papal approval to the Rule of Saint Clare through the bull *Solet annuere.* Saint Clare died two days later.

The Testament of Saint Clare

This text forms a beautiful autobiographical reflection of Saint Clare. No other writing of the saint—with the exception of the sixth chapter of her Rule—speaks so eloquently about the origins of the Poor Ladies of San Damiano, the bond of unity between the Poor Ladies and Saint Francis and his brothers, the love of poverty and humility that is the life of the "Little Flock" raised up by the Father to follow the footprints of Christ in the Church. Yet the Testament of Saint Clare is certainly one of the most controversial texts in that its authenticity has been frequently brought into doubt.[1] Nonetheless, it is a magnificent source of the spirituality of Saint Clare from which many valuable insights can be gained.

In the name of the Lord!
1. Among all the other gifts which we have received and continue to receive daily from our benefactor, *the Father of mercies* (2 Cor

---

1. At one point in the editors' research, we were quite convinced that the *Testament* was not a genuine work of Saint Clare, but rather a careful and beautiful compilation, at least in part, from her Rule and words to the Sisters at San Damiano.

The root of the difficulty lay in the lack of early manuscripts. Until fairly recently, the tradition seemed to be limited to a Latin manuscript used without any identification by Luke Wadding in his *Annales Minorum* 1253, n.5 (cf. ed. III, Ad Claras Aquas 1931, 340–343). This was copied by the Bollandist *Acta Sanctorum* (August, tome II, 747ff). Ubald d'Alençon, O.F.M. Cap., came upon both the Latin text and a French translation of the late fifteenth century—together with the Blessing of Saint Clare and the "Privilege of Poverty" (cf. Ubald d'Alençon, O.F.M. Cap., "Le Plus ancien texte de la Bénédiction, du Privilège de pauvreté et du Testament de sainte Clare d'Assise," in *Revue d'histoire franciscaine* 1 [1924]: 469–482; 2 [1925]: 290). Manuscripts of the Testament in a Dutch version are found in various libraries of Holland (cf. *Archivum Franciscanum Historicum* 27 [1934]: 395ff.; 40 [1949]: 290ff.).

Recent scholarship has discovered the following manuscripts of the Testament: (a) a manuscript of the fourteenth century, in Latin, in the monastery of Motevergine, Messina, Sicily; (b) a fourteenth-century manuscript at Uppsala, Univ. C63, which belonged to Saint Brigid of Sweden, acquired perhaps on her visit to Assisi in July-August 1352; (c) a fifteenth-century manuscript of the Monastery of Saint Clare at Urbino, authenticated by the Assisian notary Franciscus, son of sir Benvenuti Stefani de Assisio in July 1420 (cf. *Documentazione di vita assisana*, ed. Cesare Cenci, O.F.M., tom. III, indices, 374b). For further detail, consult Diego Ciccarelli, O.F.M. Conv., "Contributi alla recensione degli scritti di S. Chiara," *Miscellanca Francescana* 78 (1978): 347–374.

1:3), and for which we must express the deepest thanks to our glorious God, our vocation is a great gift.[2] Since it is the more perfect and greater, we should be so much more thankful to Him for it. For this reason the Apostle writes: "Acknowledge your calling" (1 Cor 1:26). 2. The Son of God became for us *the Way* (cf. Jn 14:6) which our Blessed Father Francis, His true lover and imitator, has shown and taught us by word and example.

3. Therefore, beloved Sisters, we must consider the immense gifts which God has bestowed on us, especially those which He has seen fit to work in us through His beloved servant, our blessed Father Francis, not only after our conversion but also while we were still [living among] the vanities of the world.

4. For, almost immediately after his conversion, while he had neither brothers nor companions, when he was building the Church of San Damiano in which he was totally filled with divine consolation, he was led to abandon the world completely. This holy man, in the great joy and enlightenment of the Holy Spirit, made a prophecy about us which the Lord fulfilled later. Climbing the wall of that church he shouted in French to some poor people who were standing nearby: "Come and help me build the monastery of San Damiano, because ladies will dwell here who will glorify our heavenly Father throughout His holy Church by their celebrated and holy manner of life."[3]

5. In this, then, we can consider the abundant kindness of God toward us. Because of His mercy and love, He saw fit to speak these words about our vocation and selection through His saint. And our most blessed Father prophesied not only for us, but also for those who were to come to this [same] holy vocation to which the Lord has called us.

6. With what solicitude and fervor of mind and body, therefore, must we keep the commandments of our God and Father, so that, with the help of the Lord, we may return to Him an increase of His *talents* (cf. Mt 25:15–23). For the Lord Himself not only has set us as an example and mirror for others, but also for our [own] sisters whom

---

2. This opening sentence echoes the *Second Letter to Blessed Agnes of Prague*, 3, and provides an exhortation in which the vocation of Clare and the life of the Poor Ladies is seen from the perspective of the generosity of God.

3. Cf. *The Legend of the Three Companions*, 21, 24. This biography of Saint Francis is accepted by many scholars as a work of the early fourteenth century.

the Lord has called to our way of life, so that they in turn will be a mirror and example to those living in the world. Since, therefore, the Lord has called us to such great things, that those who are to be models and mirrors for others may behold themselves in us, we are truly bound to bless and praise the Lord and to be strengthened constantly in Him to do good. Therefore, if we have lived according to the form [of life] given us, we shall, by very little effort, leave others a noble example and gain the prize of eternal happiness.[4]

7. After the most high heavenly Father saw fit in His mercy and grace to enlighten my heart to do penance according to the example and teaching of our most blessed Father Francis, shortly after his own conversion, I, together with the few sisters whom the Lord had given me soon after my conversion, voluntarily promised him obedience, since the Lord had given us the Light of His grace through his holy life and teaching.

8. But when the Blessed Francis saw that, although we were physically weak and frail, we did not shirk deprivation, poverty, hard work, distress, or the shame or contempt of the world—rather, as he and his brothers often saw for themselves, we considered [all such trials] as great delights after the example of the saints and their brothers—he rejoiced greatly in the Lord. And moved by compassion for us, he promised to have always, both through himself and through his Order, the same loving care and special solicitude for us as for his own brothers.

9. And thus, by the will of God and our most blessed Father Francis, we went to dwell at the Church of San Damiano. There, in a short time, the Lord increased our number by His mercy and grace so that what He had predicted through His saint might be fulfilled. We had stayed in another place [before this], but only for a little while.

10. Later on he wrote a form of life for us, [indicating] especially that we should persevere always in holy poverty.[5] And while he was living, he was not content to encourage us by many words and exam-

---

4. Lines 4–6 reflect the Testament of Saint Francis, 1–3. There are some scholars who doubt the authenticity of the first six lines of the Testament of Saint Clare and claim that the document should begin "After the most high heavenly Father saw fit in his mercy." Cf. *Seraphicae Legislationus Textus Originales* (Quaracchi, 1897), pp. 282ff.; Livarius Oliger, O.F.M., "De Origine Regularum S. Clarae," *Archivum Franciscanum Historicum* 5 (1912): 187ff., n. 4; Engelbert Grau, O.F.M., *Leben und Schriften der Hl. Klara* (Werl/Westf, 1960), pp. 21ff.

5. Cf. *The Rule of Saint Clare*, VI, 1.

ples to love and observe holy poverty; [in addition] he also gave us many writings so that, after his death, we should in no way turn away from it. [In a similar way] the Son of God never wished to abandon this holy poverty while He lived in the world, and our most blessed Father Francis, following His footprints, never departed, either in example or teaching, from this holy poverty which he had chosen for himself and for his brothers.[6]

11. Therefore, I, Clare, the handmaid of Christ and of the Poor Sisters of the Monastery of San Damiano—although unworthy—and the little plant of the holy Father, consider together with my sisters our most high profession and the command of so great a father. [We also take note] in some [sisters] of the frailty which we feared in ourselves after the death of our holy Father Francis, [He] who was our pillar of strength and, after God, our one consolation and support. [Thus] time and again, we bound ourselves to our Lady, most holy Poverty, so that, after my death, the Sisters present and to come would never abandon her.

12. And, as I have always been most zealous and solicitous to observe and to have the other sisters observe the holy poverty which we have promised the Lord and our holy Father Francis, so, too, the others who will succeed me in office should be bound always to observe it and have it observed by the other sisters. And, for even greater security, I took care to have our profession of most holy poverty, which we promised our Father [Francis], strengthened with privileges by the Lord Pope Innocent, during whose pontificate we had our beginning, and by his other successors. [We did this] so that we would never nor in any way depart from it.[7]

---

6. Cf. *The Rule of Saint Clare*, VI, 3.

7. The text of the Privilege of Poverty given by Pope Innocent III is lost. That granted by Pope Gregory IX is: "Gregory, Bishop, Servant of the servants of God, to the beloved daughters in Christ, Clare and the other servants of Christ gathered in the monastic community of the Church of San Damiano in the Diocese of Assisi: Health and Apostolic Benediction. As it has been shown, you have renounced the desire for temporal things, desiring to be dedicated to the Lord alone. Because of this, you *have sold everything and have given it to the poor* (Mt 19:21) [and] have proposed to have no possessions whatsoever, clinging in every way to the footprints of Him Who is *the way, the truth, and the life* (Jn 14:6).

"And the lack of possessions does not deter you from this proposal, for *the left arm of the heavenly Spouse is under your head* (Cant 2:6) to support the weakness of your body which, in love, you have subordinated well to the law of the spirit.

"Finally, He who *feeds the birds of the heaven and clothes the lilies of the field* (Lk 12:37) has not failed [to provide] equally [your] food and clothing, until He may minister eter-

13. For this reason, on bended knees and with all possible respect, I commend all my sisters, both those present and those to come, to our holy Mother the Church of Rome, to the supreme Pontiff, and especially to the Lord Cardinal who has been appointed [Protector] for the Order of Friars Minor and for us. [Inspired by] the love of the Lord Who was poor as He lay in the crib, poor as He lived in the world, Who remained naked on the cross, may [our Protector] always see to it that his *little flock* (cf. Lk 12:32) observe that which [our] Lord [and] Father has begotten in His holy Church by the word and example of our blessed Father Francis, who followed the poverty and humility of His beloved Son and His glorious Virgin Mother—namely, holy poverty, which we have promised God and our most blessed Father Francis. May he always encourage and support them in these things.

14. The Lord gave us our most blessed Father Francis as Founder, Planter, and Helper in the service of Christ and in the things we have promised to God and to himself as our father. While he was living he was always solicitous in word and in deed to cherish and take care of us, his little plant. For these reasons I commend my sisters, both those present and those to come, to the successor of our blessed Father Francis and to the entire Order, so that they may always help us to progress in serving God more perfectly and above all to observe most holy poverty in a more perfect manner.

15. If these sisters should ever leave this place and go elsewhere, after my death, wherever they may be, they are bound nonetheless to observe that form of poverty which we have promised God and our most blessed Father Francis.[8] 16. Nonetheless, let both the sister who is in office and the other sisters exercise such care and farsightedness that they do not acquire or receive more land around the place than

nally in heaven to you [whom He has cared for] in time, when *His right hand will* more happily *embrace* you in the fullness of His vision (Cant 2:6).

"Therefore, as you have requested, we confirm with [our] apostolic authority your proposal of the highest poverty, giving to you by authority of this present letter the right to be compelled by no one to receive [any] possessions.

"It is forbidden for anyone to infringe upon this writing of our concession or to dare to act contrary to it. If anyone dares to attempt this, let him know that he will incur the wrath of almighty God, and of His blessed apostles Peter and Paul.

"Given at Perugia, on 15 September, in the second year of our Pontificate [1228]."

8. This became prophetic in that the Poor Ladies left San Damiano in 1257 for a new residence in the former church of San Giorgio, presently the Basilica of Saint Clare.

strict necessity requires for a vegetable garden. But if, for the integrity and privacy of the monastery, it becomes necessary to have more land beyond the limits of the garden, no more should be acquired than strict necessity demands. This land should not be cultivated or planted but always remain untouched and undeveloped.[9]

17. In the Lord Jesus Christ, I admonish and exhort all my sisters, both those present and those to come, to strive always to imitate the way of holy simplicity, humility, and poverty and [to preserve] the integrity of [our] holy manner of life, as we were taught by our blessed Father Francis from the beginning of our conversion to Christ. Thus may they always remain *in the fragrance* of a good name (cf. 2 Cor 2:15), both among those who are afar off and those who are near. [This will take place] not by our own merits but solely by the mercy and grace of our Benefactor, *the Father of mercies* (cf. 2 Cor 1:3).

18. Loving one another with the charity of Christ, let the love you have in your hearts be shown outwardly in your deeds so that, compelled by such an example, the sisters may always grow in love of God and in charity for one another.

19. I also beg that sister who will have the office [of caring for] the sisters to strive to exceed others more by her virtues and holy life than by her office so that, encouraged by her example, the Sisters may obey her not so much out of duty but rather out of love. Let her also be prudent and attentive to her sisters just as a good mother is to her daughters; and especially, let her take care to provide for them according to the needs of each one from the things which the Lord shall give. Let her also be so kind and so available that all [of them] may reveal their needs with trust and have recourse to her at any hour with confidence as they see fit, both for her sake and that of her sisters.[10]

20. But the sisters who are subjects should keep in mind that for the Lord's sake they have given up their own wills. Therefore I ask that they obey their mother as they have promised the Lord of their own free will so that, seeing the charity, humility, and unity they have toward one another, their mother might bear all the burdens of her office more lightly. Thus what is painful and bitter might be turned into sweetness for her because of their holy way of life.[11]

---

9. Cf. *The Rule of Saint Clare*, VI, 6.
10. Cf. parallel passages in the *Rule of Saint Clare*, IV, 7; X, 1–3.
11. Cf. *Testament of Saint Francis*, 1; also, *First Version of the Letter to the Faithful*, II, 11.

21. And because the way and path is straight and the gate through which one passes and enters into life is narrow (cf. Mt 7:14), there are few who walk on it and enter through it. And if there are some who walk that way for a time, there are very few who persevere in it. How blessed are those to whom it has been given to walk that way and persevere to the end!

22. Therefore, as we have set out on the path of the Lord, let us take care that we do not turn away from it by our own fault or negligence or ignorance nor that we offend so great a Lord and His Virgin Mother, and our Father, the blessed Francis, and the Church Triumphant and, indeed, the Church Militant. For it is written: *"Cursed are those who turn away from Your commandments"* (Ps 118:21).

23. *For this reason I bend my knees to the Father of our Lord Jesus Christ* (Eph 3:14), that through the prayers and merits of the glorious and holy Virgin Mary, His Mother, and of our most blessed Father Francis and all the Saints, the Lord Himself Who has given us a good beginning will [also] give the increase and constant perseverance to the end. Amen.

24. So that it may be observed better, I leave this writing for you, my dearest and most beloved Sisters, those present and those to come, as a sign of the blessing of the Lord and of our most blessed Father Francis and of my blessing—I who am your mother and servant.[12]

---

12. Cf. *Testament of Saint Francis*, 41.

The Blessing Attributed to Saint Clare

The Legend of Saint Clare, *45, portrays the last hour of the saint's earthly life. As she was dying, Clare blessed her sisters at San Damiano, as well as those in other monasteries and those who would come in the future. It is impossible to determine whether this narration gave rise to the tradition of a special blessing attributed to Saint Clare. There is also some evidence of a special blessing that Saint Clare sent to Blessed Agnes of Prague. It is similar to that blessing of the dying saint. The earliest known text of this blessing, found in a Middle High German translation, dates to about 1350.[1] No study of the work has been able to determine its authenticity.[2] Yet the tradition of the Poor Clares has always cherished this text as a precious remembrance of their foundress.[3]*

1. In the name of the Father and of the Son and of the Holy Spirit. Amen.

2. May the Lord bless you and keep you. 3. May He show His face to you and be merciful to you. 4. May He turn His countenance to you and give you peace.

5. I, Clare, a handmaid of Christ, a little plant of our holy Father Francis, a sister and mother of you and the other Poor Sisters, although unworthy, 6. ask our Lord Jesus Christ through His mercy and through the intercession of His most holy Mother Mary, of Blessed Michael the Archangel and all the holy angels of God, and of all His men and women saints, 7. that the heavenly Father give you

---

1. Cf. Walter W. Seton, "Some New Sources for the Life of Blessed Agnes of Prague, including some Chronological Notes and a New Text of the Benediction of Saint Clare," *Archivum Franciscanum Historicum* 7 (1914), 185–197.

2. Cf. Walter W. Seton, "The Oldest Text of the Benediction of Saint Clare of Assisi," *Revue d'histoire franciscaine* 2 (1925), 88–90. Also, C. Mark Borkowski, "A Second Middle High German Translation of the Benediction of Saint Clare," *Franciscan Studies* 36 (1976), 99–104.

3. Cf. Ubald d'Alençon, O.F.M. Cap., "Le plus ancien texte de la Bénédiction, du Privilège de pauvreté et du Testament de sainte Clare d'Assise," *Revue d'histoire franciscaine* 1 (1924), 469–482; 2 (1925), 290.

and confirm for you this most holy blessing in heaven and on earth. 8. On earth, may He increase [His] grace and virtues among His servants and handmaids of His Church Militant. 9. In heaven, may He exalt and glorify you in His Church Triumphant among all His men and women saints.

10. I bless you in my life and after my death as much as I can and more than I can 11. with all the blessings with which the Father of mercies has and will have blessed His sons and daughters in heaven and on earth. Amen.

12. Always be lovers of God and your souls and the souls of your Sisters, and always be eager to observe what you have promised the Lord.

13. May the Lord be with you always and, wherever you are, may you be with Him always. Amen.

Appendix

I Abbreviations

THE WRITINGS OF SAINT FRANCIS

The Admonitions: Adm

The Canticle of Brother Sun: CantSun

The Canticle of Exhortation to Saint Clare and Her Sisters: CantExh

The Exhortation to the Praise of God: ExhP

The Form of Life Given to Saint Clare and Her Sisters: FormLife

The Last Will Written for Saint Clare and Her Sisters: LastWill

A Letter to Brother Leo: LLeo

A Letter to the Clergy: LCler

The First Letter to the Custodians: ILCus

The Second Letter to the Custodians: IILCus

A Letter to the Entire Order: LOrd

The First Letter to the Faithful: ILF

The Second Letter to the Faithful: IILF

A Letter to a Minister: LMin

A Letter to the Rulers of the Peoples: LRul

A Letter to Saint Anthony: LAnt

The Office of the Passion: OP

The Parchment Given to Brother Leo:
 a. The Praises of God: PrGod
 b. The Blessing Given to Brother Leo: BlLeo

The Praises to be Said at All the Hours: PrH

The Prayer before the Crucifix: PrCruc

The Prayer Inspired by the *Our Father:* POF

The Earlier Rule: ER

The Later Rule: LR

The Rule for Hermitages: RH

The Salutation of the Blessed Virgin Mary: SalBVM

The Salutation of the Virtues: SalVirt

The Testament: Test

THE WRITINGS DICTATED BY SAINT FRANCIS

The Blessing Given to Brother Bernard: BlBern

The Blessing Sent to Saint Clare and Her Sisters: BlSCl

A Letter Written for the Citizens of Bologna: LBol

A Letter Written to Lady Jacoba: LJac

A Letter Sent to the Brothers in France: LFran

The Testament Written in Siena: TestS

True and Perfect Joy: TPJoy

THE WRITINGS OF SAINT CLARE

The First Letter to Blessed Agnes of Prague: ILCl

The Second Letter to Blessed Agnes of Prague: IILCl

The Third Letter to Blessed Agnes of Prague: IIILCl

The Fourth Letter to Blessed Agnes of Prague: IVLCl

The Letter to Ermentrude of Bruges: LEr

The Rule of Saint Clare: RCl

The Testament: TestCl

The Blessing: BlCl

II Scripture References

APPENDIX

239

18:35	RCl 9:5	1:68	OP 6:15
19:21	LR 2:5 ER 1:2	2:7	OP 15:7
19:24	I LCl 28 RCl 2:4	2:7–12	RCl 2:18
19:27	ER 8:5	2:14	OP 15:8
19:29	ER 1:5 I LCl 30	2:19;51	Adm 21:2, 28:3
20:15	Adm 8:3 ER 5:10	3:8	IILF 25 ER 21:3
20:21	ILF 1:19 II LF 60 ER 22:55	4:2	ER 3:6
20:25–26	ER 5:10–11	6:22	ER 16:15
20:28	Adm 4:1 ER 4:6	6:23	ER 16:16
22:21	Adm 11:41	6:27	IILF 38
22:37	II LF 18	6:29–30	ER 14:4–6
22:39	I LF 1:1 II LF 18:26	6:37	ER 21:5
23:8–10	ER 22:33–35	6:38	ER 21:4
24:6	ER 16:19	6:41	ER 11:11
24:13	IILF 88 ER 16:21	7:25	ER 2:14
24:45	Adm 23:3	8:5	ER 22:12
24:46	Adm 10:3 17:1 19:4	8:11	ER 22:16
25:15–23	TestCl 6	8:12–14	ER 22:12–16
25:18	Adm 18:2	8:15	ER 22:17
25:34	ER 23:4	8:18	Adm 18:2 ILF 2:16 IILF 83
25:41	ER 21:8		LRul 4
25:46	ER 16:11	8:22	ER 22:18
26:26–27	IILF 6–7	9:3	ER 14:1
26:39	IILF 10	9:24	Adm 3:2 ER 16:11
26:42	IILF 10	9:26	ER 16:9
26:50	ER 22:2	9:62	Adm 3:10 LR 2:13 ER 2:10
28:20	Adm 1:22 ER 22:38	10:4	ER 14:1
		10:5	LR 3:13 ER 14:2
Mark		10:7	ER 14:13
2:17	ER 5:8	10:8	ER 3:14 ER 3:13
2:26	ER 9:13	10:20	ER 17:6
4:15–19	ER 22 13–16	10:27	POF 5, ER 23:8
4:25	ILF 2:16 IILF 83	10:38–42	RH 2
7:21	ILF 2:12 II 69 ER 22:7	10:42	II LCl 10
7:22	ER 22:7	11:2	ER 22:28
7:23	IILF 37:69 ER 22:8	11:21	Adm 27:5
8:36	ER 7:1	11:24	ER 22:21–22
9:28	ER 3:1	11:26	ER 22:24
10:29	ER 1:5	11:42	IILF 36
11:25	ER 21:6 22:28	12:4	ER 16:17–18
12:30	ILF 1:1 ER 23:8	12:5	ER 8:1
12:33	ER 23:8	12:15	ER 10:7
12:36	ER 23:8	12:32	TestCl 13
14:22–24	Adm 1:10	13:24	ER 11:13
		14:26	ER 1:4
Luke		14:27	Adm 5:8 OP 7:8, 15:13
1:28	ExhP 4	14:33	Adm 3:1
1:32	LOrd 4	16:2	ER 16:4

241

APPENDIX

APPENDIX

Second Corinthians

1:3	TestCl 1, 17
2:15	TestCl 17
3:6	Adm 7:1 3:18 III LCl 13, 15:8 I LCl 14
3:18	III LCl 13
6:3	POF 5
8:9	IILF 5 LR 6:3 I CLl 19
12:5	Adm 5:8
11:2	I LCl 12 ILCl 24

Letter to Galatians

5:13	ER 5:14
6:2	Adm 18:1, 5:16 ILF 1:3

Letter to Ephesians

3:14	TestCl 23
3:18	POF 3
6:6	LOrd 14

Letter to Philippians

2:8	Adm 1:16 LOrd 46, 3:14 III LCl 3
4:4	ER 7:16 III LCl 10

Letter to Colossians

1:15	ER 23:6 3:5 ILF 1:3
1:17	III LCl 26
1:20	LOrd 13
1:23	ER 12:4 IILF 64
3:22	LOrd 14, 1:13 I LCl 14

First Letter to Thessalonians

1:9	PrGod 3 ILCu 7 1:6 IV LCl 7
2:7	LR 6:8 ER 9:11
5:15	POF 8
5:18	ER 21:2

Second Letter to Thessalonians

3:10	ER 7:5

First Letter to Timothy

4:5	LOrd 37
6:8	ER 9:1
6:16	Adm 1:5

Second Letter to Timothy

2:14	LR 3:10 ER 11:1

Letter to Titus

2:13	IV CL 39
3:2	ER 11:79

Letter to Hebrews

1:3	III LCl 12 IV LCl 14
10:28–29	LOrd 17–18 2:10 III LCl 1
10:31	ER 5:1
12:7	LOrd 10:11
12:2	I LCl 14

Letter to James

1:2	ER 7:8 1:17 II LCl 3
2:5	ER 6:4
2:10	SalVirt 7
2:13	IILF 29
2:18	ER 11:6
4:10	LOrd 28
5:16	ER 20:3 21:6

First Letter to Peter

1:12	LOrd 22 1:19 IV LCl 8
1:22	Adm 3:6
2:11	LR6:2 Test 24 IILF65
2:13	IILF 47 ER 16:6
2:21	IILF 13 LLeo 3, LOrd 51 1:1 OP 7:8 15:13 ER 22:2 RCL Prol 2
2:25	ER 22:32
4:9	ER 7:15
5:6	LOrd 28

Second Letter to Peter

2:22	Adm 3:10

First Letter John

3:10	ER 21:8
3:14	LCler 3
3:18	ER 11:16
4:16	ILF 2:19, IILF 87, ER 17:5, 22:26
4:18	SalVirt 13

Revelations

1:5	LOrd 3
2:11	CantSun 13
2:13	III LCl 41
3:19	ER 10:3

APPENDIX

4:8	PrH 1	14:7	ExhP 1, 14:3 IV LCl 3
4:9	CantSun 1 PrH 11	19:3	ER 23:6
4:11	CantSun 1, ExhP 2 PrH 2, 11	19:4	ER 23:6
5:12	ExhP PrH 2, 11	19:16	II LCl
5:13	IILF 61, PrH 8	19:5	PrH 6
7:9	ER 23:7	20:6	CantSun 13.

III   Selected Bibliography

CRITICAL TEXTS

Clare of Assisi, Saint. "Epistolae ad b. Agnetem." Ed. W. Seton. *Archivum Franciscanum Historicum.* Vol. 17. Quaracchi: Collegium S. Bonaventurae, 1924, pp. 513–519.

———. "Regula." *Seraphicae Legislationis Textus Originales.* Quaracchi: Collegium S. Bonaventurae, 1897, pp. 49–75.

———. "Testamentum." *Seraphicae Legislationis Textus Originales.* Quaracchi: Collegium S. Bonaventurae, 1897, pp. 273–280.

———. *Escritos de santa Clara y documentos contemporaneos.* Ed. I. Omaechevarria, O.F.M. Madrid: Biblioteca de autores christianos, 1970.

Francis of Assisi, Saint. *Die Opuscula des Hl. Franziskus von Assissi: Neue textkritische edition.* Ed. Kajetan Esser, O.F.M. *Spicilegium Bonaventurianum* cura pp. Collegii S. Bonaventurae. Vol. XIII. Grottaferrata: Collegium S. Bonaventurae, 1976.

———*Opuscula Santi Patris Francisci Assisiensis.* Ed. Caietanus Esser, O.F.M. *Bibliotheca Franciscana Ascetica Medii Aevi.* Tom. XII. Grottaferrata (Roma): Ad Claras Aquas, 1978.

———. "Parole di esortazione di S. Francesco alle 'Poverelle' di S. Damiano." Estratto da *Forma Sororum.* XIV., n. 2. Ed. P. Giovanni Boccali, O.F.M. Assisi: Protomonastero S. Chiara, 1977.

BIOGRAPHIES

Brady, Ignatius. *The Legend and Writings of Saint Clare of Assisi.* St. Bonaventure, N.Y.: The Franciscan Institute, 1953.

De Robeck, Nesta. *Saint Clare of Assisi.* Milwaukee: Bruce, 1951.

Englebert, Omer. *Saint Francis of Assisi.* Trans. Eve Marie Cooper. 2nd. English Ed. revised and augmented by Ignatius Brady, O.F.M., and Raphael Brown. Chicago: Franciscan Herald Press, 1965.

Fortini, Arnaldo. *Francis of Assisi.* Trans. Helen Moak. New York: Crossroad, 1981.

Habig, Marion A., ed. *St. Francis of Assisi: Writings and Early Biogra-*

phies, English Omnibus of the Sources for the Life of St. Francis. Chicago: Franciscan Herald Press, 1972.

CONCORDANCES

Godet, Jean-François, and Georges Mailleux, eds. *Opuscula Sancti Francisci, Scripta Sanctae Clarae. Corpus des sources franciscaines.* Vol. V. Louvain: Université Catholique de Louvain (Publications du CETEDOC), 1976.

STUDIES

Brady, Ignazio. *San Francesco uomo dello Spirito.* Vicenza: Edizioni L.I.E.F., 1976.

Cardaropoli, G. e Conti, M. *Approccio storico-critico alle Fonti Francescane.* Roma: Antonianum, 1979.

———. *Lettura biblico-theologica delle Fonti Francescane.* Roma: Antonianum, 1979.

Conti, Mattino. *Lettura biblica della Regola francescana.* Roma: Antonianum, 1977.

Esser, Cajetan, and Hardik, F.L. *The Marrow of the Gospel.* Trans. and ed. Ignatius Brady, O.F.M. Chicago: Franciscan Herald Press, 1958.

Esser, Cajetan. *Origins of the Franciscan Order.* Chicago: Franciscan Herald Press, 1965.

Gratian de Paris, O.F.M. Cap. *I Know Christ.* Trans. Paul J. Oligny, O.F.M. St. Bonaventure, N.Y.: The Franciscan Institute, 1957.

Iriarte, Lazaro. *La Regola di Santa Chiara.* Milano: Biblioteca Francescana Provinciale, 1976.

Lapsanski, Duane V. *Evangelical Perfection.* St. Bonaventure, N.Y.: The Franciscan Institute, 1977.

I. Index to Preface, Foreword, Introductions and Notes

INDEX

INDEX

INDEX

211 n 3, 212–213 n 6, 224 n 31, 228 n 4.
Olivi, Peter, 153 n 2.
Omaechevarria, Ignatio, xvi.
Ottakar of Bohemia, 189, 199 n 1.
Otto IV, 77.

Parenti, John, 54, 77.
Paul, 12, 14, 26 n 1, 31 n 10, 200 n 2, 229–230 n 7.
Paul VI, 12, 12 n 22.
Penance, 52, 62, 68 n 6, 71 n 12, 101, 125, 170, 172; life of, 66, 182.
Penitential Movement, 62, 62 n 1, 68 n 6, 120 n 27, 144 n 24.
Peter, 229–230 n 7.
1 Peter, 2:21, 172, 183.
Peter Damien, 209.
Petrarch, Francesco, 10 n 20.
Philip the Tall, 224 n 31.
Philippians, 1:19, 26 n 1; 2:6–11, 181.
Pilate, 84 n 4.
Pius IX, 189.
Pius XI, 189.
Pompei, Alfonso, 67 n 5, 68 n 6.
Poor Ladies of San Damiano, life of, 62, 171, 174, 175, 181, 182, 209, 211 n 3, 215 n 12, 222 n 26, 223 n 28; and mutual love, 174, 177, 178, 182–184, 222 n 26, 223 n 28, 226; and poverty, 44, 172–175, 178, 215 n 12, 218 n 20, 223 n 28, 226; and Rule of Hugolino, 172, 174, 178, 180, 209, 211 n 3, 212 n 6, 214 n 9, n 10, 216 n 15, 217 n 16, n 17, n 18, 223 n 29, n 30; and Rule of Innocent IV, 172, 174, 209, 212 n 6, 213 n 8, 214 n 9, n 10, 215 n 11, 216 n 15, 217 n 17, n 18, 223 n 30; and Rule of St. Clare, xii, xv, 44, 44 n 1, 45 n 3, 46, 172, 173 n 7–8, 174, 175, 178, 181, 182, 183–184, 199, 209, 209 n 1, 211 n 2, 212 n 5–6, 213 n 7–8, 214 n 9–10, 215 n 11, 217 n 17–18, 219 n 21, 221 n 25, 225 n 33–34, 226, 226 n 1, 228 n 5, 229 n 6, 231 n 9–10.
Poverty, cf. also Life; charism of, 172–179; of Christ, 46, 48 n 3, 174, 181, 183, 195, 197 n 9; and Clare, 44, 172–175, 180, 181, 183, 189, 192 n 8, 195, 201 n 10, 209, 218 n 19–20, 220 n 24, 222 n 26, 226; and Francis, 141 n 15, 164, 173, 180, 185, 193 n 13, 220

n 24; and Poor Ladies, 44, 172–175, 178, 215 n 12, 218 n 20, 223 n 28, 226; vow of, 31 n 9.
Prayer, and Father, 13; and Franciscan life, 139 n 11; and grace, 140 n 13; life of, 16, 147 n 3, 199; mystical, 10; and silence, 217 n 16; steps of, 197 n 9.
Premislaus II, 199 n 1.
Proverbs, 8:30, 179.
Psalms, 17:18, 84 n 4; 56, 84 n 4; 119:105, xi.
Pyfferoen, Hilarius, 149 n 1.

Quaglia, Armando, 136 n 1.

Rachel, 196 n 3.
Rainaldo di Segni, 172, 178, 182, 209, 225 n 32, n 33.
Ratti, Archille, cf. Pius XI.
Reidy, Gabriel, 153 n 2, n 3.
Resurrection, 87 n 7.
Revelations, 2:7, 179; 10:8–11, 65 n 5; 20:6, 39 n 8.
Richard of St. Victor, 196 n 3.
Robinson, Paschal, 209 n 1.
Roger the Abbot, 29 n 6.
Romans, 2:29, 171; 8:9, 26 n 1.
Rothweil, Audrey Marie, 136 n 1, 153 n 3.

Sabatelli, Giacomo, 37 n 3.
Sabatier, Paul, 15 n 29, 52, 62, 74 n 2.
Salvation, 49, 64 n 5, 80, 149, 184.
Schampheleer, J. de, 80, 80 n 1.
Schmucki, O., 27 n 3, 58–59 n 8, 66 n 1, 80 n 1, 101 n 1, 108 n 1, 110 n 6, 136 n 1, 146, 146 n 1, 149 n 1.
Schroeder, H.J., 50 n 2, n 3, 124 n 32, n 33, 125 n 34.
Seton, Walter, 189, 189 n 1, 233 n 1, n 2.
Simon, A., 144 n 24.
Sin, and Christ, 17; and compassion, 74; confession of, 125 n 34–35, 142 n 17; and forgiveness, 39 n 8; and Francis, 17, 18, 27, 74, 75 n 5; and friars, 17, 75 n 4–5; original, 219 n 21.
Smith, John Holland, 15 n 29.
Spirituality, Christian, xv, 38, 174, 177, 200 n 5; Cistercian-, 26 n 2; of St. Clare, xv, 226; Franciscan, xv, 5, 16, 136, 150 n 4, 174, 183, 197 n 9; medieval, 15.
Stigmata, 4, 6, 37, 99.

251

INDEX

Talbot, C.H., 147 n 5.
Thomas à Kempis, 33 n 12.
Thomas of Capua, 5, 5 n 4.
Thomas of Celano, *First Life*, xi, 3 n 2, 7
    n 13, 17 n 38, 19 n 43, n 44, 25, 26 n
    2, 62, 77, 103, 104, 141 n 16, 164, 171,
    171 n 6, 196 n 4; *Second Life*, xii, 12 n
    23, 13 n 24, 41 n 6, 44, 45 n 3, 64 n
    5, 99, 103, 116 n 20, 136, 136 n 2, 142
    n 18, n 19, 148 n 9, 149, 151, 165,
    215–216 n 13; *Tract on the Miracles*,
    162.
Thomas of Eccleston, 6, 161, 163.
Trinity, and creation, 20, 38; life in,
    12–14, 17, 38, 44, 45 n 2, 171; and
    love, 17; and man, 12; unity in, 14.

Ubertino da Casale, 10 n 20, 55, 153 n 2.
Ulrich of Augusta, 80.

Verheijn, L., 31 n 8.

Wadding, Luke, 42, 54, 77, 207, 207 n 1,
    226 n 1.
Waldensians, 68 n 6, 69 n 8, 71 n 12.
Waldo, Peter, 68 n 6.
Walker, J.H., 58–59 n 8, 111 n 11.
Wenceslaus III, 199 n 1.
William of St. Thierry, 118 n 24, 204 n 2.
William the Conqueror, xiii.
Wingene, Hilarius de, 149 n 1.
Word, 15, 21, 56 n 2, 137.

Yornick, Stephen A., 153 n 2, n 3.

Zinn, Grover, 196 n 3.

II. Index to Texts*

Adam, 27.
Agnes (sister of Clare), 206.
Agnes, Lady, 190, 195, 199, 203.
Alms, 41, 69, 115–118, 141, 147, 155, 219–221.
Amatus, Brother, 206.
Anthony, Bishop, 79.
Avarice, 144, 152, 222.

Baptism, 121.
Belief, 26, 27, 64, 128, 130, 134, 138.
Bernard, Brother, 159.
Blasphemy, 30, 119, 124.
Bonagura, Brother, 206.

Caesar, 31.
Charity, 35, 58, 69, 99, 100, 103, 114, 117, 142, 195, 201, 204, 205, 206, 208, 220, 221, 231; Lady-, 151–152.
Chastity, 109, 137, 143, 191, 211.
Christ, adoration of, 56, 154; ascension of, 89; belief in, 27, 64, 130, 134; Blood of, 26, 35, 49, 50, 53, 54, 56, 57, 63, 64, 68, 69, 71, 78, 88, 125, 130, 154; Body of, 25, 26, 35, 49, 50, 53, 54, 56, 57, 63, 64, 67, 69, 71, 78, 125, 154, 200; commands of, 56, 70, 77, 89, 98, 103, 114, 116, 119, 197, 232; covenant (testament) of, 26, 57; Cross of, 29, 68, 88, 97, 109, 130, 154, 191, 197, 205, 208, 230; crucifixion of, 29, 127, 208; and Father, 25, 26, 59, 60, 64, 67, 68, 84, 87–89, 106, 129–130, 131, 232; fear of, 56; gifts of, 201; glory of, 64, 70, 87, 131, 133, 208; humanity of, 26, 67; humility of, 26, 58, 117, 129, 199, 201, 204, 205, 225, 230; imitation of, 29, 46, 48, 61, 68, 109, 117, 127, 145, 195, 197, 199, 201, 203, 208, 210, 218, 227, 229; is with us, 27, 201; as King, 195, 199, 203, 204; love for, 32, 122, 134, 191, 196, 200, 201, 204, 208, 213, 227, 230; love of, 191, 200, 201, 204, 227; and

obedience, 60, 114; Passion of, 29, 67, 80–81, 94, 191; as servant, 28, 113; serving of, 190, 191, 193, 203, 207, 230, 234; as Shepherd, 29, 67, 80–81, 94, 191; spouse of, 191, 193, 195, 198, 199, 203, 204, 205; suffering of, 197, 205; union with, 64, 70.
Church, 35, 50–51, 53, 58, 111, 122, 132, 137, 138, 139, 145, 154, 164, 211, 212, 225, 227, 230, 232, 234.
Clare, 190, 195, 199, 203, 207, 210, 211, 229, 233; and Francis, 160, 210, 218.
Clergy, 35, 49, 53, 54, 56, 57, 58, 59, 69, 111, 125, 139, 155, 164.
Compassion, 33, 228.
Confession, 34, 59, 68, 76, 125, 126, 214, 216, 217, 224.
Consecration, 49–50, 53.
Contrition, 34, 125.
Custodians, 52, 53, 54, 56.

David, 118.

Elias, Brother, 197.
Elijah, 132.
Envy, 30, 144, 222.
Ermentrude of Bruges, 207.
Eucharist, 26, 27, 35, 49, 50, 53, 56, 57, 58, 59, 67–69, 71, 78, 125, 154, 214–215, 224.

Faith, 27, 100, 103, 125, 132, 138, 145, 154, 165, 200, 207, 212, 225.
Fasting, 69, 111, 112, 139, 202, 214.
Father, cf. also Christ, Heaven; adoration of, 68, 131; children of, 63, 70; commands of, 68; glory of, 129, 130; help of, 82, 84, 85, 87; as King, 87, 97, 99, 218; Kingdom of, 64, 71, 130, 131; knowledge of, 25, 130, 131; pleasing of, 131; and prayer, 64, 68, 71, 81, 84, 104–106; presence of, 201; seeing of, 25; servants of, 44, 82, 105, 131; thanks to, 130, 131; wisdom of, 64.

*Cf. also Appendix II: Scripture References, pp. 238–244.

253

INDEX

Feasts, 202.

Francis, 47, 52, 54, 56, 60, 67, 73, 77, 79, 80–81, 94, 108–109, 134, 137, 154, 156, 160, 161, 163, 165, 202, 210, 211, 214–215, 218, 219, 224, 227–233.

Friars Minor, cf. also Humility, Poverty; clothing of, 110–111, 138–139, 155; correction in, 113, 143; custodians of, 52–54, 56, 60, 75, 76, 140, 142, 148, 155, 156; expulsion from, 120, 125; ministers of, 55, 59, 60, 110, 112–114, 121, 122, 124, 128, 138, 140–145, 148, 155, 156, 159, 163, 197, 215; and money, 110, 116–117, 120, 140; and obedience, 109–114, 134, 137, 138, 143, 145, 148, 155, 156; and Office, 111, 139, 155, 156, 214; Pentecost Chapter of, 75–76, 113, 124, 142; and Poor Ladies, 215, 224–225, 228, 230; and possessions, 109–111, 120, 137, 138, 141, 155; and preaching, 122–124, 143, 154, 155; Rule of, 59–60, 75–76, 79, 135, 137, 138, 143, 155, 156; and women, 119–120, 143; and work, 115–116, 140, 155.

Gabriel, 67, 131.

God, cf. also Love; adoration of, 32, 68, 92, 125, 128, 129, 134; blessing of, 48, 53, 78, 91, 93, 94, 105, 117, 123, 125, 134, 139, 148, 155; children of, 32, 42; as Creator, 29, 59, 121, 125, 130, 132, 133, 134, 201; fear of, 92, 102, 126; gifts of, 195, 226–227; glory of, 85, 89, 90, 91, 97, 101, 105, 123, 134; help of, 89, 90, 92, 93, 95, 97, 227; image of, 130, 200; Kingdom of, 69, 105, 111, 122, 138, 147; knowledge of 29, 105; love for, 28, 30, 33, 68, 75, 96, 105, 128, 132, 134, 147, 193, 200, 208, 224, 231, 234; in man, 128; pleasing of, 28, 48, 61, 132; praises of, 54, 68, 81, 91, 93, 94, 99–100, 101, 123, 124, 125, 134; seeing of, 26; seeking of 61, 90, 95; servant of, 29, 31, 32, 33, 44, 54, 64, 72, 88, 96, 102, 115, 128, 132, 140, 193, 210, 227, 230; is Spirit, 26, 129; thanks to, 117, 118, 123, 125, 132, 134, 195, 227; throne of, 203; worship of, 129.

Grace, 56, 57, 60, 61, 74, 105, 117–119,

133, 140, 149, 150, 165, 195, 198, 201, 204, 207, 218, 219, 228, 231, 234.

Heaven, and Christ, 193, 195, 199, 205, 207; and Father, 88, 97, 105, 122, 129, 130; Kingdom of, 32, 116, 122, 126, 130, 141, 144, 192, 193, 197, 220, 223; and poverty, 192; and reward, 109, 122, 193, 197, 199, 207; seeking of, 32.

Henoch, 132.

Holiness, 57, 64, 123, 133, 190, 193, 195, 196, 208, 210.

Holy Spirit, and Christ, 30, 31, 59, 63, 70, 149, 192; and Father, 26, 149; and grace, 57, 150; and life, 26, 40, 67; lives in faithful, 26, 31; and man, 61, 70, 203; and prayer, 79; presence of, 63, 70, 144; as spouse, 45, 63, 82, 218.

Honorius, 137.

Hope, 88, 94, 96, 99, 100, 103, 134.

Humility, 32, 35, 69; of Christ, 26, 58, 117, 129, 199, 201, 204, 205, 225, 230; and Friars, 56, 70, 73, 123, 125, 139–141, 145; life of, 200, 208; of Lord, 99; and Poor Ladies, 219, 223, 231; of servant, 32–34; Sister-, 151–152.

Innocent III, 109, 211.
Innocent IV, 137, 225, 229.
Israel, King of, 43.

Jacob, 93.
James, 125.
Jerusalem, 204.
John the Baptist, 57, 131.
John the Evangelist, 131.
Joy, 165–166, 192, 196, 199, 200, 203, 204, 207, 227.
Judas, 57.
Judgment, day of, 39, 65, 78, 113; and Lord, 88, 89, 93; and sin, 35.
Justice, 90, 93, 100, 130, 133, 144, 147, 223.

The Lamb, 43, 57, 101, 203.
Leo, Brother, 47–48, 100, 165.
Leonard, Brother, 165.
Life, of Christ, 46; common-, 216; eternal, 26, 29, 100, 109, 118, 122, 123, 125, 127, 192, 193, 207; of Friars,

254

INDEX

110, 113, 114, 117, 135, 137, 138; of Gospel, 45, 108, 110, 137, 145, 155, 159, 211, 218; in hermitage, 147–148; of holiness, 190, 210, 224, 228, 231; of Poor Ladies, 210, 211, 213, 216, 218, 227, 228, 231; of poverty, 46, 191, 195, 200, 208, 213, 218, 224; and Scripture, 30; of Spirit, 113.

Lord, blessing of, 38, 39, 42, 43, 53, 60, 71, 83, 93, 100, 101, 102, 228; called by, 40, 196, 227, 228; enemies of, 81, 83–86, 95; fear of, 35, 42, 123; glory of, 38, 43, 53, 71, 83, 88, 90, 92, 94, 95, 97, 102; is God, 82, 83, 88, 99; is Good, 104; honor of, 38, 42, 43, 53, 57, 71, 78, 83, 88, 101, 102; image of, 38; as King, 88, 97; love for, 39, 57, 63, 104; love of, 81, 118, 119, 127; name of, 38; pleasing of, 57, 121, 122, 127; praise of, 38–39, 42, 43, 53, 56, 71, 78, 83, 84, 88, 90, 92, 94, 95, 97, 102, 202, 228; and prayer, 81, 86; presence of, 58, 63, 129; serving of, 39, 141, 195, 202, 210, 219; thanks to, 39, 78, 102.

Love, cf. also Christ, God, Lord; for brother, 34, 117, 119, 141, 143, 159, 164, 228; for enemies, 30, 70, 106, 127, 144, 223; for Father, 105; of Father, 130, 131, 201; for God, 28, 30, 33, 68, 75, 96, 105, 128, 132, 134, 147, 193, 200, 208, 224, 231, 234; is God, 65, 73, 99, 122, 128; for neighbor, 63, 69, 105; for sinners, 75; for sisters, 215, 220, 231.

Martha, 147.
Martin of Barton, 161.
Mary, 26, 41, 42, 46, 57, 59, 67, 81–98, 106, 117, 130, 131, 149–150, 193, 201, 202, 208, 213, 218, 220, 225, 230, 232, 233.
Mary (sister of Martha), 147.
Mercy, 35, 57, 69, 70, 75, 76, 84, 85, 90–94, 96, 97, 132, 133, 142, 154, 222; of Christ, 193, 194, 227, 228, 233; Father of, 226, 231, 234.
Michael the Archangel, 43, 82, 124, 131, 233.
Mortification, 32, 123, 152.
Moses, law of, 57.

Obedience, 27–29, 40, 48, 53, 56, 60, 70, 75, 109–114, 134, 137, 138, 143, 155, 156; Sister-, 151–152.

The Passion, 29, 67, 80–81, 94, 106, 191.
Patience, 32, 35, 70, 94, 99, 122, 123, 128, 144, 166, 223.
Paul, 30, 57, 115, 117, 119, 120, 132, 145, 200, 225, 227.
Penance, 34, 53, 60, 63–65, 69, 71, 76, 120, 125, 126, 131, 132, 141, 142, 154, 155, 218, 221–222, 228.
Perfection, 109, 159, 195, 196, 197, 218, 222.
Persecution, 28, 29, 30, 86, 122, 127, 128, 144, 154, 155, 223.
Peter, 132, 145, 225.
Piety, 50.
Poor Ladies of San Damiano, 190, 195, 199, 210; and Chapters, 215–216, 219; clothing of, 212–213, 216; correction of, 222, 224; Discreets of, 215–217, 220, 222; and Enclosure, 215, 223, 224; form of life of, 210, 211, 213, 216, 218, 227, 228, 231; and grille, 216–218; and obedience, 211, 213, 215, 218, 222, 228, 231; and Office, 214, 217; Offices of, 215, 229, 230, 231; and possessions, 211, 212, 218, 219–221; and poverty, 210, 213, 215, 218–220, 228–231; reception of, 211–213; and silence, 216–218; and unity of mutual love, 210, 216, 222; Visitator of, 224.
Poverty, of Christ, 46, 48, 67, 117, 192, 199, 201, 204, 205, 218, 220, 225, 229, 230; and Friars, 140, 141, 145, 155, 229; and joy, 35; Lady-, 151–152, 164, 229; life of, 46, 191, 195, 200, 208, 213, 218, 224; and Poor Ladies, 210, 213, 215, 218–220, 228–231; of spirit, 32.
Prayer, 32, 64, 68, 71, 79, 81–83, 102, 111, 115, 128–130, 139, 140, 143, 154, 193, 194, 198, 210, 219, 222, 232.
Pride, 144, 152, 200, 222.

Rachel, 196.
Raphael, 131.
Raynaldus, Bishop, 210.
Redemption, 50, 56, 88, 121, 130, 132, 133, 154, 199, 205, 208.